LIFE METAPHORS

Stories of Ordinary Survival

CATHERINE SULLIVAN NORTON

SOUTHERN ILLINOIS UNIVERSITY PRESS

Carbondale and Edwardsville

Copyright © 1989 by the Board of Trustees,
Southern Illinois University
All rights reserved
Printed in the United States of America

Edited by Kathryn Koldehoff
Designed by Duane E. Perkins
Production supervised by Natalia Nadraga

Library of Congress Cataloging-in-Publication Data

Norton, Catherine Sullivan, 1956-
  Life metaphors: stories of ordinary survival/ by
Catherine Sullivan Norton.
     p.   cm.
  Bibliography: p.
  ISBN 0-8093-1427-4
1. Adjustment (Psychology) 2. Adjustment (Psychology)
—Case studies. I. Title.
BF335.N67   1989

155.2—dc19   88-17549
                                             CIP

The paper used in this publication meets the minimum
requirements of American National Standard for Information
Sciences—Permanence of Paper for Printed Library Materials,
ANSI Z39.48-1984.

Dedication

To my husband, Robert Norton, who showed me how to hold onto the dream with unreal clarity.

And for my son, Robert Sullivan—my own life metaphor—who is the dream come true.

Contents

Figures

Acknowledgments

First, I need to applaud the people in this book—they are the real heroes. I am especially grateful to Bill, the first to be interviewed. I remember tentatively approaching him and being so surprised at his opennesss and amazed at his stories. I have tried to preserve the identity and spirit of the people about whom I have written. The names have been changed and some of the words rearranged but my intention always has been to let them speak. Looking back on this book, I see a few pages devoted to each person. Under those few pages lies thirty pages of text; and under those thirty pages lies an entire life. In some ways it seems so disproportionate.

I also want to thank some other people: Leon Trachtman who listened to many of my first rough impressions; Virgil Lokke who helped me understand the text; Jim Hughey for an early beginning; Dave Brenders who helped me understand the control dimension; Studs Terkel for an echo and encouragement; Judith Heltner for reading the manuscript, editing, proofing and providing general grammatical guidance; Bill Foster Owen for conscientous reviews and reality checks; Kenney Withers and everyone at SIU Press for their support, timing, and ingenuity; my family—Frank, Coco, Tim, Louise, Jody, Fiona, Gabrielle, Harriet, Annabel, Bruce, Peter, John, Nan, Noongi, Sarah Rose, and Clara.

Introduction

Anyone who contemplates the "meaning of life" experiences moments when the ideas of "meaninglessness" and "futility" dominate. Daily efforts to find value and purpose lead one to ask "What is the point?" and "Why bother?" Giving up and avoiding problems is easy; facing life and coping is more difficult. It seems that if one wants to endow life with meaning one must conscientiously work to do so. Even existential playwrights who dwell on life's insignificance are not passively despairing. They are writing plays, actively shaping their perceptions into works of art.[1]

I started this book because I had some nagging questions of my own. How do people survive the day? What keeps people going? Is there a guiding sense of purpose? How do people cope with ordinary life? I crafted a series of interviews to find some answers. As I listened to remarkable stories of tragedy, pain, and suffering, I witnessed the change of seasons along with my own change of consciousness. I heard complaints about injustice, indifference, and inequality. People talked about fears, futility, and hopelessness and about their need for others.

Through people's language I found out how they managed. It comes as little surprise that language shapes our thinking and influences our behavior. Words change history, create impasses, execute volatile accusations, and initiate wars. They express tender emotions, capture special moments, and preserve traditions.

As one reads what follows, one might be reminded of the oral history tradition, which presents stories about people's lives based on interviews. The tradition relays the effects of history according

to the individual's account. Studs Terkel, one of the most profi-
cient contemporary oral historians, selects diverse themes around
which to focus his stories. He has written about the Depression,
the American Dream, a Chicago neighborhood, the world of work,
and World War II.[2] He deals with average people and asks them
about their lives, he describes *Working,* the fourth in his series,
as a book "about a search for daily meaning, as well as daily bread,
for recognition as well as cash, for astonishment rather than tor-
por; in short, for a sort of life rather than a Monday through Friday
sort of dying."[3]

Inspired by Terkel's interviewing style, his choice of down-to-
earth subject matter, and his interest in workaday people, I began
my own series of interviews. In seven months I spoke to forty-
six people. I tried to find as diverse a population as possible while
still representing the "sorts of lives" ordinary people lead. Most
were strangers whom I approached informally at their place of
work.[4]

Three elements of Terkel's work impressed me. First, everyone
struggles to survive the day. In the Introduction to *Working,* he
writes that "to survive the day is triumph enough for the walking
wounded among the great many of us."[5] No matter what differences separate people, everyone shares the burden of confronting
difficulties.

Second, the interview has the capacity to draw people out about
themselves. Like the perfect dancing partner, the interviewer
should know when to hold the other and when to let go, when
to get close and when to pull back, when to move quickly and
when to move slowly, when to lead and when to be led. Dancing
the tango takes work, practice, timing, and precision: if one does
it right, it is like magic.

Third, Terkel prefers the reality of everyday life, as he chooses
to deal with ordinary, average people. At first glance, watching
people go about their daily business, there appears to be nothing
extraordinary until one hears their stories. People come alive
through their words, making it possible to imagine what their
"life is like."

After the oral historian gathers the interviews, they must be
edited and organized. Terkel likens the task to that of a gold
prospector: "I've got to sift through sixty pages of each interview
to find the gold and reduce it to eight pages without distorting

the individual's thoughts and at the same time find a form for the book."[6]

While this book differs from the strict oral history mode, it falls into an increasingly popular genre which recounts stories about ordinary life, giving voice to personal memoirs and private records. In the past, one usually associated descriptions of everyday life with cultural anthropology. The classic Margaret Mead studies of Samoa and Gregory Bateson's work with the Iatmul culture of New Guinea typify the field method.[7]

Nowadays, popularized versions of anthropological studies place stories about other cultures within easy reach of a wider audience. For example, Oscar Lewis's *Five Families* presents five days in the lives of five different Mexican families.[8] His next book *The Children of Sanchez* is an "autobiography" of a single Mexican family in which he devotes one chapter to each person's story.[9] Collectively, the stories form a detailed picture from the family's perspective.

Other popular books in the personal history genre, while less anthropological, still provide case histories of the members of specific groups. Jean McCrindle and Sheila Rowbotham edited a collection of stories called *Dutiful Daughters*, which presented the lives of fourteen women and their thoughts about childhood, school, work, and marriage.[10] In Brigid McConville's *Sisters*, women talk about their relationships with their sisters, addressing such topics as rivalry, conflict, extrasisterly perception, and the sister's bond.[11] Journalist Vivian Gornick's *Women in Science*, recounts stories of women scientists who describe their personal struggles in an essentially male-dominated profession.[12] In *The Men in Our Lives*, Elizabeth Fishel examines father-daughter relationships, arguing that a woman's relationship with her father influences her subsequent relationships with men. Based on the father image, she developed categories such as "The Charmer," "The Bystander," and "The Pal."[13] Fishel collected and arranged personal interviews, letters, and written autobiographies by women.

Habits of the Heart, a national bestseller, is written by a five-person research team consisting of one philosopher and four sociologists.[14] The authors assume a cultural standpoint to examine how American people create and preserve "a morally coherent life." The book focuses on individualism, presenting portraits of people speaking about what it means to be an "American."

Because these books typify a growing interest in the lives of the ordinary person, they are becoming the popular archives of social history. At the same time, such works indirectly influence the development of history. Ordinary people are more aware of their capacity to make, shape, and preserve history. In the age of video and the "instant camcorder," the "person on the street" can be a star for a minute, providing eyewitness testimony to a news-hungry public. To the extent that this book resembles these works, it falls within the scope of an increasingly popular body of work that studies the language of everyday life.[15]

How to Read *Life Metaphors*

When I began, I was not entirely sure where the project would lead. I soon discovered that people have remarkable ways of confronting life and clever strategies for handling problems. They possess powerful metaphors and poignant stories that help sustain their lives. By the end of the interviews I was amazed at how hard people's lives are, how easily they answer provocative questions, how well they cope, and what clear visions they have.

Chapters 1 and 2 present a framework which explains the interviews. Chapter 1 specifically asks "How does language help us cope?" It examines the relationship between metaphor and coping and introduces the concept of a life metaphor. Chapter 2 develops the idea of a life orientation, showing how it fits into the framework of this study. The next four chapters describe the life orientations, reflected by the chapter titles: "The Antagonist," "The Enthusiast," "The Fatalist," and "The Spectator." The last chapter draws some conclusions, and the book ends with an appendix explaining the methodology, including how the interviews were conducted, how the texts were analyzed, and how the framework was generated.

I interviewed people from a small Midwest college town. There are twenty-five men and twenty-one women, whose ages range from eighteen to seventy-four. Altogether I collected over one thousand pages of dialogue. The names have been changed and parts of the text rearranged but the essence of the person remains unchanged. Since I have been unable to include everything in the interviews, the brief portraits must suffice to represent the entirety of a life.

In the oral history method, the data usually speak for themselves. Studs Terkel, for example, provides no commentary on his interviews. Following this style, I have tried to balance interpretation with presentation so that my voice does not speak more loudly than the voices of those I interviewed. Their words are intended to be the key feature of this work. My commentary is meant to create a theme for the stories, draw comparisons, and make speculations.

LIFE METAPHORS
Stories of Ordinary Survival

CHAPTER 1
Life and Metaphors

If I say to you "life is like _____ (blank), how would you fill in that space?"

A riddle. Life is like a riddle. It's puzzling. It's something unknown. It takes time to solve. One piece leads to the next. Usually there's a solution. Once you solve it you feel you've accomplished something. It can be amusing, adventurous or serious. It tests how clever you are. It gives you something to work on.

In everyday life people need to organize meaning to make sense of a potentially confusing world. An ordered set of events helps us remember sequences, tidy environments help us live efficiently, a patterned melody makes it possible to recover songs, and alphabetization organizes dictionaries. One's relation to the world can often be reduced to a few words describing how one thinks and feels. Language organizes daily life so that we can make ourselves understood, coping more effectively in the process.

Things that are difficult to put into words often are easier to explain if we liken them to things we know about. Whenever we liken life to something, we use a life metaphor. To some, life metaphors sound like clichés—we hear them every day: life is like "a bowl of cherries," "a roller coaster," "a stage," "a rose garden," "riding a bicycle," "the weather," "a race," "a long and winding road," "a battle," "a journey," or a "gift."[1]

To others, life metaphors carry the wisdom of proverbs: "beauty is skin deep," "as you make your bed, so must you lie in it," "the best is yet to be," "boys will be boys," "all that glitters is not gold," "better late than never," and so on. Literary critic and theorist Kenneth Burke describes proverbs as "*strategies* for dealing with *situations*."² People develop names for recurrent situations which imply strategies for coping.

However, life metaphors differ from clichés and proverbs to the extent that individuals generate personalized interpretations. One hears less frequently that life is like "an expressway," "a song," "a large dark mansion," "an elevator," "a joke," "a sponge," "a road map," "a candle flame," "a museum," "a ball of clay," "a window," "a pendulum," or "a kaleidoscope." People have private meanings that reflect more complex perspectives or serve as guides to more complicated life orientations.

This book is about stories of life and survival, addressing such subjects as human coping, purpose, and meaning. It is about the way people use everyday language. The book recounts stories of daily heroism and presents interviews that document the language of coping. It is not about the kind of heroism that is rewarded with medals and honors. Instead, it is about the unrewarded commonplace courage that characterizes ordinary people managing the daily task of living. The people are not heroes but their plight is courageous. They are not poets but their words are eloquent. They are not philosophers but their thoughts are profound.

We are so often intrigued by the extravagant lives of the rich and famous that we forget about the ordinary lives of everyday people. For many of us, getting through the day and making ends meet are difficult tasks. Coping with everyday life has to be managed one way or another. A person often struggles to keep body and soul together, making the daily task of living frequently a matter of survival—a matter of ordinary survival.

When we think about the word *survival*, we typically think of the extreme endurance that characterizes people who live through devastating events.³ Natural disasters, unexpected personal tragedies, and life-threatening illnesses come to mind. Less frequently do we think of the perseverance needed to face daily life. How do we manage? What gets us through the day? How do we make it all work? How does language help us cope?

In facing the typical demands of everyday life, some people manage better than do others. On the whole, most people do not enter therapy to help them cope. Somehow they get by on their own. Many problems that bring a person to therapy are everyday life events that are mismanaged. Whether life's problems are managed or mismanaged depends in part on how our sense-making language helps us conceptualize problems. Sometimes the words we use to name problems can in themselves cause pain. In addition to the difficulty in coping with the problem, people face difficulties because of the stigma attached to the name associated with the problem. For example, names such as "handicapped," "deaf and dumb," "backward," "retarded," or "crippled" are now regarded as demeaning and have been replaced by "developmentally disabled," "physically challenged," "mobility impaired," "visually" or "hearing impaired," "slow learners" or "learning disabilities." These transformations help us make sense of the problems in a more productive way. In each case, a change in the language brings a change in the way we cope with the issues.[4] The new names offer a more positive, less discriminating, and less alienating perspective.

Despite varying approaches, most therapists agree that metaphor helps the healing process by encouraging a patient to make associations that provide information about possible interventions.[5] Given the impact of metaphor in therapy, I wondered if it were pervasive in everyday life in helping people cope. I began the project because I wanted to find out how metaphor relates to coping. Which metaphors enable coping and which prevent it? Before directly addressing that question, the two critical issues of metaphor and coping are discussed separately.

Metaphor

A metaphor is a figure of speech formally characterized as a trope.[6] The word *trope* means a turn or a conversion. Metaphor is a figure of change, stemming from the Greek word *meta*, which means over, across, or beyond; and *pherein*, which means to carry, to bring, or to bear. In a metaphor, the qualities of one object are carried over or transferred to another object, with the result that the second object receives the qualities of the first. In the process, the second object becomes transformed. When we say "life is like a riddle" we attribute the qualities of a riddle to the subject of life. We relate to life "as if" it were a riddle and the idea of life becomes transformed through these associations.[7]

Aristotle discusses the everyday use of metaphor in *The Rhetoric*, where he attributes much of its power to giving "names to nameless things."[8] Aristotle did not expand on this idea, however if he had, his description of metaphor might include the following subjects: (1) experiences an individual does not understand; (2) things for which names do not exist; (3) information that is unknown or unavailable; (4) parts of reality an individual does not wish to confirm; (5) parts of reality an individual questions; and (6) things for which an individual has difficulty finding the right words.

Recently, Walter Ong wrote in *Orality and Literacy* that names "give human beings power over what they name: without learning a vast store of names, one is simply powerless to understand, for example, chemistry and to practice chemical engineering."[9] We need to know the names for things to understand what they mean and how they work. Furthermore, the power we perceive we have depends as much on our skill at handling the language as on our skill at using the equipment.

Usually it is hard to cope with something without a name. Indeed, the process of naming is so powerful that it starts before birth as parents consider possible names throughout the pregnancy. The newborn is quickly identified and carries that name through life. Names help us cope. When we go to the doctor, we expect to be told what is wrong with us. We want to know the name for what we have, feeling uneasy if our illness is not called something. Similarly, declaring a situation a "national disaster" serves a number of functions: it places the situation in a category, which defines the magnitude of the problem; it tells people they have suffered an extraordinary loss; and it also qualifies them for government support.

Using metaphor gives something a name that it did not previously have. The implications of metaphoric naming are the topic of current research examining how metaphor influences thought and action. George Lakoff and Mark Johnson argue in their book *Metaphors We Live By* that metaphor is pervasive in everyday life.[10] These authors share the modern assumption that metaphor is more than a decorative figure of language.

For centuries metaphor was studied primarily for its ornamental effect. For the most part, Aristotle's analysis examined the way metaphor enhances a speaker's style. In the 1960s, I. A. Richards approached metaphor as a figure that helps develop human thinking, arguing that metaphor is "a borrowing between and intercourse of thoughts, a transaction between contexts. *Thought* is metaphoric."[11] With this transition, scholars began to focus seriously on the cognitive processes evoked by metaphor, emphasizing its power to influence reality.

Initially, I wanted to find out how people use metaphor to help them cope with daily life. My goal was to explore metaphor in its everyday context by asking people to talk about their lives. I developed a concept of a life metaphor, which can be described simply as the answer to the question "If I say to you, 'life is like _____ (blank)' how would you fill in that space?"[12] The question prompted a person's metaphorical concept, making it possible to include things one might not ordinarily count as metaphors (such as phrases and sentences).

To grasp the full meaning of a life metaphor, it is necessary to realize that I am not referring to metaphor in the traditional sense. I prefer to emphasize the relationship between metaphor and reality, to focus on metaphor at the level of the discourse, and to treat each interview as a metaphoric text.[13] Psychotherapist Cloe Madanes explains the shift in levels of metaphoric analysis in her therapeutic work. Writing in *Strategic Family Therapy* she argues:

> A system's metaphor and a metaphor in a dream are not of the same order. To focus on the metaphor expressed by a sequence of interaction is of a different order from focusing on the metaphor expressed in a message or an act. There is a shift to a different level of analysis when metaphorical communication is thought of as expressed not only by individual messages but also by relationships and systems of interaction.[14]

Understanding life metaphors involves a shift to another level of analysis, focusing on a larger unit than a single message. If we think about metaphor within the frame of "systems of interaction" then individual behaviors and relationship patterns can be seen as metaphors. For example, in many ways a couple metaphorically express its structure, rules, and organization through patterns of interaction around daily life issues. These patterns can be viewed as interactional metaphors, by which I mean the indirect and unconscious definitions of the relationship.[15] A weight problem might be a metaphor for a troubled marriage. A child's misbehavior might be a metaphor for an unhappy home life. Buying a home or deciding to have a child metaphorically comments on the level of commitment to the relationship.[16] Patterns of the marital relationship, which often cannot be communicated through literal language, are explained metaphorically.[17]

Coping

Any attempt to define coping must ask, from whose perspective is it being defined? There are several meanings: *Webster's:* "to struggle or contend with some success." *The Oxford English Dictionary:* "contend successfully with; deal competently with situation or problem." *Roget's Thesaurus:* "survive, subsist, eke out, make out, scrape along, manage, get by." *Encyclopedia and Dictionary of Medicine, Nursing and Allied Health:* "the process of contending with life difficulties in an effort to overcome or work through them." There are societal definitions and individual definitions of coping, each of which influences one's understanding of the term.

The coping process can be traced through an individual's development. Before children learn language, they communicate primarily by crying. At first it is hard to distinguish if the cry means hunger, fatigue, or boredom. The parent tries different things to correct the situation. British psychologist Andrew Lock studies the emergence of meaning: "Crying on its own leaves too much of the message unsaid, too much to be supposed by the hearer. Apparently in response to this problem the developing infant begins to modify his crying, complementing it with other, more specific, communicative actions, each with its separate developmental history."[18]

As the child experiments with sounds, the crying lessens. When language begins, crying becomes even more reduced. The change from sensory communication to verbal communication indicates the ability to organize meaning, understand the world, and be understood. The development of language establishes a framework of shared knowledge which guides everyday life and reflects reality. As the child becomes more skilled in using language, coping becomes easier. The child explains what the cries mean: "It hurts here." "I am hungry." "Play with me." Language helps the child remove much of the ambiguity in the environment.[19]

In his book *The Coping Capacity*, Avery Weisman, a medical practitioner working with cancer patients, describes the development of fluency in language and the development of skill in coping as parallel operations performed by the growing child:

> Like any other language, coping begins in infancy; a child learns from its elders, scholarly niceties are largely irrelevant, and fluency is more effective than being grammatically correct. . . . Coping is the language of existence. It has a history, grammar, etymology, and skilled practitioners. . . . The vocabulary of coping is both simple and complex, but there are rules, traditions, conventions, and customs that mark out the acceptable forms in which problems present themselves for coping.[20]

Once the child acquires enough language, the parent may tell fairy tales. They are some of the first stories a person hears, extending early coping skills by shaping one's perception of the world. Fairy tales help the child cope by answering questions about the self and one's relation to the world.[21] As the child searches for meaning, fairy tales help answer questions and often explain morality. In The Three Little Pigs, for example, the child learns that if one is industrious and does not waste time, then one will be rewarded in life. Beauty and the Beast teaches that inner beauty is more important than outward appearance. Cinderella shows that it is possible to rise from rags to riches and find Prince Charming.

On a wider scale, most cultures contain myths that explain universal patterns of experience, organize memories, and provide models for behavior.[22] For example, every society contains myths about the origin of the world.[23] Australian aborigines believe in the "dreamtime," linking the creation of the earth, rivers, mountains, and stars to the spirits of their ancestors. The Chinese creator P'an Ku, is represented as having a chisel, carving out the mountains, shaping the sky, forming the oceans, and sculpting the trees. The Egyptian God Ptah of Memphis is believed to have created the world on his potter's wheel. According to the Navajo Indians, the first gods were divine spirits whose names were represented by the sky: yellow light for sunset and blue light for dawn. Western culture relies on such theories as the "big bang," creationism, or Darwinian evolution.

In any case, the structure of the myth usually corresponds to the structure of the civilization. Internalizing the myth helps people understand their relationship to the society in which they live. Myths organize meaning and explain inconsistencies in such a way that helps people cope with potentially confusing issues.

Many researchers in the field of psychology examine how people cope with stressful situations.[24] Areas of study include the psychology of adjustment, problems of adaptation, and the effects of stress on personal growth and mental health.[25] Coping has been studied from several perspectives, covering a range of topics, such as chronic illness, physical pain, job-related stress and specific issues for minorities.[26]

There has been some reluctance to examine coping as something "normal." One exception to this general trend is the work of psychologist Norma Haan, who presents a different perspective, arguing that coping constitutes normative behavior.[27] The idea that coping is "normal" is appealing because it treats coping as something done on a daily basis, for daily events, by most people. Coping refers to the ways people manage the demands, conflicts, and crises of living. Ordinary survival requires coping with mundane issues: adjusting to changes in daily life, searching for meaning in work, overcoming the fear of not being needed, maintaining a sense of self, struggling with shattered dreams, and hoping for some other kind of life.

Haan's concept of coping has several implications. First, coping is not something invoked only in threatening situations. This means, for example, that parents cope with raising children and an individual copes with finding a job. Second, coping is not necessarily something negative; it can be positive and functional. Positive coping means adapting to change and managing a life issue. Third, an individual who copes with life does not necessarily excel. The person might manage daily issues effectively, but this effectiveness is not equivalent to mastery.

Everyone expects problems. Not only do we expect them, but we have ways to manage them. Weisman suggests that life generally involves coping with two kinds of problems. The first includes predictable, unchanging events, such as the cycles of life—birth, death, marriage, the growth of children, the aging of those we love. These transitions are perennial issues, comprising what Weisman calls "expectable" problems because no one is spared.

The second kind of problem entails unexpected and surprising events. There are no guarantees, no clear answers, no abiding certainties, and no absolute assurances. Life sometimes presents unexpected problems: freak accidents, airplane crashes, natural disasters, terminal illnesses, and mass murders. One does not expect these things to happen, but they do. Our inability to predict the future makes nothing in life completely secure.

Coping means integrating unexpected events into an expectable framework. People do not get married expecting to get divorced; however, if it happens they may cope by thinking of it as an expectable possibility in today's society. On the other hand, people who assume divorce is morally wrong or unacceptable will probably have a difficult time coping.

Coping Metaphors

To examine the relationship between metaphor and coping, I needed to decide how to determine if people are coping. Because I could not follow them around making comprehensive assessments, I relied on their expressions of coping for my evidence. I asked people to think about the most difficult time in their lives, whether they coped, and how they managed. I asked them about other times to see if they consistently applied the same strategies. The answers constitute indications of coping. I focused on people's subjective evaluation, individual perception, and self presentation.[28] To the extent that they are honest and sincere, the texts are valuable for analysis.[29]

Initially I assumed that metaphor works positively to help one cope. However, many people have life metaphors that prove unhelpful. Metaphor can be used ineffectively, incompetently, and even disastrously. The treatment of AIDS (Acquired Immune Deficiency Syndrome) by the media reflects the insidious use of metaphor. Since the crisis began, many images have been generated, attempting to describe AIDS by likening it to such things as a "time bomb," "the enemy within," a "heart that can't pump blood," a "death sentence," and so on. The chances of getting AIDS have been likened to "being struck by lightning." Allowing a child with AIDS to attend school would be like "allowing a kid to run around with a gallon of gas and a match."[30]

One of the most flagrantly unhelpful metaphors likens AIDS to a "plague," implying that it spreads like wildfire through casual contact. The fact is that AIDS cannot be passed casually or spread as easily as the plague. AIDS does not "get" the person. In the majority of cases, the person must work to "get" AIDS. If AIDS were passed as casually as the metaphor claims, we would see many more cases. Not only is it the wrong metaphor, it inappropriately contributes to mass hysteria.[31]

The image that "AIDS is like the plague" also works figuratively. We think of the plague as a symptom of moral corruption, an affliction of divine punishment. AIDS is God's wrath against sin and punishment for homosexuality. This belief, while seriously held by many, does nothing to help treat the problem. The entire metaphor creates an image that people quickly associate with AIDS, escalating their fears.

In light of this example, I cannot argue that metaphor is only helpful. The stories presented in this book, however, are recounted by people who are coping—they are life copers. The metaphors emphasize the positive, functional steps taken to manage a problem.

It became increasingly clear that people cope because they have a certain perspective on their problem. The definition of a problem, like coping, is relative to the perspective of the person doing the defining. One way of talking about and conceptualizing a problem enhances coping, while another does not.

In life, elements emerge over which the individual has little or no control. For example, one cannot change one's place of birth, one's parents, or one's height. One can, however, change one's perspective about these things. One person's dilemma might be another's challenge. What one considers an enormous problem, another might consider insignificant. I talked to people who suffered what I would describe as extraordinary problems which they considered part of life. By comparison, other people had smaller worries which they thought were large. What constitutes a problem is defined from the individual's perspective, influencing how a person copes. In the interviews, people discussed how they transformed their lives by changing noncoping behavior into coping behavior.

For example, Margaret works at a run-down hotel as a receptionist. Her son died seven years ago while he was away from home. Devastated by the loss, she remembers thinking "I was the strongest person in the world. I could do anything. There wasn't anything I couldn't accomplish—until this happened. And then I saw just how weak I was." Margaret coped gradually. At first she had no idea what to do. She kept waiting for her son to come home, expecting him to walk through the door any time. She admits that she did not cope very well, trying different things that failed: she sold her house, quit her job, and sought psychiatric help. She recalls:

> Back in 1976, nobody could talk to me. I didn't have an answer for nothin'. In other words, I really didn't care about an answer. I was just tryin' to figure out why. And I couldn't figure out why. So it's like time helped me to see. And as I've gone down these last seven years I've seen a lot, and I been able to cope with it.

She says she never reached the point where she thought "life wasn't worth living." Something kept her from giving up. Indeed, the idea of the worthlessness of life opposes Margaret's fundamental appreciation for the value in life. She explains her attitude to her son's death through her life metaphor: "Life is very precious. I've experienced losing a child. And then I see other things that happen. That people cannot see how precious life is. To me, life is very precious. It's just something that you should be grateful in having. Each day should be precious."

Eventually she realized she must accept her son's death: "And when I once learned to accept it, it was easier. I wasn't gonna accept it. But I finally had to accept it." Her son's death strengthened her beliefs, solidified her life metaphor, and affirmed the reality she knew to be true.

Fred's six-year-old daughter died of leukemia twenty-five years ago. Her photograph was on his desk, and even now tears fill his eyes as he talks about her.

> I guess you have to accept it as life. You got hit early. Kind of a hard thing to cope with. And I don't think that anyone gets by in life without some tragedy in their lives somewhere. . . . You can't say, why me? Everyone does, but you look around and something else tragic happens to another family.

His daughter's death was not the only tragedy in his life. He grew up during the Depression, survived combat in World War II, his first wife died, he suffered the loss of crops and cattle, and his house burned down. In spite of the hardships he does not feel mistreated by life. Faith in his life metaphor ("life's been good to me") has helped him survive. In many ways he copes with the bad things because there are good things:

> Life's been good to me. I guess the business is successful. But the sadness too. I've been through World War II. I guess I felt the Lord cared for me because during that time I was in combat, I was nineteen, you know, and got wounded in Okinawa, and the boy right next to me got killed with the same shell. But I feel like someone's kinda' looking out for me. Caring for me. I don't know why. But someone is right there with me and keeping me alive.

Other people were coping with more immediate issues. Pat's husband, for example, walked out on her a week before we had our interview. She started a new job two days earlier, finding it frustrating and overwhelming. She lost the seniority she enjoyed before she quit to get married:

> I guess this kinda' scares me. At my age. It's harder as you get older. . . . It scares me, and I become very much afraid and anxious. I keep telling myself that it'll work out and something will happen. You just have to have patience and not try to make your way through in one day's time. You have to sleep on it and not make a decision immediately.

Pat was beginning to cope with a major life change. I asked her what life is like, and she said, "It's kind of a bad time to be asking. I thought I had it all together until my husband decided to move out. I would say it almost destroyed me." Although difficult, she wanted to continue the interview, talking about her life "before" and how well she used to cope. As she continued talking she reminded herself that she usually thinks of life as a "challenge." The memory seemed to strengthen her. By the end of the interview, she was determined that she would handle this problem in the same way. "I like a challenge. I like to get ahead. And I like to be organized and plan and know where I'm going. And I thought I did know where I was going. But you just get a lot of obstacles in your life that you have to overcome. And I'll overcome this too."

It is appropriate to return to Aristotle. We are now in a better position to understand why he assigned metaphor to manage the issues in our lives for which literal language is inadequate.[32] Issues that are contingent, controversial, or complex directly concern metaphor.[33] More recently, Weisman argues that many of an individual's "least-readily communicated experiences" involve the use of metaphor.[34] Earl MacCormac similarly claims that "ordinary language rests upon well-confirmed experiences, usually so well confirmed that we call the descriptions provided by it literal."[35] Literal language typically conveys easily communicated or well-confirmed experiences. If metaphoric language expresses the least-readily communicated, the not-so-readily-confirmed, and the more bewildering experiences, then it should work to help people cope with difficult issues.

CHAPTER 2
Life Orientations

> It is in us. The drama is in us, and we are the
> drama. We are impatient to play it. Our inner
> passion drives us on to this.
> Luigi Pirandello, *Six Characters in Search of an Author.*

Once the interviews were completed, they were ready to be analyzed. As I began the process of searching for representative themes and recurrent issues, I needed to find a way to explain the patterns that emerged throughout. I also needed a model that would separate the different life metaphors. With these two criteria in mind (exhaustiveness and mutual exclusivity), two factors-activity and evaluation-consistently surfaced.

It is not surprising that these dimensions should emerge.[1] Whenever we wish to find out what something means, we typically ask people if they think the subject is good or bad. This dimension (evaluation) gauges the way people rate something. A second question we might ask is whether the subject is active or passive. This dimension (activity) assesses the action associated with the subject. For example, the concept of "father" could be rated as follows:[2]

Father

happy ___:___: X :___:___:___:___: sad
slow   ___:___:___:___: X :___:___: fast

Many behavioral researchers have used this technique to measure the meaning of a variety of concepts, including people, objects, and situations. Indeed, hundreds of studies have been conducted supporting the presence of three major components of

14

meaning.[3] The recurrent dimensions are evaluation of some sort (good-bad), potency of some sort (strong-weak), and activity of some sort (fast-slow). Any person reacting to the concept of *life*, for example, can respond along the three dimensions. One person might rate it as good, passive, and weak; another might rate life as bad, active, and strong. Although potency did not stand out in the present study, the other factors, namely, evaluation and activity, did.

Evaluation

Every life metaphor can be described according to how an individual evaluates life. A continuum ranging from positive to negative expresses the degree to which the life metaphor assesses the quality of life. Evaluative statements range from "life's fantastic," "life's great," "life's pretty good," "life's OK," to "life stinks."

Evaluation refers to a rating, a judgment, or an analysis. Some characteristic adjective pairs for the evaluative dimension include:

good-bad	pleasant-unpleasant
fair-unfair	wise-foolish
honest-dishonest	valuable-worthless

Nunnally writes that "the evaluative factor almost serves as a definition for the term *attitude.* . . ."[4] Most adjective pairs suggest some degree of evaluation. Nunnally points out that even words such as "wet-dry, long-short, and up-down hint of evaluation."[5] Psychologist Robert Freed Bales developed a sophisticated three-dimensional model and method known as the Interaction Process Analysis, which interprets interpersonal behavior within groups.[6] Explaining how to analyze value statements, he provides another definition of evaluation: "Social evaluation involves the application of abstract concepts, rules, attitudes, feelings, and values to ongoing behavior. . . . All human beings presumably evaluate, to some extent, their own and other persons' behavior and attempt to control or change it. . . ."[7]

Evaluations about life derive from an individual's attitudes, which may be explicit or implicit, conscious or unconscious, abstract or tangible. Bales describes a person's evaluative capacity:

"He can develop values, ideas of 'the good,' with regard to anything he can symbolize, and he can then apply the values to new cases."[8]

In this study, the evaluative continuum indicates the excitement or enthusiasm with which an individual judges life (anchored by positive-negative). Individuals who rate it positively accept life as something worthwhile, affirming it as inherently good. Appreciating others, they usually elicit positive reactions. They are emotionally supportive, warm, and friendly. For example, Jan says, "I look at growth as a positive experience rather than a negative experience." Val says, "If you wanna make it fantastic, it can be fantastic. Every day can be wonderful." Teresa says, "The best thing in life is laughter."

Individuals who rate life less positively express a lack of enthusiasm for life, rejecting it as something worthless. Feeling alienated and alone they deny any goodness in life. Restricting their involvement with others, they fear they will get too close. Their general attitude often makes them disagreeable. Thelma says, "I know I have to come back [to work]. I don't have any alternatives." Dave says, "Life may not get any better at all. But you learn to cope with things." Becky says, "Life stinks. It gets harder and harder."

Activity

The activity dimension indicates the mental and physical energy an individual puts into life, characterized in this study by active-passive. Some action categories follow.

fast-slow	extrovert-introvert
sharp-dull	excitable-calm
busy-lazy	impetuous-quiet

Although the activity dimension is not meant to reflect any evaluation, it is sometimes difficult to avoid, as Nunnally points out. In our society, most people tend to regard activity positively, just as the less active life-style is devalued in our society. We think active people are happy people, and we expect them to be positive. Similarly, we expect less active people to be less positive.

The most active individuals typically say, "you can make your life anything you want." They are extroverted, dramatic, entertaining, frequently interactive and success oriented (materially, socially or personally). Active people make their lives the way they choose. Acting upon life, they work hard. Some of the more active comments were made by Glenda, who says, "I wanna grow old being vibrant and young." Sue says, "You take the opportunity and make of it what you want." George says, "You just can't stand still. 'Cause when you're standing still, you're going backwards."

The least active people say, "it's just the way it is. I just take it as it comes." They tend to be passive, submissive, and in search of security. They perceive themselves as acted upon by life, taking what it offers. Cheryl, one of the least active people, says, "You just kinda' have to live through it. There's not a whole lot you can do about it. . . . Everything changes and there's nothing you can do to stop it." Dan says, "You don't have to work at life, it's just there." Joe says, "We're just going along, you have no choice on whether you want to be here."

Combining the dimensions led to the development of four life-orientation categories: (1) most active–least positive; (2) most active–most positive; (3) least active–least positive; and (4) least active–most positive. The active-positive and passive-negative groups include the most people, reflecting a general expectation about the relationship between the dimensions. Psychologist Herbert Lefcourt studied the link between control and vitality and reached the following conclusions:

> If one feels helpless to affect important events, then resignation or at least benign indifference should become evident with fewer signs of concern, involvement, and vitality. . . . When one believes that hope is possible, that there is opportunity to act in one's own behest, then he becomes more "determined" and "alive to all his own powers and resources," or in a word, vital.[9]

In other words, someone who believes he or she controls what happens in life is probably a vital person. By contrast, someone who thinks it is pointless to try to change what happens probably lacks vitality.

The categories suggest a model of four life orientations, constituted from some quantity and quality of activity and evaluation. Figure 2–1 shows people's location on the model, and figure 2–2 shows the life metaphors. I have termed the categories "The

Figure 2–1.   Individual Ratings by Quadrant

Most Active	ANTAGONIST			ENTHUSIAST		
6	Harry					Jan Bonnie Teresa George Val Ron
5	Rick Phil	Dennis			Arlene Joanna Dorcas Glenda Sue	Peggy
4	Becky	Dave		Fr. Dave Evelynn	Norman Rudy Karen	
	FATALIST			SPECTATOR		
3		Carol Lynn Keith Pat		Leonard Joan Janet		
2	Claude	Steve Edward	Bill Bryan Fred	John Joe	Margaret	
1	Chuck Cheryl	Mike	Mac Dan Clem Thelma			
Least Active	1	2	3	4	5	6
	Least Positive					Most Positive

Antagonist," "The Enthusiast," "The Fatalist," and "The Spectator." Before describing them, it is helpful to explain what I mean by a life orientation.

Context

In a life metaphor a person says, "life is like x." How are we to understand this statement, which has the form of connecting life to some attribute or object? It would have been possible simply to ask people what life is like and categorize those short replies.

Figure 2–2. Life Metaphors by Quadrant

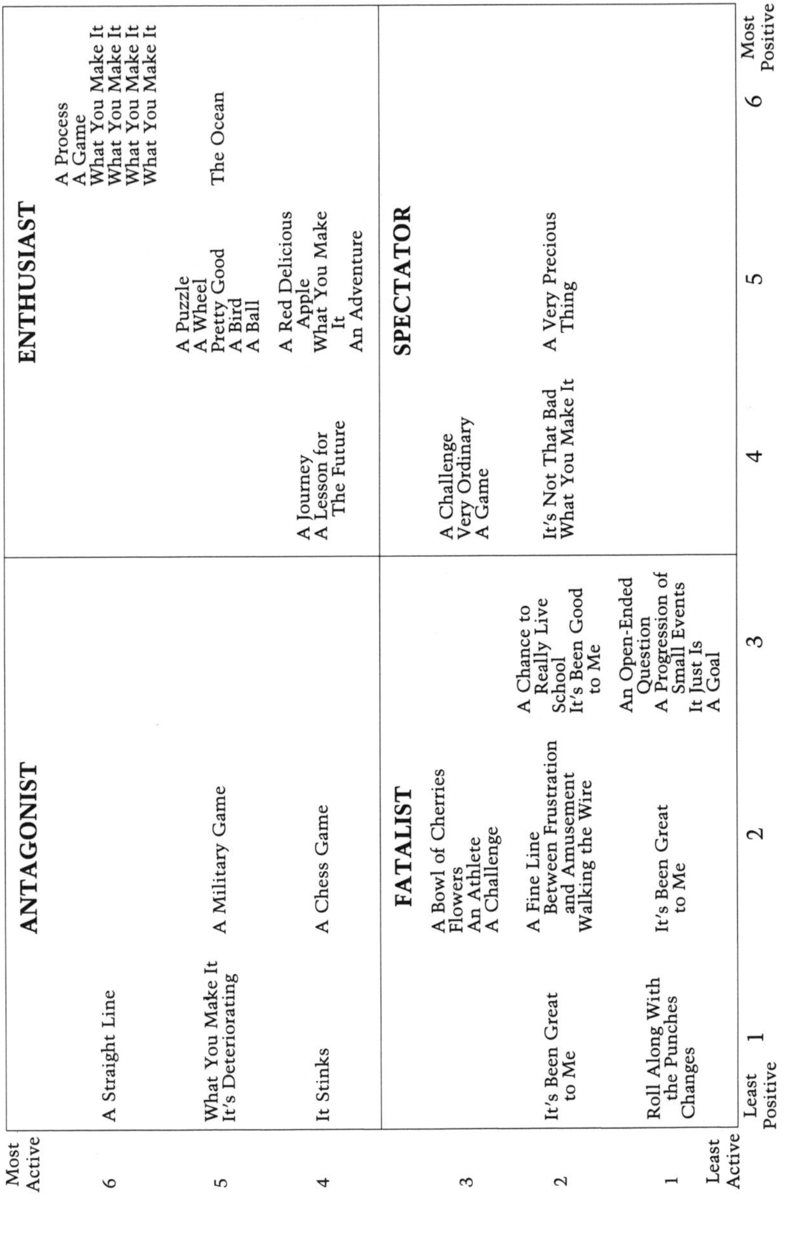
Most Active
6
5
4
3
2
1
Least Active
Least Positive
1
2
3
4
5
6
Most Positive
ANTAGONIST
A Straight Line
What You Make It
It's Deteriorating
A Military Game
It Stinks
A Chess Game
ENTHUSIAST
A Process
A Game
What You Make It
What You Make It
What You Make It
What You Make It
A Puzzle
A Wheel
Pretty Good
A Bird
A Ball
The Ocean
A Journey
A Lesson for The Future
A Red Delicious Apple
What You Make It
An Adventure
FATALIST
A Bowl of Cherries
Flowers
An Athlete
A Challenge
It's Been Great to Me
A Fine Line Between Frustration and Amusement
Walking the Wire
A Chance to Really Live
School
It's Been Good to Me
Roll Along With the Punches
Changes
It's Been Great to Me
An Open-Ended Question
A Progression of Small Events
It Just Is
A Goal
SPECTATOR
A Challenge
Very Ordinary
A Game
It's Not That Bad
What You Make It
A Very Precious Thing

The answers, however, would be incomplete and not explain what the person means. The statement "life is like x" can be understood only by linking it to the rest of a person's life. Someone can say that "life is like a game" and have an extremely cynical, sarcastic orientation. Another can say that "life is like a game" and have a sensitive, loving orientation. In each case, to get from "game" to the orientation, the bridge to the person's life must be found.

The interview connects the life metaphor to the life orientation by providing a context within which the details of a person's life may be understood. Each person has an outlook on life or a view of the world—consisting of an infinite number of possible life issues, such as one's attitude towards work, religion, society, the economy, politics, and so on. By providing a context, the interview frames the life metaphor, which otherwise would be impossible to decipher. Arlene, for example, answered that life is like "a puzzle." Dan said that life is "a progression of small events." And Steve said life is like "a fine line between frustration and amusement." On their own, these replies are ambiguous. It is possible to guess what they mean, but we do not know for sure that our hunches are correct.

The information needed to decipher the meaning of the life metaphor is held within the life orientation—a person's total behavior pattern, consisting of the sum of one's values, beliefs, and attitudes. A life orientation refers to the way one approaches life and relates to reality. It acts as a blueprint for life, providing a sense of direction. The life orientation refers to the disposition to which a person is psychologically and emotionally committed, providing the vocabulary, the central concepts, and the plans of action.

Each of the life metaphors has been placed within one of the four major life orientations. The structure is organized to form the human life system, guiding and reflecting a person's thoughts and actions.

Implications

Having established the framework, some interesting scenarios emerge. Two people may have the same life orientation but different life metaphors. For example, Bill and Steve, both characterized as Fatalists, have different life metaphors. Bill says that life is "a chance to really live"; Steve says that life is "a fine line between frustration and amusement." Each life metaphor entails a different perspective. Bill is elderly and works at the college gym distributing sports equipment. He believes in a God who plans his life and has a reason for everything. Steve is a young musician working as a cook to save money to move to the big city and become famous. He believes in a kind of cosmic mysticism and transcendental equality. Although they have different life metaphors, both Bill and Steve are Fatalists because they believe in a powerful guiding force.

Harry and Phil, both Antagonists, have different life metaphors: Harry says life is "a straight line"; Phil says life is "deteriorating." Not only are their life metaphors different, they have extremely different moral aspirations: Harry is a hard-drinking man who does not believe in religion; Phil is a devout Jehovah's Witness. They are Antagonists because they share a general active-negative orientation to life.

At the same time, two people may share the same life metaphor, using exactly the same language, but serving different long-term life orientations. Dennis and Bonnie both say life is like "a game." Dennis specifies the kind of game—a military game. Bonnie is less specific, referring to a "game" in general. Dennis, an Antagonist, feels the rules are unfair and he was mistreated. Bonnie, an Enthusiast, treats the game less seriously, believing you can make it anything you want it to be.

Jan and Joe agree that life is "what you make it"; however, they make it different things. Jan, an Enthusiast, aggressively pursues her goals, going after everything she wants. Joe, a Spectator, treats life delicately, quietly waiting for things to come his way. In these cases people share the same expression about life, but it works for different long-term goals.

People usually maintain the same life orientation throughout their lives. Just as values are relatively difficult to change, so are life orientations. However, life, like coping, is a process in which there must be room for inconsistency. One does not wholly and constantly cope with life. There are times when even the most solid coper falters. Likewise, someone with a history of ineffective coping may show surprising fortitude in times of great stress.

Typically, a change in the life orientation reflects a serious life change. John, a campus postal worker, became a Buddhist, marking a radical shift for him.

> I used to be an old grouch. I mean I did. Everybody hated me. I mean all the secretaries were scared of me. Well I been doing this [Buddhism] for about two weeks, and one of the ladies came up to me one day, and said, "What have you done differently?" I said, "Oh, I don't know. Why?" She said, "Whatever it is don't ever go back. 'Cause," she says, "we can talk to you now, and you don't snap our heads off." Before you'd say anything to me and I'd snap right back at 'em. And then I told 'em that I was a Buddhist. And she said, "Don't ever go back. You keep that up."

Even though this conversation took place over twenty years ago, John speaks as if he recalls it verbatim. The recollection keeps him going and helps him maintain the change. Most people whose life orientations have been altered have a clear picture of the event that changed their lives. Teresa remembers the effect of her brother's suicide:

> I used to think everything had to be just perfect. Then one day my brother killed himself. And you always think you're gonna do this tomorrow or you're gonna do that tomorrow and you never do it. And I guess when that happened it made me realize it. You should do it now because you may not be able to do it. It's a strange thing. And it changed my way of thinking about a lot of things.

She changed from being a perfectionist to being more flexible, from being timid to being willing to try anything, and from procrastinating to seizing every opportunity. She now believes life is "what you make it." If I were to interview the same people today, they might make different statements. Depending on one's life experiences, one's life metaphor at fifty may differ from one's life metaphor at twenty, but it nonetheless influences the way a person copes.

The life metaphor and the life orientation interact in surprising ways, reinforcing the need to locate the context of each person's life. This book could possibly have been called *Life Orientations: Ways to Cope.*[10] The move to focus on the metaphor was intended to suggest the smallest possible unit of analysis within the scheme to provide a starting point to understanding a person. Before discussing the specific life metaphors, the remainder of this chapter presents general portraits of each life orientation.

The Antagonist

The Oxford English Dictionary defines antagonism as "active opposition" or "resistance." It means an "opposing agent or principle"; and Antagonists actively oppose life. For every story of success they have two of failure; for every story of hope, three of despair. When asked, "why bother," or "what's the point?" they answer, "there is no point," and "there is no use in bothering." They make active efforts to deny anything positive in life.

Antagonists repeatedly describe life with words like "difficult," "tough," and "struggle." They think of themselves as fighters in the "battle" of life, actively complaining, actively provoking, and actively championing their cause. They tell you life is "unfair" and "full of problems" as they loudly moan about how bad everything is. They relate aggressively to the world because they know what it is like to fend for themselves. They expect little and firmly believe that the natural condition is intrinsically negative—"life is hard" and supposed to be hazardous and frustrating.

Betrayed so many times, Antagonists are distrustful of others and believe they must rely on themselves. They expect people to take advantage of them. Anticipating deception, they prefer to be isolated rather than embrace the risks of intimacy. Stoically claiming that they do not need anyone to make them happy, they are unwilling to make commitments. They say that they don't need people and that they are "all alone in this world." Their bad faith relieves them of responsibility for anything. If a relationship does not work, it is not their fault. If life does not go their way, it merely confirms their expectations.

In spite of the unfairness, Antagonists believe in a dream of a better world, which actively encourages them to persevere and continue the struggle. In the dream, they have what they lack in reality; life's injustice seems less severe, the unfairness seems to disappear, and the inequity seems inconsequential. All the agents and forces that threaten them are absent. They become energized as they escape to their dreamworld because it provides an escape from reality, which gives them hope. In spite of how bad every-thing is, they believe that one day they will find their ideal world. The dream reflects the most positive element in their lives and keeps them from being extremely negative. They cling to it be-cause it is *theirs:* no one can take their vision away. As they create the dream, they create an illusion that sustains them. To break the illusion would shatter their hope.

Antagonists have a clear picture of what constitutes fair and just treatment. Although they do not have an elaborate system of rights mapped out, they intuitively understand what they mean. Their expectations are not extravagant, but they know their basic constitutional rights and will not tolerate their violation. On the job, for example, they know what should be permitted. An An-tagonist will not stand for any breach of personal rights; he or she will protest vigorously and aggressively defend himself or herself, his or her family, and his or her territory.

Antagonists focus on money, believing it to be the way out of their problems. The idea of wealth appeals because they think it would solve everything. If they had money, they would have what they want. They would be happy, life would be easy, they would be more positive, they would have freedom, and the world would change for them. They perceive money to be a source of power linked to their struggles and dreams: "If only I had money, life would be different. . . ."

The Enthusiast

The word *Enthusiast* refers to people who are positively active. Eager to learn, interested in life, and willing to work; the words *making, doing,* and *working* characterize their life-style. They are action-oriented people, energetic actors, and irrepressible opti-mists. Concerned with making their own fate, they try to take advantage of everything life has to offer. Priding themselves on being inquisitive means finding the answer is not as important as asking the question. Although they have discovered many per-sonal answers, they believe there are no final solutions. Life, like the yin and the yang, is both positive and negative. They balance the two sides, searching for the positive, healthy side rather than dwelling on the negative, destructive side. Not only do they seek the positive in life, they believe they can transform negative situations into positive ones. They say "even things that seem negative at the time, can be turned around into positive things, and you can learn from them."

Enthusiasts create a positive picture of life, emphasizing the "process of personal growth" within which the most important goal is the quest for self-knowledge. They constantly analyze themselves in an effort to improve their disposition. They possess a solid self-image together with a strong, confident personality. Enthusiasts are not burdened by self-consciousness and are uninhibited by what others think as they work to better themselves. Making the most of strengths and minimizing weaknesses, knowing what to do to achieve goals, and being willing to make sacrifices help them get what they want. Personal satisfaction motivates them more than material success.

Enthusiasts are upbeat, friendly, and dynamic. They are talkative, happy, not self-destructive, and rarely do they yield to depression. Always looking for ways to make the best of any situation, they believe in the power of positive thinking. They constantly tell themselves "I can be anything I want." Their personality is infectious and people like to be around them. They usually have a good story to tell, inspiring others with their *joie de vivre*. Unlike the Antagonist, whose energy moves towards the negative end of the continuum, the Enthusiast's energy moves in a positive direction.

Enthusiasts not only believe their perspective is important but act on the basis of that perspective. Success stems from positive thinking combined with positive action. They make the most of whatever happens, believing one must actively participate in one's fate. The adage "life is what you make it" helps them think of themselves as powerful individuals, able to guide their own destinies. Enthusiasts are not likely to sit around waiting for things to happen, passively accepting life. Energetically working at getting what they want, they choose to make life a good, positive experience.

Enthusiasts are so active they are likely to say that they never have enough time, or that there are not enough hours in the day. They are always busy and willing to try new things, meaning they often add unplanned events to a schedule already full. The daily routine is largely unpredictable. They seldom procrastinate because their sense of urgency about life compels them to seize the moment.

Enthusiasts perceive a directly proportionate relationship between what they put into life and what they get out of it. Life represents the sum of a person's contributions. If one puts nothing in, then one can expect nothing in return. On the other hand, if one exerts substantial effort and makes the most of things, then one should expect much.

Enthusiasts believe everyone has opportunities available, which provide experience and knowledge. Experience teaches Enthusiasts how to alter their lives by giving them information to plan ahead. They are expert planners, relying on well-developed organization skills. They know their goals, objectives, and follow things step-by-step. They carefully choose exactly where they want to direct their energies.

The Fatalist

The word *Fatalist* describes people who believe in a scheme of things larger and more powerful than the individual. They think of themselves as fairly "normal" and "average" and of their lives as "ordinary." They also like to think of themselves as people who do not philosophize, seldom wondering why something happens since they are convinced that there are no answers to perennial questions about life.

There are as many different kinds of Fatalist as there are branches of fatalism. Each one depends on the perceived source of power, which ranges from a religious God, or other supernatural being, to the Tarot, the I-ching, or astrology. A dominant person, or guru-type figure, might be the controlling force. Events could happen by chance, luck, or accident. Regardless of the expression of fatalism, it rests on the assumption that a powerful external force controls one's life, making one powerless to control one's destiny. Fatalists are characterized as the least active and the least positive of the orientations. Their portrait consists of essentially negative characteristics: not worrying, not thinking about life, not exerting energy, and not having freedom.

Fatalists express their acceptance of fate by saying: they are "going along" through life; they "go through" things and "go with" whatever happens. To survive, they say that "you have to keep going." They "take life as it comes." As they proceed through life, they exert minimal energy, shrugging their shoulders and expressing little enthusiasm. They lack exuberance and rarely get excited. Being quiet, shy, and withdrawn, they tend to be inconspicuous and nonassertive.

The word *takes* typifies their approach to life: they "take life easy," "take things as they come," and "take it in their stride." They use the word *take* in the sense of "accept," "put up with," "submit to," and "accommodate." The word suggests receptivity and drawing the self in. In their eagerness to take from life, they become predominantly self-directed rather than other-directed.

Fatalists respect an underlying order that provides explanations about life, clarifies difficult subjects, and justifies inconsistencies. An individual needs order to organize the world and make sense of what happens. The idea of order implies that events are linked together to form a progression in which everything relates to everything else.

Within this order, Fatalists perceive almost no freedom of choice. Their options are limited because they believe they have no power in shaping their own destinies. Without any direct control, there is no reason to alter events or deviate from a life plan. When people perceive that they have little or no choice about altering their lives, they tend to become lethargic. Fatalists inevitably tolerate the bad, accept what happens, and lack any desire to make significant changes. Moreover, they find solace in knowing they are unable to control what happens.

The distinction between internal and external perceptions of control describes the difference between Enthusiasts and Fatalists. Enthusiasts, who clearly perceive a sense of internal control, view themselves as active and self-controlling. The word *makes* typifies their lives. Fatalists, who perceive a sense of external control, view themselves as passive and controlled *takers.*

Fatalists know what to expect from life, and they like it that way because it makes their life-style predictable and certain. They are satisfied that nothing extreme or unusual happens. The daily routine is steady and reliable; the days, weeks, and months are much the same, mirroring the cycle of their lives. They are reluctant to try anything new or leave themselves open to explore variations.

Fatalists rationalize their tendency to avoid worrying in a number of ways: "it ages a person"; "it shortens one's life"; "it serves no purpose"; "it wastes time;" and "it takes too much energy." Essentially, they argue that they are not going to worry because there is nothing they can do anyway. Coping by not worrying, they do not perceive any insurmountable problems. They do not wish to get upset by worrying. They prefer instead to go through life ignoring problems.

The Spectator

The word *Spectator* is intended to capture the qualities of the least active and the most positive individual. Spectators "look on," "watch," and "observe." They believe "everything happens for a reason" and "the answer will come in time." Although detached from life, they approach it positively. They are not participators, initiators, or activators. Instead, they are recipients, accepters, and bystanders. They combine a positive perspective with a pervasive acceptance of what happens. They do not actively initiate or pursue change because they believe they are unable to alter the course of life in any significant way. Patiently expecting things to be taken care of and problems to be resolved, they typically comment that "the future will be better" and that "things are gonna get better, if not tomorrow then the next day." Seeing others in difficult situations makes them feel extremely lucky. By comparison, their situation does not seem too bad. They take nothing for granted, believing life is too fragile to waste. They appreciate life, treating it delicately and respectfully, elevating the "value" in life. The important things are "loving, caring, and sharing with one another."

Like Fatalists, Spectators believe in a fateful existence marked by an underlying order. Since fate determines the order, and life consists of situations beyond human control, people of both orientations do not feel responsible for taking action. Knowing that an omnipotent force guides them is most satisfying. Fate, order, and control interconnect in the form of a powerful force outside the person, which directs life. Unlike Fatalists, however, Spectators' belief in order does not make them pessimistic. While Fatalists resign themselves to what happens, Spectators happily coexist with their fate. They cannot change fate, so they accept what happens.

Spectators typically find jobs working with the public. Helping others is a hobby. They like to help because it makes them feel useful. They will put their own work down to help someone else and feel pride in how well they work with people. Helping others helps them understand themselves, keep their minds off their problems, and appreciate how fortunate they are.

Spectators seem to have a special insight into death. As you read the chapter you will find stories about how each person survives the death of someone close. It seems that Spectators learned that how one looks at death influences how one copes with life. One never knows when one might die, when one's loved ones might die, or even when one might be touched by a stranger's death. Spectators do not like to waste valuable time.

With a clear vision of where death fits into the scheme of things, Spectators cope knowing that death is part of a predetermined plan, part of a natural progression. The inevitability of death is another reason they believe one should not take life for granted. Understanding Spectators' special insight into death may be the key to understanding their character since it influences so many other dimensions of their lives.

As I mentioned in the last chapter, I treat each interview as a metaphoric text, showing how the life metaphor relates to the life orientation. The presentation of people's stories throughout the book is guided by their ratings on the active and positive dimensions.[11] You will find out how these dimensions interact in a person's life and discover what makes someone an Antagonist or a Fatalist. Each life metaphor entails an implicit organization and an intricate set of assumptions. I have selected passages from the texts of the interviews that show the impact of the life metaphor on a person's view of reality.[12] Every metaphor does not have a detailed analysis; instead one finds passages which contribute to understanding each person's life orientation.

CHAPTER 3

The Antagonist

> We repeat old stories over and over, like a
> repetition compulsion, a spiraling circle, a web
> in which we trap ourselves.
>
> Edward Sampson, *Ego at The Threshold.*

> He that wrestles with us strengthens our
> nerves, and sharpens our skill. Our antagonist
> is our helper.
>
> Edmund Burke, *Reflections on the
> Revolution in France.*

Antagonists think of themselves as energetic fighters committed to a life of conflict, confronting daily life as if it were a battle.
Most of their lives, they have been taught that life is hard and
they must fight for what they want. Antagonists relate to the
world as if it were a struggle, an idea so entrenched that it has
become a self-fulfilling prophecy: the message creates the expectation, and the expectation creates the reality. Everywhere they
look, Antagonists find reasons to be negative, and they see no
reason to change.

The purpose of many dramatic plots in literature and drama is
to create friction and disharmony, which can be achieved effectively through the character of an antagonist. Pitted against the
main character, the protagonist, the antagonist's presence creates
stress between the characters and produces conflict in the plot.
As the story unfolds the antagonist helps lay the groundwork for
the tension, which must later be resolved. The antagonist provides
contrast, giving added meaning and poignancy to the protagonist's

plight by amplifying the character's dignity and power and other admirable traits.

Shakespeare's plays are full of antagonists, acting as foils to the main character, who represent the opposite of the hero or heroine. In *Hamlet*, King Claudius (the antagonist) incites Hamlet (the protagonist) to avenge his father's death. Plagued by procrastination, Hamlet finally confronts Claudius by devising a play, which reenacts his father's death. Claudius creates the pressure necessary to permit Hamlet to take action and do the right thing.

Through the narrative, the audience establishes bonds with the characters and is eager for the antagonist to receive his or her just reward. Because antagonists are so openly hostile and provocative, we want them to be punished accordingly. In Hamlet's case, we want Claudius to be shown up for the fraudulent murderer that he is. We want retribution for his killing Hamlet's father and for marrying and deceiving Hamlet's mother.

Everyday Antagonists are not as evil as such dramatic characters as Claudius, but they possess similar traits. Antagonists live in a world of spiraling negative expectations, which form their frame of reference. Based on the assumption that life consists of problems and obstacles, Antagonists expect adversity from life, just as they expect to encounter resistance from other people.

Antagonists demonstrate their activity through their hard-working nature. Their approach to work is pragmatic—work means money, which means that the bills are paid. For most, there is little personal reward, and they separate their work from their personal life. In addition to paying the bills, money represents an idealized vision. With money, they would not be so antagonistic. Money, representing freedom, is linked to their struggles and their dreams. Nothing in life is free or given away without implications: "everything costs something."

Antagonists can be characterized by an aggressive perseverance. They keep on trying despite the expectation that life will not improve. In spite of the unfairness and the inequity they see everywhere, they believe they can never give up. Part of their plight means continuing the fight. Antagonists possess a dream or a vision of a way out, which helps make life bearable.

Generally suspicious of others' motives, Antagonists are untrusting. They seldom accept anything at face value, making even friendship a precarious undertaking. They have even been let down by their families which adds to their disillusionment. On the whole, Antagonists believe they have to rely on their own resources.

Rarely passive about anything, Antagonists speak out when their personal rights are violated. Their sense of fairness forces them to stand up for themselves and others who are less fortunate. They are passionate about protecting their identity and refuse to take abuse from anyone.

Defined as "active opposition," antagonism reflects blatant animosity. The Antagonist combines a negative attitude with an active approach. Within the present series of interviews, these ratings are the most extreme in the negative direction. Overall, the Antagonist represents a relatively small portion of society. Of the forty-six people I interviewed, only six are classified as Antagonists.[1] This is not too surprising since we typically expect active people to be positive rather than negative in outlook.

Each person's life unfolds through selections from the interviews. The chapter begins with a discussion of Harry, a factory worker, who thinks life is like "a straight line." Next is Rick, a Vietnam veteran, whose life metaphor ("what you make it") carries antagonistic overtones. Phil, an active Jehovah's Witness, forecasts doom and believes life is "deteriorating." Becky, the aging massage parlor worker, thinks "life stinks." Dennis, the rigid fire fighter, likens life to a "military game." Finally there is Dave, a laid-off factory worker, who has a temporary job in an adult bookstore. He thinks life is like "a chess game." Starting with Harry, the chapter shows how Antagonists make their ways through life.

Harry: "A Straight Line"

Life is like a straight line. It never ends until you're dead. . . . You know you just gotta keep going. You can't let things bother you. . . . Life sucks. . . . Everybody's got their problems. . . . As long as you got problems, it's gotta be hell.

I thought a factory would be a good place to talk to people. It was appealing because I wondered how someone copes with the monotony of the routine. How does a person keep going back?

What could I understand about the invisible people who work in factories? My interview with Harry, a worker in a grain factory, begins to answer these questions.

The factory stands at the south end of town in a reputedly dangerous area. It is separated from the rest of the community and located in an old, wooden building that looks like it should be condemned. Like most factories, it shows constant signs of activity, although the movement seems more mechanical than human. Trucks pull in and out, smoke streams from the chimneys, wheels turn, and generators pound. In the daylight it looks desolate and alienating. At night it seems strange and surreal.

I went to a local tavern where the workers go at quitting time. The dark bar contrasted sharply with the brightness of the day outside. It was very quiet, as there were only a few people inside. I introduced myself to the bartender in a voice loud enough for everyone to hear. I asked if anyone would be interested in being interviewed. Harry, who had just finished work and was feeling good, volunteered.

Harry, twenty-seven, has worked in the same factory for seven years. He was the least positive and the most active individual I interviewed. He was also the most volatile. He struggles fiercely to survive and frequently uses images of death to describe life. He fights for life as a matter of daily survival.

Harry works as a meal transfer operator, which means: "You grind the product up and you load it. You just push buttons and let the equipment do the work." He had few positive things to say about the job. The Antagonist typically dissociates himself from his work because it brings little personal satisfaction. "It's just a job and you gotta put up with it. That's it. I just do it. I put in my eight hours and leave. You got responsibilities. There ain't no way you can back out of them. After I leave here, the shop's done."

Not surprisingly, Harry complains about management. He hates the system but he needs it. He needs something to work against; something to fight. "I buck the system. I don't like the system. The system's not right. That's why this plant's in bad shape. They need a lot of new equipment. I been preaching for seven years, and they come up with anything they could to try and fire me. But luckily the union stood behind me, and I got my job back."

Harry works shifts. Although the night shift is the best paying, it is the most demanding.

> Your eleven-to-seven or your twelve-to-eight is the worst. I work four weeks one shift, four weeks another shift. It tears you up. Tears you up. Can't get your sleep down. No way. Like this friend of mine. I'm twenty-seven, so he's probably twenty-nine. And he looks like he's thirty-nine. The doctor told him shift work will put twenty years on you.

Harry describes the effect of working the night shift with images of "tearing." His language mirrors his attitude; "ripping," "destroying," "demolishing," and "injuring" reflect his destructive perspective.

In many cases factory work is not only physically unhealthy for a person, but can injure mental health. Harry worries about losing his temper. According to him, he works with "a bunch of backstabbers." The conditions of the plant and the monotony of the job add to the problem. He believes any one of these things could "set" him off in a minute. He uses explosive, fiery language to describe the rage that burns inside him. The torment is real. He knows he needs to keep his temper under control.

> When I get that mad I usually go out and get drunk. I try and find a real good close friend of mine where I can talk to him, you know. Or I get mad enough where I gotta hit somebody. It's that simple. I just go out and pick a fight with somebody. It's usually a bar. . . . It's *always* a bar. I go someplace where I don't frequent very much, you know. And I make sure there ain't too many people there. I feel real good after that.

There have been fights, and there have been confrontations with the law, but so far none has been too serious. Harry believes he has been lucky to stay out of jail. The physical fighting complements the psychological fighting. Studs Terkel identifies violence as a part of everyday life in the introduction to his book *Working:*

> This book, being about work, is, by its very nature, about violence—to the spirit as well as to the body. It is about ulcers as well as accidents, about shouting matches as well as fistfights, about nervous breakdowns as well as kicking the dog around. It is, above all (or beneath all), about daily humiliations. To survive

the day is triumph enough for the walking wounded among the
great many of us.[2]

Not all Antagonists are as actively negative as Harry. He is the
most physically aggressive of the six I interviewed. Typically the
Antagonist expresses his frustration through psychological rebellion and emotional fighting. The tendency to move towards
physical violence characterizes the *extremely* active and *extremely* negative individual.

The Antagonist has a deep sense of alienation. He believes he
cannot count on anyone. Harry expresses his isolation by saying,
"You have to look out for yourself all your life. You got to cover
your butt. 'Cause if you don't do it, you're dead." He is dramatic,
perhaps extreme, but he believes what he says. He will die before
his time if he is not careful.

Harry values friendship. One of the basics in life is having "a
shoulder to cry on. 'Cause if you ain't got a friend, you ain't got
nothin.' That's basically what all this means." He recalls the
words of his favorite aunt: "You only have one true friend in your
whole life. My aunt told me that years ago. You have a lot of
friends. But you only have one true friend in your life time. And
I believe her. She was a smart lady. She taught me a lot."

Harry seems to contradict himself. On the one hand, he believes
he cannot depend on people, since no one can be trusted. On the
other hand, he believes he must have at least one friend for personal validation. He wants to protect himself and save face if
anything happens. Harry copes with success and failure in life by
holding ambivalent views.

Although Harry had never thought about a life metaphor before,
he was quite articulate and passionate in his answer.

> Couldn't say it was a merry-go-round. 'Cause the ends never
> meet. I don't know. Life is like a straight line. It never ends.
> Until you're dead. You know? The ends never meet, 'cause it's
> just a straight line. There's always a lot of obstacles that you're
> gonna find. You got to. 'Cause if you don't, you're gonna be
> down. I mean you're gonna stop dead. You're gonna die. And
> you're gonna be nothin'. You just gotta keep goin'. You can't let
> things bother you. You gotta try and put it out of your mind.
> . . . Well to me, you gotta keep going forward. You don't wanna
> make no turns, 'cause if you make a turn you're gonna be off

course. And you're not gonna go any further. So you just stay on a straight line. Sure, you're gonna run into some obstacles. But it's just temporary. There's gonna be some obstacles but you gotta jump back on track.

In trying to explain that life is like a straight line, he starts out by saying that it is not a merry-go-round. On a merry-go-round there are no boundaries—no beginning and no end. The ends meet to form a circle. On a straight line, however, there is a distinct beginning and an ending. The ends literally never meet. There is also something frivolous about a merry-go-round, whereas a straight line sounds more serious. Later in his explanation, Harry contrasts the direction of a merry-go-round with that of a straight line: on a straight line, one goes "forward"; on a merry-go-round, one goes in circles.

"The ends never meet," is also a cliché, which can refer to one's financial situation. When people complain that "the ends never meet" they usually mean that no matter how hard they work, they cannot earn enough money to cover expenses. Clearly, the cliché implies that life is a struggle.

Harry expects problems. He anticipates difficulties and counts on obstacles. He prepares himself for anything life offers. His general attitude towards life is not very positive. "It sucks. Everybody's got their problems. Like I said before, whether it's money, or whether it's your marriage, everybody's got their problems. If there was no problems it wouldn't suck. But as long as you got a problem, it's gotta be hell."

The Antagonist uses a number of strategies to cope. First, he ignores inconsistent information. If something disagrees with his frame of reference or interferes with his perception of the world, he puts it out of his mind. The way Antagonists actively try to not let things bother them illustrates this strategy. Harry quickly chooses not to worry about things if he assumes they cannot be changed.

Second, the Antagonist copes by remembering responsibilities. Without his memory, Harry has no guide, no conscience, and no advisor to direct him. If he forgets his responsibilities he gets off track, falls off the "straight line," and becomes overwhelmed by his problems. He cannot cope and the consequences are devastating. "You get to thinkin' about your responsibilities. That's

the main thing. You can't forget them. I mean, sure you can go
to sleep. But they're gonna be there when you wake up. There
ain't no way of avoiding your responsibilities, no way at all."
   Each Antagonist has different responsibilities. It is not the responsibility per se, but facing the responsibility that helps him.
As much as Harry would like to forget his obligations he cannot.
He has been married and divorced twice and has a child from each
relationship.

> I got two kids. One lives just about twenty-five miles west of
> here. And the other lives out in Iowa. I go out and get her every
> summer. And then I go down and pick my son up. And we spend
> the summer together. Go camping, you know. . . . They're with
> their mothers. . . . They each have different mothers. . . . I been
> married twice.

He pays child support and alimony to both families. They constitute his inescapable responsibilities. If he ignores these duties
he will be held in contempt of court and possibly face other charges.
The risk is too great to forget his commitments.
   Money emerges as a recurrent preoccupation with each Antagonist. When Harry says, "I know what money means," he speaks
for all Antagonists. The phrase works on a number of levels. *Means*
refers to a definition. We say that something has a meaning. *Means*
also refers to money, property, or wealth, as in the phrase "she
has independent means." *Means* is also a way of getting what we
want, as in the phrase "a means to an end." By saying he "knows
what money means," Harry implies each of these significations.
   The preoccupation with money intrudes on Harry's earliest
childhood memories.

> My mom's the one that taught me how to play ball. She was
> with me all the time. My dad always had two jobs to make ends
> meet and everything. She's the one that taught me right from
> wrong. She was always there. My dad, he was never there. You
> know, I only got to see him on Sundays. . . . My family always
> had a business of their own. They had a bar since Prohibition.
> I grew up in a bar. It was interesting, 'cause my dad never really
> drank. Strictly business. My grandpa too. When I was in kin-
> dergarten, I would go to the storeroom and lay down on a case
> of beer and go to sleep. My mom, she always worked in the
> kitchen. They struggled real hard. So I know what money means.

> And I know what you can buy with it. And I know what you can't. I know if I ever have a lot of money, I'm gonna get custody of my kids right away.

Harry knows what money means from having seen his family struggle. His father, who tried to "make ends meet," attempted to teach his son the same lesson. But experience taught Harry that the ends never meet, no matter how hard you work. He watched his father work hard and suffer a debilitating heart attack, which Harry believes was caused by too much work. No amount of money can salvage the loss of activity and the change in his father's life. Inevitably, Harry developed his work ethic from his family.

> You can't be lazy. You gotta work. You gotta work all your life. But you don't necessarily have to work hard at it. Just make ends meet. Well right now I'm at the plant. I don't wanna be there all my life. I'd like to make somethin' out of myself. But if it don't happen, it don't happen. Dad worked for forty dollars a week. I make three hundred. It don't mean nothin'. Money don't mean nothin' at all. My mom always told me that.

While Harry vows he will not be like his father, he continues to work the night shift and lives a life that "tears" him up emotionally and physically. Even though he says "the ends never meet," he struggles to try to make them meet.

Later in the interview, after thinking about how he manages his life, Harry uses another life metaphor:

> What can you do? You can't change it. There's nothin' you can do to change it. You just gotta go with the flow. You know, you're on the straight line. If that flow goes to the right, you're gonna have to go, you know, until you find some place where you can cross. Just like a river. You gotta go with the flow. If it goes to your right, you gotta go. You try and go to the left, you're gonna drown. . . . There's obstacles all along the way. And if that sucker turns right you gotta go with it until it comes back. Well, life's a river. Instead of a straight line, it's like a river. You gotta go with the flow. You come home free. If you don't you're gonna drown.

To "go with the flow" means freedom; to go against the flow means death. Harry copes with life by simply accepting its conditions because nothing can be done to change the course of events.

Even though he knows he cannot change his life, he dreams of a way out. The dream helps him cope. He eagerly talks about his vision of another world where problems are minimized and he lives happily. Although he says he does not need money, he believes that it would make his dream come true. Harry gets a faraway look in his eyes as he talks about what it would be like to have money.

> I dream about gettin' the lottery. A bunch of money to where I can take my kids. Buy a Winnebago. Hire me a tutor. And take off for five years. And I wanna go to Ireland. That's where my ancestors are from and where I wanna go. Cork County Ireland. I've already read about it in the *National Geographic*. My sister traced the family tree for a school project. That's my dream.

Rick also has a dream of returning to a normal life. Fighting in Vietnam changed his entire outlook, his personality, and his relationships. Although he manages better now than when he first returned, he still suffers the nightmares of the war, and not a day passes that he does not think about it.

Rick: "What You Make It"

> *I really believe what you are and what you end up, after a period of time, is what you put into it. . . . I know what has to be done each day and what it takes to do it. . . . In the last four or five years I've been able to deal with it [Vietnam] a little better. It's still tough.*

Rick has been in the restaurant business for twenty years. Four years ago he bought his own restaurant, which he now operates. He is thirty-five and the fifteen months he spent in Vietnam changed his life radically. Only in the past few years has he been able to cope with many of the issues he was forced to confront. With the help of a local support group, Rick has been able to get himself back on his feet and direct his life in a healthy way.

He is a very serious man, laughing only once during the interview. He looks directly at me as he answers, speaking slowly and deliberately, structuring his replies carefully and emphasizing particular words. His pace, which reflects his personality, is both thoughtful and forceful. He is extremely articulate, and he punctuates his speech precisely.

Rick finds working in the restaurant business extremely satisfying. On one level, work represents his ability to guide his own destiny. It is not so much the work he enjoys, as the fact that he owns the business. The whole Vietnam experience created a sense of utter helplessness for him. He had little control over anything associated with the war: he had no choice about going and he had no choice about fighting. Killing people was a matter of survival. Once he was there, he had no way out. Buying the business helped restore his faith in himself and brought him in touch with a world in which people have a measure of control over their lives. "What I like about this place is that I own it. It's for me. So all the time and effort I put into it is for me. It's what I want to do. If you work for someone else it's a thankless job."

Rick underscores his contempt for the war by describing Vietnam as a "thankless job." In this metaphor, he associates essentially negative qualities with the war, just as one does with a thankless job. Vietnam was not for him: he did not work for himself; he received no thanks when he was there or when he returned; and the effort he put into the war gave him no personal satisfaction. The pleasure his present job gives him is the antithesis of his dissatisfaction with Vietnam. Owning his business represents more than a job. It represents the positive things in life: he owns it; the time and effort is for him; it is what he wants; and it brings personal satisfaction.

On another level, Rick likes the fact he owns the business because it gives him independence. He can get away whenever he wants. Sometimes his memories of the war overwhelm him so much that he needs to take a break without having to give any explanations or reasons. "If this thing occasionally builds up to where I gotta get away, I can do that and not draw attention to it. If you work for somebody else, they don't understand it."

Finally, he copes by working. Rick gets more satisfaction from his work than the typical Antagonist because he knows that it gives him a healthy way to occupy his time. He does not want to be tormented by his thoughts, and working occupies his time and his mind. "I just work. I know what has to be done here, so that keeps me pretty well occupied. . . . As long as I keep busy, keep my mind occupied. That's been the best therapy for me, working fourteen hours a day. It doesn't bother me. But I don't take vacations. I can't."

People usually take vacations to relax and forget about everything, but not Rick. If he has too much spare time, he thinks about the war and all of the problems associated with it. He gets angry and frustrated and the tension builds. He feels self-destructive. Public holidays are the most difficult times.

> They're like having a birthday, but you couldn't participate. Memorial Day, Veterans Day, the Fourth of July. I know they're coming up. I know that they bother me. So now I'm involved in this group and we confront it—parades, all that kind of stuff. And it seems to help a little more than it did before. Before, I never went to any parades. I never was around anybody else. A lot of times, on Memorial Day, I'd just take off in my car or motorcycle or something and just be alone. It was something, like most people, World War II vets, and Korean vets look forward to. We didn't.

Antagonists tend to rely only on themselves—Rick is no exception. Like Harry, he believes he can only count on himself. When he returned from the war, facing many problems, friends and family abandoned him. He sought counseling from a Veteran's Administration hospital but found the help inadequate. After going for over a year he eventually realized it was up to him to change.

> I was there to be helped, not to help other people. So finally, after about a year and a half, I came to the conclusion that if I felt like being helped, I'd better do it myself. You can't rely on anybody. The government. They'd all let me down again. And your own people do after a while—friends, relatives—because they don't want to be confronted with something they don't know. It scares them to be around you, so they stay away from you.

Rick remembers coming home from Vietnam wanting to feel like a hero. He had spent the last fifteen months defending his country. His feelings of pride quickly changed as he saw people's reactions. After awhile, he could not bring himself to admit he had even been in the war. "When I first came home, I was proud of it. And then after a couple of months, when somebody you ran into who hadn't seen you in a while, they'd say 'where have you been?' I'd tell them, 'Oh, I was out in California for a couple of years.' Just to stop that. It was like telling them you had cancer."

When you tell someone you have cancer, you immediately become stigmatized.[3] You become marked by the label. The stigma of cancer equals the stigma of Vietnam. Cancer, like Vietnam, is taboo. It is not talked about, and it is avoided if possible. The label evokes other associations. Cancer is a disease. Vietnam is a disease. When you have cancer you become a "victim." In many ways, if you fought in Vietnam, you were also a "victim." You need treatment, psychological and physiological. Indeed, the cancer metaphor is extremely powerful because cancer is a major devil term in modern society that conjures up associations of unrelenting evil and pain.

Rick's denial of being in Vietnam parallels many cancer patients' denials of their diagnoses. Just as Rick tells people he was out in California, so does the cancer patient conceal the truth. Both want no one to know their secrets because they fear the reaction. The inclination is to hide the pain and remove the outward signs.

The metaphor is especially potent because it provides a dual perspective. The emphasis on the "telling" part of the metaphor explains the interaction between Rick and the public. The subject is a difficult one for the receiver. When people tell us that they have cancer or that they were in Vietnam, most of us do not know how to react or what to say. These subjects still arouse fears.

Rick feels removed from society at a deeply personal level: "I've lived in neighborhoods and worked with people before that I didn't know were Vietnam vets. And they didn't know I was. Just because you didn't want anybody to know." He senses the fear that people project onto him. The whole experience represents an enormous, ongoing struggle. "It really hurts you mentally. It takes a long time to recover from it. I've just now, in the last four or five years, been able to deal with it a little better. It's still tough sometimes. . . . Very seldom a day goes by that you're not confronted with it."

Rick has a clear philosophy about what the war means, why it happened, and who caused it. Although his personal analyses are endless, he does not voice them in public very often. Instead, he shares them with a local support group. He tries to leave the pain and frustration and anger at the meetings, rarely discussing the war outside that safe environment. More than anything, he appreciates the feeling that he is not alone. The group helps him cope. "It's a local chapter of Vietnam Veterans of America. We get together mainly for a social type of thing. You get together with people who've had the same experiences. We all understand each other. It's just a lot easier to accept. You know that you're not the only one like that."

Like Harry, Rick describes experience in terms of life and death. Both are survivors who work to overcome the threat of death. However, Rick believes that perfection was the only thing that kept him alive, and now he relies on it for daily survival.

> I'm more of a perfectionist than I ever was before, because perfection keeps you alive. If you didn't do things right, perfect, the way they were supposed to be done, you were dead. You didn't survive. It would come down to doing your job. You couldn't be thinking about something else. You can't do that. Because you don't get a second chance. That's why I deal with precision. I like things done exactly the way I do it. And I base almost my whole life and my family on that.

Rick demands perfection from those close to him, including his staff, and he manages the restaurant efficiently. "I know what has to be done each day and what it takes to do it, so that has to be done first." He believes his method is necessary and correct. "I can tell you exactly the way to do it, the easiest, most efficient way. And I'll explain it to you so you know how. So there's no reason for you to do it any other way. If you don't do it that way and mess up, that irritates me. Because there is no reason. I make things as easy as possible for you."

Rick's dogmatism creates complications for his wife and two sons. He knows his obsession causes problems and he tries to control himself at home. He does not react with physical violence, as Harry does, but emotionally. With his wife's help, Rick copes with that dimension of his life. He describes his wife as a very special person who consistently gives him the understanding he so greatly needs. "A lot of times it was a lot more than my wife could handle. The biggest part of it has to do with her. If I had not met her, and she's the person she is, I would not have turned out the way I am now."

Rick's memory of returning from Vietnam helps him cope with the present. The thought of living the way he did when he first came home terrifies him. He was tormented by guilt, questions, lack of acceptance, and alienation. It drove him to alcohol. "I have the memory of what I can be like. An alcoholic. Don't really care about anything. Family, friends, tomorrow. There's no worry, no pain. And I have that in the back of my mind all the time. It works probably eighty to eighty-five percent."

Rick uses the memory of what he used to be like as a way of making it through the present. There are times, however, when this strategy fails, and he questions how he will survive. At such times he needs to be alone. "There's still some bad times. I get away by myself. It's the easiest way. Because if there's anybody around to argue with or ask questions or to have to justify something to, it usually just ends up in a fight or an argument. So if I just get away by myself, it eventually goes away."

The Antagonist often deals with problems by ignoring them. Occasionally, Rick chooses to forget about his difficulties. Like Harry, he believes that avoiding the issue helps it disappear. Just as Harry believes he must keep going forward on the river, Rick believes he must always look ahead. "I always look forward. I don't think much about the past. Except when I have to. I build for the future, and the past is done. There's really nothing you can change."

Although Rick feels he has recovered the self-confidence the government took away, he has not lost his anger. He believes "kids are drafted at eighteen to twenty-one years old because they're easy to brainwash and it's easy to change their morals." Learning to kill changes an individual's entire moral structure. Right and wrong become blurred, good and bad become indistinguishable. Values are lost and forfeited.

Like Harry, responsibilities anchor Rick, and in Vietnam, his responsibilities were the men under his command. He was obligated to protect them.

> I was the squad leader. I had several men under me, and I never lost a man. A few wounded, but never any killed. In fifteen months. And I know that that's because I did my job one hundred and ten percent all the time. And they knew it. That's why whenever I went on patrol, I had no problems whatsoever.

Part of the problem with Vietnam is the difficulty the veterans have making their experience understood. One of Rick's greatest complaints is the lack of understanding people have about what happened.

> There's a lot of people that say they care. But it's still something that I can't explain to you, because you'll never understand. You'll never feel it. And in relation to something, maybe that's easier to understand. It's like your best friend tells you that they have cancer and that they are gonna die in a year. What do you say to them? You can feel for them. You can cry for them. You can pray for them. But you never know what that feels like. Until it happens to you.

When I asked Rick to describe what Vietnam was like for him, he was adamant that I would not understand. Why should he bother to explain? It was pointless. He had tried many times. People simply did not understand. Rick was angry about being misunderstood by the American public. In his mind, attempts to explain the war to people who had not experienced it were useless.

> I can tell you experiences, I can tell you visions that are wrong, and everything else. But it still doesn't mean anything because you don't know how it feels. You don't know how it feels to be out in the jungle at night and hear things and have that adrenaline going through you, as if someone is here to kill me, or is it friendly? Or what am I doing here? Is this what it's all about? Is this life? You know? All these things go through your mind constantly. And then you go and take somebody else's life and see them lay there. And say "I wonder if he hated this as much as I do." You don't know how that feels. So you can't understand. That's the whole problem with everyone who came home. You can listen, and you can write books, but you can't feel it. Unless you were there. My wife has gone through a wholesale meat house up north, and she was robbed at gunpoint. She knows what it's like to be in question of her life. Is this the end? Is he gonna pull the trigger? Here's a person I don't know, but he wants something, and he's gonna do anything he can to get it. She knows what that feels like, and she went through hell and still has nightmares about it. And that's just one incident. Now, could you handle that every day of your life? For fifteen months? You have to compensate and learn to live with yourself and you have to make different morals in life. I guess that's one thing that really hurts. You have to change your morals. No matter

what you believe in. Because once you're there, it's a live or die situation. If you don't want to go with the system, fine. But you're gonna die. And if you stay with the system, then you'll stay alive. You may lose an arm, you may lose a leg, or an eye, or be screwed up the rest of your life mentally, but you'll live. So you have to make that decision.

In telling me what I could not understand and what I could not know, Rick explained what Vietnam meant. He described what the war was like and how he felt most eloquently. As he said, a person may never truly understand Vietnam without having been there, but hearing Rick's story helps one come closer to knowing. In telling the story, he actively organized meaning in such a way that the experience was made understandable for himself and me. In the process of telling the story, he was coping with what happened there.

Survivors of devastating events, natural disasters, and personal tragedies stress the need to speak about their tragedies. Terence Des Pres recounts such stories in his book *The Survivor.*[4] The Holocaust, for example, is a tragic tribute to human survival in its most extreme form. For many of the survivors, the goal of their struggle was to live to tell about the horror. Des Pres quotes one survivor, Nadezhda Mandelstam, who wrote that "it later turned out that there were people who made it their aim not only to save themselves, but to survive as witnesses."[5] A survivor of Treblinka stated that "I had to live, to give the world the story of this depravity, this bestial depravity."[6] Another survivor of Dachau wrote:

> The SS guards took pleasure in telling us that we had no chance in coming out alive, a point they emphasized with particular relish by insisting that after the war the rest of the world would not believe what happened; there would be rumors, speculations, but no clear evidence, and people would conclude that evil on such a scale was just not possible.[7]

Des Pres suggests that survival grew out of the individual's "passionate will to preserve the memory of the horror he has witnessed."[8] Those who experienced the nightmare could not let the Nazis get away with it. The survivors could not let the story be buried in the mass graves. That would be an even greater injustice. Des Pres argues forcefully that "the final guilt is not to bear witness. The survivor's worst torment is not to be able to speak."[9] They had to survive. They had to speak.

To tell the story and bear witness helps the person cope with what happened. Part of the terror for veterans following Vietnam was their inability to speak about it. Rick, and many other veterans, were denied that catharsis. They were tormented by the lack of understanding and acceptance by the American public. They were deprived of the thing that might have helped them cope better. Given these circumstances, it is not surprising that so many veterans suffer post-traumatic stress disorders.

The foregoing components contribute to Rick's life metaphor. "Life is what you make it. I really believe that what you are, and what you end up, after a period of time, is what you put into it. So after a period of ten years, if you don't put something into life, you won't get anything out of it." At first glance, this statement does not seem to be a life metaphor. Yet how can we understand this literally? When we look at it more closely, we realize that Rick means the phrase metaphorically. He perceives a relation of equivalence between individual effort and life. "What you make it" equals "what you put into it." When Rick did not put anything into life, it was a hopeless mess. He was an alcoholic with no direction or purpose. He reached a point when he realized he needed to turn things around and change his life. He made it entirely different. Owning the restaurant demonstrates to Rick that if he puts work into life, then he will get tangible rewards, just as putting energy into his group meetings gives him peace.

"Life is what you make it" is not the exclusive property of the Antagonist. As we will see in the next section, the Enthusiast uses the same expression. Indeed, I found that "what you make it" was the most frequently used life metaphor. Enthusiasts believe that they have the capacity to turn negative experiences into positive ones. Antagonists assume life is hard and accept the status quo without trying to change anything. Spectators treat life delicately and cannot understand why others do not treat it the same way. Fatalists are least likely to believe that "life is what you make it" since they believe in predestined order with little room for personal control.

Rick believes people need what he was denied—understanding.

Understanding is what people need most. And a lot of communication. That's the most important thing that marriages need. In fact, without it, you have nothing. You have no marriage. You have no life. You have no future. If you're not able to deal with what happens to you, and change that, or want to change it, you really have nothing, and never will.

When he equates communication with life, he is speaking both metaphorically and literally. In Vietnam, a lack of communication or miscommunication meant possible death. Effective communication prolonged life. Like Vietnam, everyday life has situations that depend on communication. A marriage, for example, will not survive if there is no communication; the relationship will die. On the other hand, if there is communication, the relationship will thrive. Rick knows it is difficult to survive in a world without understanding. He has survived using communication—with his platoon in Vietnam, with his wife, with his children, and with his support group.

Perhaps the most frightening issue Rick faces concerns his identity. "Sometimes I have trouble sorting out, 'Is this really me?' or 'Would I have done it the same way had I not been in Vietnam?'" He knows the answer: "I can look back at the last fifteen years and figure out, 'Yeah, I did this because I was in Vietnam. It's not really me.' And it's a lot easier to accept now." Rick copes with life knowing he is a different person from the one who did not go to Vietnam. He wonders about what he might have been like, but he does not dwell on it. He will never really know that other person. He is a realist who believes "you only have one life. You do the best you can with what you got."

He believes he "never lost consciousness" with himself. He retained a quiet strength, which was "part of the real Rick." He believes his strong sense of self kept him from going crazy. Regardless of Vietnam, that part of him would have turned out the same.

One of the positive results of the war is that Rick learned about his identity. He knows who he is and acquired an inner power from this understanding. He uses Vietnam as a metaphor for learning to discover oneself:

One thing I can really look back and enjoy about Vietnam, the one good thing that happened to me is that I met myself. I know myself. I know what I'm capable of and what I can do. And very few people know that. They go through their whole life, and know a lot of people but they don't even know theirself. But I know what kind of a person I am. All the pressures and mental strain, physical strain that you go through. . . . I'm self-confident. I know now that if I set my mind to do something, I can do it. There's nothing to hold me back. If I want to do something, I'll do it. Someway, sometime, somehow. I'll accomplish it. And that comes from knowing yourself. Knowing how to reach that goal. And what you can put yourself through to get to it. So I never set goals that I can't reach. All my goals, I know, can be reached because I think them out before I ever reach that plateau. I never do anything that I know I can't do.

He says he wants to "get away from the city," live in the country, and "grow up with my boys and teach them life." I wondered what he meant by "teach them life."

I'm gonna teach them basics of life. How to survive. Things they'll have to deal with. Just general education. Why birds fly, why leaves fall off the trees. Simple things, you know. A lot of people go through life and don't even think about them. I think that's more important than college education and stuff life that. . . . I want my kids to learn to live with themself. And then meet theirself. See what they're capable of. And then you have to face the rest of your life on that. If you're not able to handle independence, you may be weak when it comes to being alone. You have to learn what you are before you're able to do anything. . . . I'm gonna tell them what happened to me. And why it happened. I hope there's no other wars. But I hope that they can relate that situation to their lives. It may not have to be as drastic as mine. Just knowing what I went through and what happened to me and how I've turned out. . . . I'll teach them basic skills. How to use their hands. You know, build things. Not to expect a lot from other people. Be able to do things yourself. Or at least have the knowledge of what it takes to do them. Mechanics. Why things work. No one ever explains those things to you. Simple things.

Just as Rick believes that life consists of simple values that fast-paced city life cannot give, so Phil resents being part of a disintegrating society. As a member of Jehovahs' Witnesses, Phil prophesies the impending demise of civilization.

Phil: "Deteriorating"

Life in general is deteriorating. It's going down the drain.
. . . All you can do is just grit your teeth and growl and
hang on and work. . . . We go door to door. I'm preaching
to you right now. . . .

I met Phil at a mall. He was sitting on a bench, and we talked
as we waited for his wife. He is seventy-four, retired, and spends
his time working on his home. He does all the remodeling and
decorating, including the plumbing, the electrical work, and the
carpentry. He tries to keep busy.

Phil worked for forty-seven years as an engineer in Detroit. He
recently moved away because he felt unsafe. "But I'm happy down
here. We're away from the crime. I can sit out in my yard without
being afraid of somebody running up and sticking a knife in my
back. And that means something to me."

The Antagonist trusts very few people and seriously doubts that
he can rely on others. He suspects people will take advantage of
him. Phil openly discusses his distrust. He believes "people are
not what they profess to be." After his life was threatened by
violence and crime, he felt forced to leave Detroit. The violence
and crime make him angry, and he still feels bitter.

> I learned that when I first went there it was a nice place to live
> and work. Conditions have deteriorated. Detroit used to be the
> motor capital of the world. It'll never be the motor capital of
> the world again. Working conditions are not what they were.
> Things are bad. They call it "murder city." That's the reason
> we moved out. It was getting so bad in our neighborhood that
> we had to sell out and get out.

Phil sees Detroit's deterioration as symptomatic of global deterioration. As a Jehovah's Witness he believes that problems in
the world will lead to its destruction. The religion prophesies
impending doom and its disciples actively preach beliefs that
endorse an essentially negative view of the world. Phil forecasts
an ominous future. He believes that people have fallen on evil
times and have sunk to the depths of depravity. His life metaphor
reflects the deterioration he sees in the world.

> Life is deteriorating. It's going down the drain. After Armaged-
> don, when the new order's established, there'll be a mess because

there'll be a lot of people killed. The wicked will be destroyed. There will be a lot of things that will be destroyed. It'll take seven years to clean up that mess. Then after that we start to study. And the dead will be resurrected. We have already studied that if we're good enough we'll be teachers. Teach them. There's a lot of people that's classed as unrighteous. Unrighteous doesn't mean that they are wicked. It means that they have never had a chance to know what Jehovah wants them to do. We'll have a chance to educate them. Then at the end of a thousand years, mankind will be educated to the point of perfection again. Like man started.

In this case, the life metaphor equally expresses beliefs about life and about religion. For Phil, they are one. He applies Jehovah's teachings to life and follows the doctrine literally. According to Jehovah, "Life is deteriorating," and Phil believes it.

In his book *Apocalypse Delayed: The Story of Jehovah's Witnesses*, M. James Penton records that the worldwide movement has 2.7 million active members in the United States.[10] Its sophistication matches that of any multinational corporation.

The Witnesses have established a highly sophisticated printing and publishing empire, have developed a world-wide missionary program, and a highly structured hierarchical organization to govern their community, all of which has been done by their principal legal association, the Watch Tower Bible and Tract Society of Pennsylvania.[11]

The religion imposes a rigid life-style on its members. The movement guides, directs, and disciplines them. The proponents are alienated from the rest of the world. Penton, himself a Witness, writes:

No major Christian sectarian movement has been so insistent on prophesying the end of the present world in such definite ways and on such definite dates as have Jehovah's Witnesses. . . . Since, for over a hundred years, the end of this world has been delayed for them—something which they never expected would happen—they have not been able to adjust satisfactorily to world events or to a world which, in their view, goes "groaning on."[12]

The struggle for perfection characterizes Jehovah's Witnesses. The path is difficult. They must pass through the "great tribulation" and wait for Armageddon, which will be the ultimate war, the global war, the war to end all wars. Then the new order will be established, which will bring salvation and perfection.

Again, the desire for perfection haunts Antagonists, providing a standard of judgment against which they evaluate life. While Phil and Rick differ in how they interpret perfection, both strive to achieve it. For Rick, one attains perfection if one follows a series of clearly specified directions and rules. He believes perfection keeps you alive. For Phil, the world must be destroyed before perfection can be reached. In the mean time, he believes people live in an imperfect state. "We're imperfect. We inherited imperfection from Adam and Eve. They didn't know how to behave. They thought that what they did wouldn't matter. They believed in Satan the Devil. And there are a lot of people today that believe in Satin the Devil."

Antagonists transcend a negative orientation with the help of dreams that preserve their lives and offer hope and a way out of a troubled world. Phil's sustaining vision is that he will survive the deteriorating conditions because he has a hope of living forever. "The Bible tells us that if we do what the Almighty God wants us to do we can live on through this terrible mess and he'll eventually straighten things out. In his new order, after Armageddon. And if we shape up and do what he wants us to do we can live forever. Do you believe that?"

Phil waits for God's order to be established. He endures the adversity of the present because he anticipates the glorious afterlife that awaits him. He copes because he believes in this vision. He faced difficult times in his life and remembers the early years as the hardest. "I guess when I got married the first time. I had to scratch to get along. And pay the mortgage and so forth." He managed. "Just grit your teeth and hang on and work. That's it." Today he still grits his teeth and endures life.

Phil criticizes people's obsession with worldly goods. He emphasizes that Jehovah's Witnesses operate on poverty. "There are no paid ministers. All the work is carried out on a contribution basis." He says he is not interested in wealth and commends his religion for its reliance on little money.

Surprisingly, Phil repeatedly uses monetary language. He urged me to visit a meeting because "it doesn't cost you a dime." When he finds fault with other religions, he comments, "If people don't get their ears tickled the right way, why there's no money in the plate." He checks himself, "Of course we don't have a plate." He remembers when he sold his house in Detroit: "It didn't disappoint me really because I happened to sell my house at the right time. I got top dollar for it, which I wouldn't have got if I'd have waited a little while."

He admits he could use some more money: "I'm happy with my second wife. I have two stepsons that I'm happy with. I could use a little more money, but I don't know how I'm gonna get it." For someone who professes to be uninterested in money, he seems preoccupied with the subject.

Phil's ambivalence about money is not surprising. Money preoccupies the Antagonist. It symbolizes a person's desires, wishes, and goals. It represents unattainable objects, such as freedom, security, and possessions. Money symbolizes the possibility of an alternative way of life. It belongs to the dream world.

Phil believes the Bible is the truth. He also believes that through most of his life he was indoctrinated. Like so many people, he was wrongly educated about the way of the Lord. He believes he succumbed to the misconceptions of ignorant people about the true way of Jesus Christ. By studying the Bible, he perceived many distortions. "Everything that I believe comes right out of the Bible. My wife started studying, and I finally sat in on the study and realized that a lot of the things I learned were distorted."

Phil now reeducates people as he was reeducated. He teaches the truth and helps others overcome their learned limitations. All the members believe they are ministers whose duty is to educate people. Just as the religion is founded on education, so the lives of its members are founded on their role as teachers.

Antagonists typically voice their opinions, and Phil demonstrates his outspokenness through his ministering. He likes to talk and he likes to argue. He takes every opportunity to preach to people, claiming during our interview "I'm preaching to you now." Religion keeps him going and energizes him. "Sometimes I feel like I was about fifty-five and raring to go out and tell people the news." By talking about the destitute state of the world, he fulfills a mission and finds a purpose. He teaches others and proudly goes door-to-door spreading the word. Ironically, the thought of the inevitable destruction of the world keeps him going.

Dennis is not as disillusioned about the future as he is about the past. He suffered personal losses as a child that changed his life. Although he accepts the tragedy and tries not to let his resentment build up, he cannot help but approach life bitterly.

Dennis: "A Military Game"

> *I think of the military. I thought of that as a game. And I won that game. . . . Life is a challenge. . . . It's like hitting your head against a brick wall. You back up and regroup and do it again. . . . I'm getting paid back for the things I lost when I was younger.*

Among the three people I interviewed who work at one of the main fire stations in town, Dennis is the only Antagonist. A captain at only twenty-nine, he is considered by his fellow officers young to hold such a senior position. He has an impeccable record, which he has worked hard to achieve.

Dennis' mother died when he was twelve, and his father died when he was fourteen. Although he does not think about them often, the memory of their loss is vivid.

> I, ah, lost both my parents when I was a teenager. My mother when I was twelve and my father when I was fourteen. So growing up was pretty tough. I got a brother a year and a half older and a sister five years older. And she more or less raised us. And I think, by us three kids sticking together, helped more than anything.

Dennis learned to rely on himself at an early age. "Most of the things I have to go out and get on my own. It's not like it was exactly handed to me. You gotta work for 'em. You gotta prove to somebody that you're worthy of them." The early tragedy influenced everything that was to happen in later life. The three children grew up quickly. Although they worked together, his sister took over as head of the family; he knows the deaths demanded a lot from her.

> It had to be a lot harder on her than us because it just didn't seem fair. A nineteen-year-old girl that had to play mother right off the bat. She had to do that even in high school, when she was seventeen and eighteen. So it was really tough on her. But

we pulled through it all. Once I got out of high school I didn't know what I wanted to do, I wasn't sure about goin' to school or not, so I thought I'd go in the service for a couple of years and give that a try. And I'm glad I did, I don't regret that at all.

The most difficult effect of his parents' death was the loneliness he felt as a teenager growing up without them. He missed the guidance they would have given.

Not having somebody really to turn to. We had a grandmother living in town at the time. And a lot of close friends from the family always kept track of us. If we had a problem we'd always go to them. But it was difficult. There was a lot of things I kept inside me. From age fourteen to seventeen, those three or four years, I just kind of don't think about. You know, they weren't bad. It's just difficult.

Dennis copes with this time by blocking it out of his mind. It is easier if he forgets. He is able to shut off his feelings and not think about things that bother him. This style of coping entails consciously ignoring something. Antagonists frequently use this strategy: they choose not to think about the hard times; they rationalize life as containing uncontrollable events; and they dismiss the what-would-it-have-been-like-if attitude held by many people.

Overall, Dennis has made remarkable progress in his life. He holds a senior position in the fire department with job security and a pension plan. He makes investments and owns property to insure his security in the future. He believes in a model of moral justice: "sometimes I wonder if I'm getting paid back this way for the things I lost when I was younger." He knows that no amount of restitution can bring his parents back. Nothing can make up for the loss he suffered from their untimely deaths. While he tries to put this behind him, it influences how he looks at life. He is not morbid, but he does not expect positive things from life either. He thinks it is unfair.

Recently, Dennis experienced another tragedy when his father-in-law died. He married young and adopted his father-in-law as his own father. "I lost my father-in-law. He was awful close to me, not having a father. I let him take my father's place, and came really close to him and he taught me a lot. I guess it's like an on-off switch. You just have to forget about it. You have to think about the good times and try not to feel sorry for yourself."

Dennis has thought much about dying. He makes his most negative statement about life as he considers what death is like: "I imagine it's peaceful. You hear people say 'pronounced dead.' That's about all that you can think. I don't know. As long as you think it's gotta be better than what we're going through now."

At eighteen, Dennis joined the marine corps wondering what to do with his life. It was a good environment for him and he prospered, learning how to climb the ranks quickly. He was promoted to squad leader and then to sergeant. Many of the skills he learned made a lasting impression on him. In fact, he explains his life metaphor in terms of his experiences in the military.

> A game. A military game. I won that game. It was funny the day I got out. Like I said before, I tried to do what I was told and get along, and I picked up rank pretty fast in the military. And I was sergeant within a year and a half. It's usually a three-year step, and the day I got out there was a gunnery sergeant asked me "what do you think of the military?" And I said, "well, it's kinda' like a game, and I feel like I've won." You know, so life is, it's a challenge. It's not a game 'cause it's not fun to play at all. There's a lot of rules I don't like. It's just like losing my parents when I was so young. But you've just gotta try to. I think you just have to try to win.

By describing life as a military game, Dennis implies that life is, at once, like a game and like the military. To understand the life metaphor we must discover how he relates to the military and what he thinks about games. The service taught Dennis much of what he knows about life. The few years he spent there provided him with valuable experiences that gave him confidence and brought him out of himself. It encouraged him to face the world at a time when he had grave self-doubts. The military indirectly helped him overcome the loss of his parents. He attributes his present success, professionally and personally, to the military. He believes the military helped him become the person he is today. Dennis uses the "military metaphor" to explain his present job, which for him resembles the service.

> The closest captain to me has nine years' seniority on me. I try to think of it like the military again and do a really good job.

And motivation's a big thing. The job motivates me. . . . That's
the way it was in the military too. I was in artillery, and we had
the best gun crew. I guess it's just self-satisfaction. The chief
must think something of me too. He put me in the hottest engine
house in the city. We make the most runs of the city. That's a
compliment. I don't know what makes me tick sometimes.

Dennis also associates his life metaphor with a game. A game
has a clearly defined pattern and structure. The military was a
game in which he did well. As he says, he feels that he won that
game. He transfers this positive experience to life in general, finding that life also provides the challenge of a game. A game must
be played according to rules. By following the rules, Dennis has
succeeded. He describes his time in the military: "I just tried to
do what I was told and keep my nose clean." Acquiescence to the
rules eliminates choice and provides a well-defined frame within
which to live. On the whole, Dennis likes to "go by the rules. I
learned that from the military." He is the kind of person who
likes the rigid structure of a disciplined life. Dennis appreciates
that the game of life is not always fun. The more serious and even
tragic parts of life are not pleasurable at all. He feels that he started
off trailing behind other players with the loss of his parents. But
his loss motivates him to win, and he struggles to balance that
loss.

In *Games People Play*, Eric Berne describes the way people play
games throughout their lives.[13] As children, we learn what games
to play and how to play them. As adults, we develop versatility
and acquire expertise in the games we play. Claude Steiner, one
of Berne's students, wrote *Scripts People Live*, in which he argues
that a person plays out an unconscious life plan called a script,
which is "the blueprint for a life course."[14] In each of these books,
the authors assume that the idea of a game provides an excellent
explanation for human behavior. Steiner states that "a *game* is a
behavioral sequence which (1) is an orderly series of transactions
with a beginning and an end; (2) contains an ulterior motive, that
is, a psychological level different from the social level; and (3)
results in a payoff for both players."[15]

The game metaphor has been discussed by a variety of scholars.
Michael Billig recently traced its progress as an explanation for
social life. In his book *Arguing and Thinking: A Rhetorical Ap-*

proach to Social Psychology, he summarizes how the metaphor works. "Social life, therefore, is more like a game, in which there are general rules which have to be obeyed; however, the rules provide the latitude for the players to develop their own individual strategies and styles of play." Billig treats rules as the salient characteristic of metaphor.[16] "The metaphor concentrates upon the importance of rules in games. The person playing a game follows certain rules and attempts to win the prize within the agreed framework of these rules. So it is with ordinary life: we follow the social rules."[17] Although Billig has in mind sports like football and baseball when he refers to games, he emphasizes the way metaphors "provide insight into the routines of everyday life and the properties of human cognitive processes."[18]

The game metaphor is the second-most frequently used in my study (the other is "what you make it"). Four people believe that life is like "a game," and it can be found in three of the groups. The Enthusiast wants to participate, the Antagonist suspects the play, and the Spectator wants to watch.

Not surprisingly, the Fatalist is the only group in which the game metaphor is absent. Intuitively, it is incongruous to imagine a Fatalist who thinks that life is like "a game." The idea seems too frivolous for the serious Fatalist. Also, a predetermined world precludes the role of chance, an essential element in games.

The game metaphor is extremely adaptable and can be applied by people in different ways. Its presence in three of the four groups suggests its versatility. It easily accommodates a variety of attitudes towards life. One person might be excited about the game and eager to play, while another might be overwhelmed by the rules and hesitant to play. Someone else might treat it as a joke and take nothing seriously.

Although Dennis describes life as a game, he is deadly serious when it comes to work. Being a fire fighter involves more than controlling fires. He must engage in practice drills, preventative maintenance, cleaning equipment, and studying manuals and textbooks. The inconsistency of the work causes physical problems.

> The only thing physically bad about this job is you go from sitting in a chair to full blast within five minutes, and that's just bad when that happens at nighttime. Dead asleep and the

next thing you know you're climbing a ladder. There's a challenge right there. It's almost like going to sleep with one eye open. You don't wanna really let yourself go when you fall asleep, but I have.

All the fire fighters at this particular station live there while on duty. The days can be long and monotonous, and the nights even longer. Not the type of person to sit around, Dennis keeps active and finds ways to break the monotony:

> We've got our chores we do around here. Like this morning we spent probably two hours studying streets. It's kinda' hard in the wintertime. Because you can't go out. In the summertime we do a lot of training outside. And then on nicer days we may go out and do some driving. Drive our territory. Learn it, familiarize the new men with the streets and where the fire hydrants are at.

Like Rick, Dennis is committed to his fellow "soldiers." He describes how he made it to the rank of sergeant.

> Leading the squad and taking care of and keeping track of the men. I felt that if somebody feels that I'm good enough to do it, I wanna do it to the best of my ability. And not let the person down. And I think when I'm here I'm the same way. With the chief. I don't wanna let him down, so I'm gonna do it to the utmost of my ability.

The successful work of the fire fighter demands perfection. Dennis cannot afford imprecision. Timing is critical and literally means the difference between life and death. There are seldom any second chances. Perfection means organization and teamwork: it means accuracy and coordination. Like Rick, Dennis is constantly aware of his responsibilities. Both know what it takes to survive. Mistakes and errors cost lives. Fire, like war, must be handled accurately—both must be faced with courage.

Becky, the only woman in this group, uses her own style of courage to face the day. Working at a massage parlor, she spends long, unrewarding hours trying to please others. Although she says she will quit, she stays there because she needs the money.

Becky: "Life Stinks"

*Life stinks. . . . It gets harder and harder. It's hard emo-
tionally having a job like this and having a home life too.
. . . I just put up with it you know. What else can I do.
. . . I've always wanted a horse farm. Maybe some day.
I'm working toward it. . . . I take it one day at a time.*

Becky is the only female Antagonist in the present study. She
is thirty-nine and works in a massage parlor. I interviewed her in
the small trailer where she operates. It was isolated on a main
road on the outskirts of town. I walked in late at night and found
three women sitting, watching television. One was filing her nails,
one was knitting, and the other was reading a magazine. Their
ages varied. None was under thirty. There was also a man sitting
with them. They looked bored and were not talking. The room
was brightly lit, cozy, and warm.

It was the second parlor I entered; the first was about a block
away. The woman there would not talk to me because the parlors
were undergoing a state investigation; she was worried that I
might be an undercover agent. Becky, on the other hand, was
happy to talk to me, saying it would break the monotony.

In his book *The Prostitute and Her Clients*, Lewis Diana examines prostitution from a range of angles, including the prostitute's character, life, and sexuality and provides a profile of the
client.[19] He examines the organizational structure of prostitution
and presents a hierarchy that ascends from street prostitution,
brothels, truck stops, hotels and motels, and roadside lounges, to
residential homes, massage parlors, and call girls.

Diana places massage parlors high on the scale because the
atmosphere is "more relaxed and superficially less commercial-
ized, [and] there was more time for a woman to engage her client
in conversation."[20] In contrast to the previous categories, many
women working at massage parlors are amateurs. Not everyone
includes "intercourse in their repertoire of sexual services."[21] Some
massage parlors operate a legitimate business, but Diana's study
found most to be "fronts" for prostitution.

The atmosphere at massage parlors varies. Diana writes "some
were cheap, sordid fleabags with only the barest of accoutrements.
Others were sumptuous if not lavish with a lounge, exercise rooms
and saunas."[22] The small trailer where I met Becky was by no

means lavish. It was cheaply furnished, but clean. She led me into the back. There were two rooms with long tables. We went into another room and sat on a waterbed. There was not much furniture: a mirror behind the bed, a bedside table, a closet. A horse's harness hung on the wall. She began by describing her work:

> We call it "light touch and talk." They come in, and they get a rub on the back and legs. Not massage because we can't use that word. We don't "massage," just "light touch." There's no sexual release of any kind. Everybody has their own idea of massage parlors. Some people think of them as whorehouses. Every place is different. I've worked in a lot of them and some of them are and some of them aren't.

Becky has three children: one fourteen, one five, and one two. They have grown up knowing about her work since she said she has never hidden it from them. She is in her third marriage, which is not going the way she expected. The last three years have been extremely difficult emotionally. Her husband has trouble dealing with her job and is not as understanding as she would like. They cope by ignoring their problems.

> We don't talk about it. We just ignore what's happening. Whenever we do, he blows up. It gets all distorted and out of proportion. I got out of this business right when we got married, for about a year and a half. I thought he would get involved with the children and everything would be rosy. And I could get back to being a normal person. It just didn't work out that way. And finally it was necessary for me to go back to work. He's back working again now, and I'm really grateful for that.

Becky, like Harry, tries to separate her work from her personal life. She thinks it might help reduce the problems. "I put my time in and then I leave. I put my eight hours in here and then I forget about it. There's my whole life away from here, separate from this. This is my job. I make the money to survive on, and that's it. I put it behind me. I try not to let it affect my home life."

Becky and her husband stay home most of the time. She wears blue jeans around the house and lives a quiet life. She likes the contrast her job gives. "It's nice to dress up and have people notice you. 'Oh, you look nice tonight.' Put makeup on. Things like that." She likes the "money and the dressing up." She dislikes "putting up with the drunks and the perverts."

Becky's life metaphor indicates her dissatisfaction with life. She says, "Life stinks. It does. It gets harder and harder." Throughout the interview she expressed her belief that everything about her life is difficult. She equates life with hardship. For example, she searches for love, which she believes is the most important thing in life. So far it has been elusive, but she continues to dream of an ideal loving relationship.

> I've always sort of had this fantasy in the back of my mind that when my kids were older and I was in my later thirties that I would be living out in Colorado. And I would find someone there that I'd be very happy with. I guess all through my life I've never felt I would be really happy. Until I am more mature.

Becky still searches for love. The lack of love is one reason she thinks her life stinks. Being dissatisfied in her love relationships has left her feeling unfulfilled. She sounds like Rick who thinks understanding is the most important thing in life but who never received enough of it. Becky wants love as much as Rick wants understanding. Both know that love and understanding make communication and relationships possible. For both, the world is cold and lonely without love.

One would think that the temptation to become involved with her clients might be great, but Becky said she could never be romantically interested in them.

> Men have come into the parlors and I've thought they were really appealing and I've thought I'd like to go out with them. But I've never done that. I've always felt that there's gotta be a reason for them to come here in the first place. Whether they're married or have some kind of sexual problem or just being shy or whatever. And I've never wanted to date a person who's come into the parlor. Because I've always felt that if I got involved with them, then I wouldn't want them to go anywhere else. 'Cause once a guy comes into a parlor he doesn't stop. They always come back. Maybe it's years later but they always come back.

Although Becky prefers men, she has been sexually involved with women. "When two women are together, there is compassion. In most cases you don't feel it between a man and a woman." Although she does not actively seek relationships with women, she accepts them. She believes that women's attraction toward other women is more widespread than they like to admit. "Women are afraid to talk about it. They don't want to admit it. I was like that for years. I often wondered what it would be like. I guess I was a closet case."

The Antagonist knows life is hard. Becky thinks life stinks because it is so hard. She uses the word difficult to describe much of her life—"it's difficult emotionally"; things are "more difficult" than they used to be; and it is "difficult" for her husband's ego to deal with the work she does. Life is also difficult because Becky believes that she cannot change things. "I just put up with it you know. What else can I do?" The Antagonist often copes with life by accepting things as they are. Becky does not anguish over trying to change life. She is a staunch realist. Her perspective tends to be less positive because she believes that she cannot overcome the obstacles.

The Antagonist usually stands up for personal rights. Becky speaks her mind. She tells clients to behave or leave. She says what she thinks and knows where she stands on most issues. She says, "I don't put up with bullshit anymore. I'm too old. This has hardened me and my relationships at home. My personal life is hard."

Becky likes to watch people's reactions when she tells them what she does. "I enjoy telling people that I work in a massage parlor, because I like to see their reaction. They drop the subject. It doesn't bother me. Why should I have to deal with it? If they can't accept me for who I am, I don't need 'em. I'm not ashamed of what I do."

She does not trust people, commenting sadly that "you can't trust anybody. Not even your best friend. I don't respect people very much." The Antagonist embeds a lack of trust into expectations about the world. The expectation becomes part of a self-fulfilling prophecy. By expecting distrust, the Antagonist discovers distrust, reinforcing the expectation and prompting more discoveries. The belief creates an endless spiral.

Money stimulates Becky and is central to her struggle. Money means freedom. The desire for money keeps her going. The Antagonist's preoccupation with money is symptomatic of a prevailing orientation toward the future. Becky lives in the present through her dream of the future. Her vision sustains her. It would be difficult to go on without it. Her goal is "the outcome." She says that "with that outcome I would have the money to give me the freedom that I need." Becky is convinced that the only way she can get the money is by working in a massage parlor.

Part of her dream involves owning a horse farm and being a nationally known trainer. Having the dream "keeps my sanity intact. . . . That'll be my fame. . . . That's what I'm working for." For Becky, horses symbolize freedom and her life "the way I wish it would be." She needs money to buy her dreams: her horses and her freedom.

Becky also daydreams about her past. She remembers her youth: "I was young and I had it all. Had the figure. Had the money. Had the looks." The business is "not as exciting as it was years ago when I was young and had it all." In many ways, the memory of the past carries her through the present. She holds onto a memory that is a retrospective vision. She also looks forward to the future with the help of her dream, which provides a projective vision.

She has tried other jobs. Before her present line of work, she worked as a supervisor at a department store, and before that job, she worked in a carpet store. She disliked them because the pay was not very good. "It was very hard for me to adjust to that. Most of the girls get lazy in this line of business because of all the free time that you have and the money that you do make. And working a normal job is hard. You know, the time and being on your feet for eight hours a day."

Becky works in the massage business so that she can "invest in another line of work. I've often thought of opening a restaurant." This dream is part of Becky's goal to get "back to being a normal person." Like Harry, she talks about finding some other work for herself. Harry dreams of a "career." He wants to "find a good job with a steady shift. Where the money's good."

Becky continually contrasts her "line of business" with a "normal" job. She wants a normal life, but admits she probably could not live with it. "I would go absolutely berserk if I had to go to a job. Eight hours a day and make maybe twenty, twenty-five dollars a day and maybe have enough to pay my bills." Just as Becky realizes she may never have her normal job, Harry accepts the improbability of his having a career. "I don't wanna be here all my life. I'd like to make something out of myself. But if it don't happen, it don't happen."

The dream helps Antagonists put up with life. Realistically, the dream will not come true, and the vision of another way of life will not amount to anything. Harry will never go to Ireland, and Becky will never be a famous horse trainer. Deep down, they know this but rarely admit it because that would leave little reason to live. They pretend that the dream will come true because it helps them cope with an otherwise uncompromising world. Antagonists transcend life's hardships by holding onto an illusion, which keeps them going: to shatter their illusions would be to shatter their world.

Dave's dream is to find a job in a high-paying factory. He likes factory work and feels comfortable with a stable routine. Life is rough and he knows he has to work for what he wants. Dave is the least extreme Antagonist and falls in the center of the sample.

Dave: "A Chess Game"

> *A chess game. It's always changing. . . . You have a choice all your life of moves to make and moves to not make. Just whatever happens. . . . May not get any better at all. But you learn to cope with things. . . . You could lose a chess game. . . .*

Although classified as an Antagonist, Dave is the least extreme. His let-things-be attitude places him near the center of the active and the positive dimensions. At twenty-five he usually works as a machine operator in one of the local factories. Currently, he is laid-off and employed in an adult bookstore. There was not much activity in the store when I approached him. He was glad to talk to break the monotony of the day. He began talking about his work; "It's a plastic factory and we make things like CB radios. The machines do all the work. We just do the packaging. . . . Twelve hours a day, just sitting there, turning parts and packing them can get pretty boring after a while."

Like Harry, Dave complains that management makes the work difficult. But Dave accepts it more than does Harry. "That goes along with it. A lot of times the right hand doesn't know what the left is doing." He knows he cannot interfere with management: "What's the use? Who really cares? They couldn't care if your job is done right. You think, what the hell's the use? To hell with it."

In spite of these complaints, Dave likes factory work and feels well suited to it.

> I done factory work since I got out of school. I'd rather be in another factory. A higher paying factory. Maybe I'm in a rut. It's just that I'd rather be in a factory. . . . I work four days on and three off. I'd rather do it that way than I would work five days a week. . . . To me that's just a drag. I mean with two days off. I get an extra day that most people don't get. I get fifteen days off a month. It's great in the summertime. Gives you more things to do.

Working in the adult bookstore has opened his eyes.

> The first couple of days are a real eye-opening experience. But after that you become immune to it. It doesn't matter what anybody's buying or what anybody does. Every once in a while you see something and you say, what was that? . . . . Some of the guys come in here, they're cross-dressers. That's the freak-out. They dress as women. . . . Culture shock—that's what I call it. . . . I'm pretty open-minded. Whatever they wanna do is their business. It doesn't really bother me.

Dave answered the life metaphor question easily. He had ideas about life; life is like "a chess game. It's always changing. In a chess game, the odds are always changing for you or against you— no matter what. You have a choice all your life of moves to make and moves not to make. Sometimes you make the right ones, sometimes you don't. I've always thought of it that way."

It is interesting to compare Dave's interpretation of a game with Dennis's. Dennis thinks of a *military* game, while Dave thinks of a *chess* game. Each requires ingenuity. Dennis and Dave believe that an individual must play the game, rules must be followed, and competition is critical. They know that winning is the goal, but they expect a certain number of losses. We typically think of chess as an intellectual exercise and of the military more as a test of physical endurance. The military is much more physical and violent than chess. In chess, there are a finite number of moves; in the military, the number seems unlimited. Clearly, each person make moves to counteract the opponent but those moves are qualitatively different.

Dave takes time to explain how winning and losing are the key components in his life metaphor. He believes that they are determined by the individual's point of view.

> It depends on your own perspective and how you think you did. I mean, sure, you might have lost something, say material or otherwise. But that doesn't mean that necessarily you've lost. You may have lost something materially but have gained something else. I don't know. A piece of wisdom. Whatever. It doesn't mean you've really lost. A fine line so far as I'm concerned.

Harry and Dave both talk about their lives in terms of lines. For Dave, it is a "fine line"; for Harry, it is a "straight line." Are these lines similar? Dave believes that "somewhere along the line, things get better. You don't think it will, but it does. When you least expect it. That's the way it usually runs. The bad things happen when you least expect them. So do the good things." This statement seems to echo Harry's feelings about not getting off the line. He believes he needs to stay on track and jump back on that line to maintain the good things in life.

Even though Dave is more optimistic than most Antagonists, he gravitates toward the less positive end of the scale. He thinks "life just happens." He explains, "I guess you keep trying. It doesn't mean it's gonna get any better right away. May not get any better at all. But you learn to cope with things." Dave's complacency makes him somewhat less active than most Antagonists, but like most Antagonists, he believes life is hard. "Nothin' comes easy anymore. You have to work for what you want. They won't hand you anything on a silver platter. . . . Nothin' is handed to you. You can't have something just because you want it."

Although Dave's distrust is not as strong as that of the other Antagonists, he does not like to rely on people. "It's up to yourself to make you happy. Nobody else can do it for you." His most difficult times have come recently, during his two-year-old marriage. Part of the difficulty has been learning to trust his wife and to rely on her. "If I have something bothering me I usually keep it to myself. It's hard to rely on somebody else. After you've been relying on yourself all your life."

Like Harry and Rick, Dave feels the burden of responsibility. "When you want something, you can't just go and get it like when you're single. You have to stop and think. You have ten thousand times more responsibility when you're married. You can't just go out and get whatever you want."

Antagonists know their obligations. Responsibility motivates them, anchors them, and warrants their life-style. They care about their responsibilities even though they often choose to ignore other dimensions of their lives. If they did not have their responsibilities, they would have nothing but dreams. Life would be purposeless and disorganized. They would not be accountable for anything.

Both Dave and Harry talk about getting "fired up," but each handles himself differently. Dave is less extreme than Harry. He is not as negative and has taught himself to control his temper. Where Harry might go to a bar and start a fight, Dave expresses his anger less physically.

> I can be pretty calm. But I can get fired up real quick. I mean at the drop of a hat. Most times I'm pretty easygoing. But when I get mad, I mean when I get fired up, I get real mad. I don't get physical. It's just that I get boiling. I yell mostly. If I get mad enough I'll be yelling. . . . It doesn't last very long. There have been times that I've picked up and thrown a few things. Mostly over something you couldn't control. Where you felt like maybe you should have been able to.

Dave consciously tries to minimize how much he worries. He clearly expresses the strategy most often used by the Antagonist:

> You can only worry so much. I just say, to hell with it. No matter how much you worry, nothin' is gonna change what you're worrying about. Some things you can't change. You just have to live with it. You learn how to do that. It's not easy for me. 'Cause when I want something I want it now. I'm very impatient. But I've had to learn to be more patient, but it's not always easy for me.

Ambiguity characterizes his style of coping. He has a take-it-or-leave-it attitude, which gets him through the day and through life. The Antagonist commonly employs this strategy. Dave's ambivalence towards life might be summed up in his attitude towards the seasons: "I like the fall best of all. It's changing leaves, things like that. It's not really cold, but it's not really warm. That's my favorite time of year. If it could be like that all year round I'd love it."

Taken together, these six individuals indicate the predispositions of the Antagonist—playing the "game" (a military game and a chess game); realistically "making" life what it is; making the "ends meet"; and struggling with the rank "deterioration" and stench of life. Antagonists assume that life is bad and express their life orientation through maximum activity and minimum evaluation.

The next chapter presents the Enthusiast, who is as active as the Antagonist but represents opposite personality characteristics on the evaluative dimension. Enthusiasts reflect optimism and exuberant praise for life.

CHAPTER 4

The Enthusiast

> Nothing great was ever achieved without
> enthusiasm.
> > Emerson, *Circles.*

> Opposition always inflames the enthusiast,
> never converts him.
> > J. C. F. Schiller, *Kabale und Liebe, III.*

> The world belongs to the Enthusiast who
> keeps cool.
> > William McFee, *Casuals of the Sea.*

When we think of enthusiastic people, we generally think of happy, energetic individuals whose liveliness seems infectious. Enthusiasts are animated actors, who possess an irrepressible *joie de vivre* that sometimes verges on mania. They are vivacious, have a robust zest for life, and eagerly participate in everything they do.

Communication researcher Robert Norton developed the idea of "communicator style" to explain the *way* people communicate.[1] He associates enthusiasm with an animated style, indicated by specific behaviors, such as engaging another in eye contact and using a variety of facial expressions and gestures, behaviors typically used by Enthusiasts.[2] People's psychological orientation also helps predict enthusiasm. Bales' typology of personality traits, for example, uses the word *extrovert* to represent enthusiasm.[3] Enthusiasts are most likely to be outspoken.

Enthusiasts rate highly on both the evaluative and the active dimensions. They approach life positively, which means they enjoy living, tend to feel optimistic, and find daily activities re-warding. For the most part, life is a good experience in which negative situations are quickly transformed into positive ones. Activity is indicated by physical and psychological movement. Enthusiasts are most active and are motivated by progress and change as they "make," "set," and "achieve" their goals. They perceive few external limitations that they cannot control because they believe they are directly responsible for what happens in their lives. They believe opportunities are available to everyone if the individual is willing to take advantage of them. They echo these premises in the following typical expressions: "you get out of life what you put into it"; "you shape life the way you want"; "you are the only one responsible for getting along in life."

Compared with Antagonists, Enthusiasts represent a relatively larger population. This should not be too surprising given the way society positively values active and affirmative people. In my study, seventeen people are classified as Enthusiasts.[4] Because this number is too unwieldy to allow the presentation of detailed portraits, the format used in the last chapter, I have organized the present chapter according to four common attributes: activity, evaluation, control, and motivation.

These attributes are not the same as the dimensions. An at-tribute is a characteristic or a quality selected as appropriate for a particular individual or group. There are many ways to talk about Enthusiasts, and I have chosen four features because they provide useful distinctions for explanation. My intention in sep-arating them in this way has simply been to break up the pres-entation. In real life, the attributes cannot be separated this easily; indeed, it is difficult to separate them even for anlaysis. As one reads about activity, one will find instances of evaluation. When reading about motivation, one should not be surprised to find that it overlaps control. The integrated Enthusiast is someone who combines the attributes. In addition, there are numerous rela-tionships between the attributes that I have not discussed. As always, it is important to keep in mind that the details are nec-essarily brief, and much more could be said about each individual than is written here.

A number of individuals have been selected to illustrate each attribute. In some cases, the connection between the life metaphor and the attribute is clear. For example, it seems appropriate that the idea of an adventure should fall into a discussion of activity. At other times, one might think that the life metaphor is not directly related to the attribute. At first glance, it might be unclear how a bird or a wheel relates to evaluation. On their own, life metaphors cannot always be precisely interpreted. To make an accurate assessment, every life metaphor must be placed within a context. The game metaphor, for example, might be used in a number of different ways, depending on one's perspective. Some people think of life as a game in which they set the rules and are continually winning. Other individuals might think of life as a game, but treat it as restrictive because the rules do not allow them enough freedom. In each case, the context is necessary to decipher the meaning.

The following discussion explains how the life metaphor relates to the attribute by placing it in the appropriate context. The meanings of life metaphors do not always match our expectations. In some cases, the way a person interprets the life metaphor might not coincide with our usual assumptions and might even include some surprising connections. A notable example is life is "what you make it." This sounds as though it could only belong to an enthusiastic person because we expect people who make life what they want to get out and do things. Indeed, five Enthusiasts will be discussed who do use this life metaphor. Imagine another case, however, where an individual claims that life is "what you make it," but makes it something quite passive, or perhaps even negative. In this instance, the same life metaphor, "what you make it," has been used differently and can only be understood when placed in the overall context of the person's life. The first attribute, activity, is one of the two dimensions on which all the life metaphors are rated.

Activity

"You just can't stand still. 'Cause when you're standing still, you're going backwards." "There's just too many things to do. I'd like to be about four of me, maybe even six of me. I never have enough time."

Activity refers to the physical and mental energy one exerts in life. Enthusiasts believe they can do anything they want if they put their minds to it and persevere and work hard. Things do not just happen to Enthusiasts, they make them happen. They are active initiators of their fate who believe opportunities are everywhere if people are willing to take advantage of them.

Because they are so active, most Enthusiasts are preoccupied with time. This obsession takes different forms. Some worry about getting older, being forced to slow down, and having their physical activity limited. Others are afraid they are running out of time and will not be able to finish everything. Enthusiasts rarely postpone anything because they feel compelled to make the most of the present.

To a large extent, activity involves interacting with people, and Enthusiasts love working with people. Often successfully self-employed, they like being the aggressive energizer, taking the active role, and getting things going. They like to motivate others, and Fatalists are likely to be the recipients of their encouragement.

Four of the interviewees illustrate activity. George, a Greek-American who owns a family restaurant, is never idle at business or at home. Peggy manages two branches of a photocopying chain and loves the challenge of making the business a success. Karen has just bought a bar with her husband, one of several ventures they have undertaken without any experience but with the hope of success. Sue is a self-employed cosmetic consultant who enjoys getting out and meeting different people. Each one talks explicitly about the need to keep busy and to stay active.

George: "What You Make It"

George owns a small, busy, downtown restaurant that specializes in home-style cooking. He is a jack-of-all-trades, who does most of the work from cooking to hiring the staff and ordering the food. The business is more than a job. "I grew up here. It's part of my life. It's been in the family for sixty years. It's part of me." At forty-seven, George remembers his mother working by his father's side. Following the family tradition, he and his wife have worked together for twenty-eight years, and his five children have worked there at various times, supporting themselves through college.

Like most Enthusiasts, George believes time is too short. "I'm always working. If I'm not working here, I'm working at home, on my house. Or doing things with my children. Or work on my cars. I've never got enough time." George thrives on work, and he finds ways to stay busy, sometimes, he admits, too many ways. "I get a little busy. I get too many things going at the same time. I get hyper, you know." Laughing at his own impatience, he says, "When I want something done, I don't want it done tomorrow. I want it done yesterday. . . . I'm like a tiger. I go after 'em. I go. I start to do something. I just jump right into it. I get it done. I don't hesitate. I do it the fastest and the best way I can."

George's "tiger" metaphor characterizes his drive. Although there are "too many things to do," he would not have it any other way. He knows that "if people really get out and work at it, they can get a pretty good business going." He expresses his strong work ethic in his life metaphor.

> I wouldn't say a bowl of cherries. It's what you make it. Life is actually tough. You gotta work at it to make it good. I know a lot of people that's educated that hasn't got much on the ball. And the reverse, I know them that's educated can get out and do good. So it's just what you wanna do. If you got the make-up to get out and get busy and work at it.

His advice to his children echoes his sense of personal determination and commitment to hard work.

> Get as much education as you possibly can. And don't be afraid to work. It's really up to the parents, I think, to teach their kids how to work. I think we did a pretty good job. All of our kids worked while they were in high school and through college. They haven't had a free ride. They worked at it. And they've done well. They're good workers.

Activity is such a priority that the prospect of slowing down as he gets older inspires the only regretful reflections in George's otherwise optimistic outlook. "It bothers me. I can't do near as much now as I could before, and I just been realizing that in the last few years. It takes twice as long to do some things as I think it should take. You gotta slow down a bit. You get a little older. You don't move as fast."

Peggy: "The Ocean"

Peggy, twenty-six, is a regional manager for a national photocopying company. An energetic individual, she copes by staying active. "My stamina and my energy keep me going. I don't tire out easily. I'm still young, plus I have something that I'm responsible for and committed to. That carries me through the day." Like many Enthusiasts, she talks about life in terms of "growth," "change," "accomplishments," "challenges," and "learning." Peggy is activated by personal ideals, such as "self-fulfillment," "self-achievement," and "self-esteem."

Peggy's job is "to motivate people to perform, to set goals, and to create different ideas." Like most Enthusiasts, she worries about the shortage of time. "There's never enough time. I wish I could improve my time management. I think a lot of it has to do with my husband working here. If one of us isn't done with their stuff, the other tends to stick around and help out. And that's good and at the same time, that's where the time keeps lagging on and on."

Peggy emphasizes physical energy and loves to exercise. "I feel rejuvenated. Released. The energy's out." Her work also requires psychological energy, which stimulates her creativity and intellect. "I'm a motivator. . . . I am a sort of a guide for people. A lot of people come to me to just talk. And they respect what I have to say. I'm one that is willing to listen and learn, and people trust me in that respect." Her life metaphor stresses the motion she associates with life:

> Life is like the ocean. I lived on the ocean for a few years. It's constantly moving. It's constantly changing. Every day at the beach was different. Some days the waves are real big and it's furious and strong. And usually there's not just one day, it goes for about a week, and then calms down. It's beautiful, and the sun comes out and it's very tranquil and restful. That's what usually happens when something big or major happens in my life. That is either very challenging or very hurtful. And then all of a sudden I overcome it and a lot of energy has been put into that. And it's calm and tranquil afterwards, and it will develop back into its regular flow of power.

The ocean metaphor relies on the image of a cycle, which is common among Enthusiasts. From Peggy's perspective, the calm is followed by the storm, which subsides into another period of calm, and so on. The weather reflects the unceasing but everchanging demands of life that stimulate one's energy. For Peggy, even the "flow of power" is cyclical. She accepts that things are never as constant as one would like, but she remains convinced that they can always get better. Just as the ocean changes, so does life, and for Peggy, the ultimate question is "What do I do next? And that's an ever-changing question-and-answer procedure. [It is] constantly being answered and constantly being asked again."

Karen: "An Adventure"

Karen, a forty-one-year-old retired schoolteacher, works in the bar that she and her husband recently bought. Although the work is quite different from her previous occupation, she is getting used to it and enjoys learning about the new life-style. As with most things, she adjusts by being active. "I generally keep moving, keep busy. . . . And if you wanna be happy, you're the one that has to do it. Nobody else makes you happy. You have to find out what makes you happy and you have to do that."

Like many Enthusiasts, Karen finds jobs in which she can work closely with people. "I like their personalities. Their experiences. Sharing experiences. And finding out what they do. You learn a lot of things. The more people you're involved with, the more you learn." Her life's goal is to learn as much as she can, which reflects the sense of "adventure" expressed by her life metaphor. "Life is like an adventure. A new adventure every day. Sometimes it's good adventures. Sometimes it's bad adventures. But most of the time, it's good and interesting."

By treating life as an adventure, Karen welcomes change and takes advantage of opportunities. She likes variety in her routine and enjoys adjusting to different things. She meets new situations with excitement because of the challenges they pose. She tries to find experiences that will enrich her understanding of the world. Throughout her life, she has lived in a number of different places, held a variety of jobs, and made many friends. She remembers the businesses she and her husband have managed over the past twenty years: "We've farmed, had rental properties. And this is something else. We'll do this and then chances are that in ten or fifteen years we'll probably have some other project." She approaches each new situation as a "new adventure."

> I like different situations and learning how to handle them or how to cope with them and the results. Sometimes things happen and you handle them in a certain way, and you don't see the

results right away. But eventually you get a result. Say you work hard, eventually you get a reward. Sometimes it's a little farther off than other times.

Enthusiasts evaluate life positively and respond to it actively. Karen explains how optimism and activity are directly related:

> I'm really a very positive person. I am always trying to look for something positive, even when maybe it doesn't look like there is to other people. ... I think, maybe there's something I can learn from this and go on. I always try to find something positive. If you're always dwelling on the negative, you get very tired and very depressed. And when you're tired and depressed, you feel old. And then it's wasted energy. It really is very wasted. So if you're thinking positive things, then you have a lot more energy.

Karen states emphatically, "I just never had time to spend with negative things. Somebody always had something worse than I did. You have to go on. Keep busy. Look for something else." She does not have enough time to be depressed. Karen realizes that the goodness in life does not simply happen and that she must work to make it so. "You have to work on it. It's hard work. You have to be willing to take the slaps. You're gonna get some rejections and some negative things. But, if you work at it really hard, your positive attitude will usually overcome. Eventually you'll just wear people down. That's where your patience pays off."

Sue: "A Ball"

Sue, a cosmetic salesperson who works from her home, conveys her commitment to action in her athletic life metaphor. "Life to me is like a ball. Because the more that you bounce that ball, and the harder you work at learning to bounce it, the higher the ball goes. The more you learn to manage the ball in the game, the better you are at the game, the better you are at life."

When she says life is "like a ball," she seems to use a double metaphor. On one level, she equates life with a "game," and on another level she sees herself as a "ball" that "bounces" within that game. Like a ball bouncing in the game, Sue moves through life: sometimes quickly, sometimes slowly; sometimes up, sometimes down. She sounds like Peggy as she talks about the cycles of life. Success comes from actively engaging in "hard work," "learning," and "accomplishments," all of which are necessary to play the game well. Sue believes she can "choose the opportunity" and "make of it" what she wants.

The one part of life that Sue feels she cannot control is the aging process, and at thirty, she worries about getting old. She does not fear being alone as much as "the loss of mobility, the loss of physicalness." Characteristically, she copes by keeping active. "Getting out" and "meeting people" help her to overcome her fear of aging.

> I've learned in life to always get out the door. Don't sit back and think, what if? Just go do it. Because I used to be like that, really protected. Like I'd stay within this little zone and not too much can happen. I'm not that way anymore. I just go on out and see what happens. Don't sit there and procrastinate 'cause it's not gonna do you any good.

Her fundamental optimism enables her to transform her preoccupation with age into ambitious goals, and the passing of time motivates her to do more.

> I feel that the clock is ticking more for me. I wanna do more with my life. I'm a lot more ready to do things on the moment. I used to procrastinate. I'm not like that now. When I have a delivery to make I go do it now. If you're on rhythm with yourself, you get a lot done. It's a cycle. . . . Somebody might say, we could go do it tomorrow, or we could go next week. I'd go today. Because you never know what tomorrow or next week will bring. The older you get the more you should take the opportunity.

Sue tries to make the most of the present and does not like to postpone things. Like the other Enthusiasts, she actively seizes the potential of every day. "I make changes daily. The older I get, the more I live day-by-day. And I meet someone new every day. . . . That's what makes me happy. If someone were to make me miserable, put me in a house and don't let me outside. As long as I can go out and meet people."

Unmarried and presently not involved in a romantic relationship, Sue makes satisfying bonds. Interacting with others reminds her that she is not isolated.

You know that your life can be a little bit better if you can get out the door. I think too many people sit back and daydream about what life could be like. The first year my roommate lived with me she never wanted to do anything. Now she's going out all the time. She can see what she's missing. And it's much better than sitting in her room and dreaming about what it could be. Going out and really doing it.

A tiger voraciously consuming each moment; a swimmer in the restless ocean; an adventurer in a series of imposing challenges; and an athlete perfecting skills with tireless dedication—each of these metaphors vividly conveys the Enthusiast's ideal self-image as a person who actively and energetically forges a meaningful existence in the face of an all-too-brief span of days.

Evaluation

"I think you can turn things that seem negative at the time around into positives and learn from them." "Sure, there's good and bad, but never let the bad outweigh the good." "If you're not happy doing what you're doing, then don't do it."

People's assessment of the quality of life ranges from positive to negative. Those who rate life positively typically feel happy, enjoy living, and treat life as something worthwhile. Those who rate it negatively usually feel bitter and pessimistic. People in the middle tend to feel nonchalant and unconcerned and are generally likely to rate life neither positively nor negatively.

Without a doubt, Enthusiasts are positively oriented toward life: they find it challenging and embrace it wholeheartedly and optimistically. They are neither tentative about their excitement for life, nor reluctant to take chances. They believe it is possible to make the most of any situation. Typical Enthusiasts say that "life consists of good and bad, but I'm going to make it good." In this respect, they differ from Antagonists and Fatalists who emphasize the negative.

Enthusiasts often describe life as a process of discovery. For most of them, life is a continuous cycle of learning, and one of the most important tasks is to ask questions. Regardless of the answer, asking the question is what counts. Equating life with learning helps them turn negative situations into positive ones because they think of everything as a lesson.

Enthusiasts accentuate personal growth, positive energy, and productive outcomes. They do not like to waste time with negative thoughts, and some even feel it is hazardous to their health to feel depressed. They actively search for the positive path as a way to stay healthy.

Five Enthusiasts have been selected to characterize evaluation. Jan, who directs a health program at the YWCA, maintains a positive attitude in spite of the enormous responsibility and long hours. Joanna and Glenda work in a craft store that Glenda owns. With Carol, a Fatalist, they form a trio of working women who gain confidence from their independence. Norman, a car salesperson, has felt enthusiastic about life ever since he changed jobs. Evelynn recently graduated from law school and finds that working with low-income people makes her appreciate everything she has. These people feel good about themselves and what they are doing, reflecting the positive energy that Enthusiasts generate.

Jan: "A Process"

Jan directs a crisis program for women at the YWCA which offers help to battered women in the form of shelter, legal aid, food, and emotional support. At thirty, she is the administrator; her work involves "writing the grants, getting the money, supervising the program, and making sure everything is going well." Her personal organization helps increase her efficiency. "I'm a really well-organized person. I keep it straight by knowing what my goals and objectives are, writing out an action plan, and taking things step-by-step. That's the way I have to function."

She describes her approach metaphorically: "You need to have your finger in the pot, so to speak, so that you can feel the pulse of what's going on. Not only the people who work for you but the people you are serving." Jan loves work that involves service to others because she empathizes with people's problems and is able to help them discover alternatives. Her talent lies in sharing her vision with people who have difficulty seeing any way out of their problems:

> I always wanted to be somebody who worked with people. I
> remember going through it—the teacher, the nurse, and that

sort of thing. And then when I started college, I really wanted
to go to Arizona and work with the Indians. I was extremely
idealistic. But I always wanted to be in some sort of helping
profession.

Part of Jan's skill lies in her intuitive abilities. "I've always been
real perceptive. I can talk to people and almost know what they
are feeling. It comes from the gut, and I'm not usually wrong."
She balances the language of feeling and emotion with the language of thinking and logic. Although careful not to let one outweigh the other in her work, her own language reflects the way
"feeling" and "perception" guide her.

> First, I'm a raw-feeling person. And it starts from the gut. Then
> I'm analytical. I know I usually go with my gut feeling. I think
> that's an asset. But I also know that I can tend to be very im-
> pulsive. And those are good qualities. But they have to be tem-
> pered a little bit. . . . When they get confused, I just have to take
> a step back, and I have to look again at my purpose.

"Choice," "opportunity," and "personal control" help Jan in
her efforts to be positive. "We have choices. And to constantly
realize that and know that I have a choice in the matter. And to
exercise that choice. You do have the opportunity to be able to
choose and have options."

Her life metaphor incorporates an intricate philosophy about
"growth," "challenges," "goals," and "learning."

> Life is a process. It means physical change, always moving. Al-
> ways meeting different people. Always growing in a personal-
> growth sense. Challenging myself. Doing new things. To realize
> that you have a choice in life—that's my big secret. Everybody
> has those opportunities, if they would just key into it. To realize
> life's a process. It's growth. And I look at growth as a positive
> experience rather than a negative experience. Knowing that along
> the way, growth means change, and sometimes change means
> pain. But that's OK. I manage pain because my mind-set is that
> growth sometimes means pain, and I don't think pain's always
> bad. . . . If you believe that growth is a process and that life is
> a process, you don't ever work anything out absolutely. My own
> truth is that it's a process, and therefore there is no truth. It
> kind of flows back and forth.

The "flow" of energy sounds like the "cycle" Peggy described in her ocean metaphor, and the "bouncing" rhythm Sue described in her ball metaphor. These women manage negative energy just as effectively as positive energy. Jan comments, "I can accept it or not accept it. And if you don't choose to accept it, then I think you can turn it around. But I'm not gonna sit around and have you tell me, or anybody outside of me, what to do." She works at making her experiences positive.

> How do I cope? I know I'm here for a reason, and I might as well put as much positive energy into the experience as I can. . . . What makes life worth living to me is I never know what's gonna happen in the next second. It's real exciting to me. . . . I seem to attract a lot of opportunities to me and a lot of positive things. It's that excitement and positive energy.

The ability to make the most of any situation distinguishes Enthusiasts from the other life orientations. Jan expresses the characteristic strength and will: "I think you can turn things that seem negative at the time around into positives and learn from them." Jan is a perennial optimist who believes that anything can be framed positively. "I don't think you can set yourself up not to grow. And in growth, maybe you make some mistakes or continue to work things through. Because if it doesn't happen today, it's gonna happen sometime down the line. And there was something you needed to learn in that process to get to someplace else."

Joanna: "A Wheel"

Joanna works in a craft store run by three women. Her response to her work is characteristic of her positive disposition. She likes "the fact women can make a go of it. They've all had families and they understand. You know, if your children are sick or whatever. Some places wouldn't understand that a mother needs off." At thirty-nine she describes herself as "independent," "opinionated," and "creative." Devoted to her family—her husband and two teenage sons—she places them at the forefront of her life. "I have a very good family. My children and my husband. They're very important in my life, and they also give me a lot to look forward to. I have a lot to live for really. We do a lot of things together. We keep busy and active."

Content with her life, satisfaction keeps Joanna going. "I enjoy living. I think part of the secret is doing things that you enjoy doing. And you feel you do well." Believing in the power of positive thinking, she faces problems calmly by relaxing.

> You just sit down and rest for a few minutes and then get going again. Take a little break. 'Cause if you can't seem to solve your problems, just put it aside, and then think about it while you're doing something that you don't have to think hard on. Sort of unconsciously you eventually figure it out. That usually works.

Time has treated Joanna well. Since her children have grown, she has become more independent, more self-assured, and more professional. She enjoys working outside the home, socializing with friends, and making her life a pleasurable process of discovery. "Life is fun and exciting—just finding out who I am, what I can do, my ability, and also watching my children grow. I guess I'm just finding out more about myself. I'm taking time to develop my own interests in life. And it's fun." Joanna realizes that much of what she has learned over the years has changed her. Many of her current attitudes represent her own personal development.

> My thoughts have evolved over several years of maturing. I've been through a difficult time for myself. I probably feel more comfortable answering these questions today than if you'd asked me at twenty-five. I wouldn't have near the answers that I have today. I know why more than I did before. I've asked myself why and found answers.

One of the major difficulties she faced was the divorce of her parents after their thirty-nine-year marriage. Their separation triggered many questions, not only from Joanna, but from her children. "My most obvious question was, why, after so many years. It didn't make sense. But then after I talked to my parents, I understood why. The biggest effect was on my children." The family's efforts to understand the divorce resulted in turmoil. Different family members took sides, judging the morality of the situation, wondering about the reasons. The solution finally came when Joanna accepted her parents as individuals, with the right to live their own lives. She convinced her sons that they also needed to accept their grandparents' decision. "We all learned to accept them for what they are." The experience helped shape her life metaphor: "Life is sort of like a wheel, and I'm at the center. And all these spokes are still coming out of the center. That's me. If that makes sense or not? That's just how I perceive myself. As the center. And I'm no different. The spokes are just different parts of the center."

Feeling like the center of the wheel gives Joanna much satisfaction. She believes she is the heart of her family, keeping everyone together. At work, she is also part of the nucleus; the other women need her skills to complement the trio. To feel needed in this way brings Joanna a feeling of importance. She is not *just* a mother, or *just* a working woman, but proud of every job she has. Just as the spokes are different parts of the wheel, so are Joanna's different roles part of her personality.

> I wear a lot of different hats in my jobs: as a mother, as a spouse, as a daughter. Different things require different hats. I think I'm always the same person. In other words, I don't feel that I change. I guess I perceive myself as one whole person. I don't see myself reacting to something differently because I'm doing something differently. Like, if I'm married at one job, I'm married at another job. Or if I'm a mother at one job, I'm a mother at my other jobs.

Some people feel divided, conflicted, at odds, or torn by the many roles they must play, but for Joanna they all harmonize into a single direction. A wheel is a perfect circle. The idea of a wheel is not something threatening, and she does not feel that she is "going round in circles" or that she is caught in a "vicious circle"; she feels more like she has "come full circle," which provides a sense of completeness and satisfaction in her life.

Glenda: "A Bird"

Glenda owns the craft shop in which she teaches. She enjoys working with people and sharing her knowledge and experience. At fifty-five, she stresses creativity. "I love being able to create something myself. To design it and then see it finished and then getting the reward. Not only the emotion of knowing that I have done something, but financially seeing returns from what I've done."

Time speeds by for Glenda, as it does for so many Enthusiasts, as she tries to fit everything into her day. "There's just too many things to do. I'd like to be about four of me. Maybe even six of me. I never have enough time, even though I need very little sleep, like four hours a night. I enjoy everything I do."

She teaches people to macramé, sketch, make silk flowers, paint folk art, paint landscapes, as well as a variety of other activities, and she proudly commends her own talents. "I can teach anybody anything, and if I don't know how to do it, give me a week, and then I'll teach you how to do it." Glenda attributes this ability to having been raised on a farm where she had to amuse herself. "I've always been a loner. I was an only child. I was self-sufficient and didn't need someone else around to keep me entertained." She has maintained this independence throughout her life.

Her life metaphor matches her love of freedom: "Life is like a bird. I'm a free spirit or a free bird and no one can change me. Free to go float and do what it chooses. But yet to reach high expectations." Glenda has never really felt trapped or caged in.

> It's because of one of the philosophies of my father. He always said, "If you're not happy doing what you're doing, then don't do it." You know, get rid of it. Do what you want to do. And so basically I guess that has been my attitude. That if I wasn't happy doing what I was doing then I'd either see that it got changed or I quit doing whatever it was.

Believing herself to be a "free spirit" entails following a path that makes her happy. Her relationship with her husband reflects the importance of freedom. "He never changed me. I was free and he accepted it. I am a free person even though I am married."

Glenda's attitude towards marriage coincides with her larger attitude towards life. She believes that much of what people think depends on attitude. "Basically, I think that a person's attitude about themselves, about what is happening between themselves and other relationships, they make themselves miserable." Explaining what she means, she says:

> It's just like a person who hasn't enough sense that, when they have an argument with their husband, that when they walk out that door, and they shut the door, they carry it to work with them, and they let it spill over onto the work, over onto whoever they associate with. Instead of, when that door shuts, that attitude is left behind that shut door. . . . Staying mad is not affecting the person you're mad at. It's not making them miserable.

They're punishing themselves. You close that door and you have it behind you, and for some reason I have the capability within myself to accomplish this.

Glenda refuses to get discouraged. "I can't say that I ever was depressed. I was saddened or sorrowful, like when I lost my parents. But I can't say I was really depressed about it." She remarks quite seriously that "the only time that I could say that I have a depressed attitude and that's when you have to make out all the checks and there isn't enough money to cover them." She links depression to poor health. "Becoming depressed is detrimental. And physical well-being and mental well-being to me is most important, so you don't do something that's gonna tear you down physically or mentally." Depression works against the individual. "I don't brood over it. I have this inner-built thing that's within me that says all that's gonna do is age me. And I don't wanna age. It's not that I don't wanna grow old. But I wanna grow old being vibrant and young. I wanna be how-many-years-young, not how-many-years-old."

Glenda describes the way she manages problems as "a pendulum that swings back and forth." Sometimes things are the way she wants and other times they are not. The pendulum image conjures ideas of the cyclical ebb and flow of the process of life. In any case, Glenda, like many Enthusiasts, believes that the real barometer for success is personal satisfaction.

> I think being happy with yourself and your own self-esteem, being satisfied with you is the important thing. . . . As long as you feel that way about yourself. That to me is more important than anything. I've always been very egotistical in the fact that I think I'm a pretty terrific person. In other words, I'm very satisfied with myself and my accomplishments.

Her definition of happiness, coupled with her conviction that we are all free to achieve it, accounts for Glenda's positive life evaluation.

Norman: "A Red Delicious Apple"

Norman, tired of his job in management in a grocery store, recently began selling cars. At twenty-nine, it was a big risk to leave the secure management job he had held for ten years and to take up the precarious occupation of selling cars. Since making the change, Norman loves his work and faces each day with excitement. He remembers the frustration of the previous job:

> Day-by-day you go back to the same job, and if you're not happy, you're not gonna do what you need to do and it's gonna reflect on your work and it's gonna reflect on you personally. And so it's a driving subject. Do I wanna wake up tomorrow and be there twenty years and not do something with my life? Or do I take a chance? It's a type of situation where time goes so fast before you realize and you can be there ten years, twenty years, and then you'd say, God! And I can't leave after twenty years.

Honesty and a realistic life assessment convinced him that the only way to manage career dissatisfaction was to take the risk and try something else. On the days when selling cars does not go very well, he encourages himself by saying, "You can't let it get you down. There's always tomorrow." His cheerfulness helps his selling technique.

> I have a deep desire to believe that I can do good. And I don't let it bother me if don't sell something. I'm a happy person. You have to put on your smiling face every day. Not a fake face, but a face where you can go out and be honest with everybody. And put your ability right up front and do what you can do best. Talk to people. Be honest with people. Selling yourself is probably the most important thing. The product is nothing if the person doesn't like you. If you can't come across on an even keel with a customer, you'll never be able to sell anything.

Committed to the values of integrity and truth, Norman realizes that people despise phoniness and can easily detect false friendliness.

> If you don't really have it in your heart, you can't fake it 'cause people know. Not judging people has always been important to me. I take people under my wings, and I've had people work for me that had nothing. I enjoyed giving. And yet, there's takers in this world and there's givers. And you've got to be both, really, to feel good about life itself. You've got to be a giver and you've got to be a taker if you're gonna survive. There are sole takers, and there are sole givers.

Norman's life metaphor reflects the common proposition that Enthusiasts make life the way they want.

> Life is like a red delicious apple. It revolves. It's fresh. And you can either eat of that life or let it spoil. You can either go out and be successful and do the things that you oughta do, go to the places that you oughta go to. Or at twenty-five or thirty years old sit at home with your mother and father and get on the welfare line and get food stamps and sap up the gravy of life. So that's what I'm saying. Either be spoiled, and do nothing, or be something. A red delicious apple is fresh and crisp, and you can either eat of that apple and do what you wanna do or let it spoil.

Norman's desire to be something inspires him to move forward onto greater things. His determination to make something of himself stems from his belief that life will be better. He also knows he is responsible for personal satisfaction and no one else can live his life.

"I don't think there's any books that are able to control your personal destiny. You get out of life what you put into it. Each person has their own feelings, their own thoughts, their own drives, their own goals, will accomplish their own feats, in their own time, at their own pace." Books cannot tell a person how to live. Instead, Norman believes people have to write their own stories and make their own histories, based on their own experiences.

> It's like each person has their own plane to fly. And you go with the flow. I feel like things happen for a reason, like this job, and I have to give it a chance. I've always sold stuff. And if I didn't give this opportunity a chance there would be a nagging question. Now I feel like I can go out and be my own boss. And I can survive. I think I'm a survivor.

One of the experiences Norman was forced to face and survive was his father's death five years ago. Although difficult, he coped, and the experience changed Norman's attitude towards death.

> I just accepted it. No other way. A loved one's gone, and I think about it every day. That's just a mountain you gotta climb, and if you don't climb it, you'll never get over it. You just gotta climb the mountain and look for a new horizon. And accept,

what will be, will be. There's still not a day goes by I don't think about it. But that's happened, and thing's happen for a reason. . . . I think death is a happy experience. Because you're born to die. You start dying the day you're born. A lot of people look on death as ugly. But I try to make something happy out of it. I try to think positive about any negative situation. That way I can cope with it. I have to believe death is a happy experience. 'Cause nobody knows. You might as well make a happy experience out of it and feel like you've fulfilled your life. Life on the other side.

Norman created a positive attitude towards death, which reinforced his ideas about life. Thinking about death as something happy makes life all the more enjoyable. His father's death also influenced how he approaches day-to-day living, inspiring him to appreciate life, just as one appreciates eating a red delicious apple.

Evelynn: "A Lesson for the Future"

Evelynn is a twenty-seven-year-old attorney for a legal-aid center. The work involves her in the problems of low-income clients—how to obtain the basic necessities of life—food, clothing, and shelter. Working with desperate individuals makes Evelynn truly appreciate the good things in her life. She knows the impact of her work on low-income people could be great if she can bring change through legislation. The potential for reform helps her to decide which cases to take. "How significant is the impact of your representation for each individual case for other people having similar problems? Is it gonna have some effect on them? And you take cases which have a long-range, a large-scale effect."

Although she sees problems within the legal system, Evelynn believes it has a built-in mechanism that allows the poor to receive fair treatment. "There's always another landlord, another trustee, another application. There's always a way. Nothing is so critical that you can't restore it. The system is not that bad where there's not something that these people can get from it."

Vivacious and energetic, she is dedicated to helping the people she represents. "It's always a good feeling to help those people who really have no other means of help or support." Unfortunately, some people fall outside the agency's guidelines. Although upsetting, Evelynn copes by accepting the fact that she cannot help everyone.

On other occasions, when she does not win, she rationalizes the lost cases with her optimistic philosophy: "There's always hope that maybe the legislature will change. Because generally when you lose a case, the law is bad. And you can never give up on that." She believes community education would help solve the problem. "Unless you've experienced poverty you really don't understand."

Evelynn's interest in education extends beyond her formal training to daily life. Her life metaphor affirms the importance of learning.

> Life is a lesson for the future. Everything I learn from day to day is valuable to me. My life today and the problems that I experience in these times will prepare me for the future. I don't expect to have these same type of problems, because I'll know how to deal with them. Life today is preparation for life tomorrow.

Part of the education process means facing problems and solving them. "I like being alive. I like having to work out life experiences. . . . You know, the different things that happen. On the job, working out problems as they come through. Working out personal problems. I really enjoy dealing with those kind of problems."

Unrealistic expectations can undermine one's optimism and even one's health. Evelynn's positive life evaluation includes acknowledging that not all problems can be solved.

> If you don't achieve a small goal that you set for yourself, then at that point is psychological destruction. I work with a lot of clients who have medical problems, and what it appears to me has happened to many of them is that they've set these goals for themselves, and they're inflexible goals, and then they couldn't attain these goals. Or say they achieve a goal, and something happens that they take a step backwards. They're not able to cope with that.

Evelynn maintains her optimism by carefully assessing which problems are worth working on. "I usually take things in their stride. As long as there's something that I can do about it. I gotta decide if I'm gonna face my problem or ignore it and forget about it." She balances the priorities in her personal life the same way and acts accordingly.

I look at what the alternatives are. How difficult will it be to overcome what it is. And if it looks like it's just practically impossible, or if it's gonna take too much from me emotionally, and timewise, then I might say forget it. So there's not much I can do about it. If it's something that's really important to me, I'll say I don't care what it takes, or how much time or how much money it takes, I'll do it.

Her positive attitude, then, results from her ability to regard problems as a means for her growth and to avoid fixating on them. For instance, her husband, a policeman, works one hundred miles away in a large city. The distance has been difficult, but she tries to make the most of it. "I look at it as a challenge. We'll get out of this. I believe you get out what you put into it. If you fight something, you'll come out of it feeling pretty good."

Sometimes it is essential to leave a problem for a while, to block it out mentally. For instance, Evelynn is learning to leave her clients' problems at work. "I still haven't totally adjusted. I'll wake up at night thinking about a client's problems. And think of some great idea. It's not easy to make that separation." Fortunately, she has a busy home life and a three-year-old daughter who demands her attention, making it easy to push the day's cases out of her mind.

A process providing endless experience; a wheel forming a perfect circle; a bird flying freely; a tasty red delicious apple; and a continuous lesson—animate and inanimate objects alike reflect the Enthusiast's positive evaluation and optimistic assessment. Cycles and growth make life a happy experience.

Control

"I believe that I can make anything happen." "Life can be as good or as bad as I want, it's entirely up to me." "Everyone has opportunities available to them if they want to use them."

Control refers to the *perception* of one's power to influence one's destiny. Seldom is control a constant in our lives. Even those who think themselves in command experience moments or phases when they feel weak and vulnerable. Sometimes it is natural to question our influence. Facing death, for example, leaves most of us with a sense of powerlessness to control anything completely. At other times we seem to have more control. When our well-laid plans work out and our goals are being achieved we say that things are falling into place. We feel that we are in control and that life is as it ought to be.

Although control was not one of the dimensions by which the life metaphors were rated, it emerged indirectly as a recurrent concern for most people.[5] Like activity and evaluation, control is measured along a continuum. The range extends from believing one is solely responsible for directing one's life and deciding one's destiny, to believing one has no control and is entirely at the mercy of fate.

Enthusiasts believe that they are responsible for making life the way they want it to be. They seldom rely on others to change their lives, realizing that the motivation must come from within. Even Enthusiasts who believe in God (or some other external power) assume they are responsible for the way they live their lives. They do not leave it up to God to get them their promotion or to help solve the family's problems (as Fatalists might).

Four individuals illustrate the Enthusiast's sense of control. Val, a graduate student and a drum majorette for a college band, believes that "the more pressure you're under, the more control you have." Rudy is an ex-serviceman, returning to school to get a better job. Fascinated by computers, he studies them because of their potentially unlimited control. Arlene is a housewife struggling with a weight problem, which metaphorically represents the amount of control she has. Bonnie, a working student, struggled with an awkward self-image for many years. Marrying to escape the home life she hated has turned out to be the best thing she could have done. Each story demonstrates how Enthusiasts believe they can take charge of their lives. Val sees herself as constantly in control and describes how she excels at everything she does. Rudy, Arlene, and Bonnie, on the other hand, can quickly recall times when they have felt out of control, and they use that wisdom to guide and maintain their present control.

Val: "What You Make It"

Val believes she has total control over what happens. An unforgettable experience she had in the sixth grade taught her that it is possible to change anything to make it the way you want it to be.

> My handwriting was slanted backwards. I was somewhat ambidextrous. But I had been given the pen in my right hand. I started writing my letters backwards. Well, they told me, "You can't do that, and we're giving you a B in handwriting because of that." And I said, "I'm not gonna take this B. This is ridiculous. Handwriting is easy to do." And so I worked and worked. And I practiced my handwriting and I made it. I mean, I did every style you could imagine. Made huge letters and little teeny ones and every kind of handwriting until one of my teachers said, "That's good handwriting. That's the one that will give you an A in handwriting." And then I used that from then on. And I still write that way. So that was something that was difficult to change that I really worked at.

Her life metaphor reflects her philosophy that the individual can achieve anything.

> Life is what you make it. Life is right there and it's fantastic. It can be fantastic. It can also be bad. Maybe a lemon. It just depends on how you look at it. It depends on how you wanna treat it. Because you make it the way it is. If you wanna make it rotten, it's gonna be rotten. I wanna make it fantastic, and it is fantastic. Every day can be wonderful.

Like everything else in her life, Val believes she can get it if she wants it enough. If she wants life to be fantastic, then it must be so. A twenty-four-year-old student, she is working on a master's degree in counseling, but her first love is baton twirling. Her success in twirling for the college band is another reason life is so fantastic, which reinforces her belief that "dreams can come true."

> I wanted to twirl for the band ever since, oh, ever since I was born practically and was old enough to understand what that was. My father went to the college and I heard him and my mother talk about twirling. It didn't mean a whole lot to me until about the age of ten. At that time I started twirling. And then it became more of a reality.

Being part of the band is the most important, fulfilling part of her life. "Right now I'm being the best I can be. . . . I can understand what you must be saying. 'She's got everything.' And that's how I feel. I've got everything." Val believes she is the best.

> There's so many things that are appealing. I like being in the public eye, and to make people happy, to help the sport of twirling for one thing. I think the most important thing for me is that every time I perform I do my best. And I think people appreciate it. I feel the excitement. It's incredible. It's hard to explain. But you can imagine. You can feel they are with you.

Twirling is such an integral part of living that it becomes a metaphor for her life.

> As far as life goes, I think it's the same as twirling. I deal with things in the same way. The more pressure you're under, the more control you have to have. Sometimes you don't have it. . . . I do what I can, and that's all I can do. As long as I'm being the best that I can be. It's all that I can expect of myself.

Val thrives under pressure, which means putting herself on the line. The more pressure there is, the more control she has. She chooses challenging situations to test herself and her control. "I've been in competition twirling for fourteen years now and I can handle the pressure. I know what it takes to do your best."

She believes she succeeds because she takes advantage of every opportunity that comes her way. She remembers psyching herself up for the twirling trials. "I want it. I've worked for it." Believing that she controls her life helps her achieve the goals she sets.

> I really feel like if there's something I want, I'm gonna get it. If there's something I really wanna go after and it's my number-one priority, I'm gonna make it happen. And that's such a good feeling. I don't wanna come off like I'm always up and always happy and things always go right for me. Most of the time they do. And I try and focus on that. Things go wrong for sure, but as long as you don't focus on that, you're OK.

Rudy: "What You Make It"

Rudy, a thirty-two-year-old veteran, took control of his life when he returned to school as a full-time student to study electronics. He had been in the service for six years and then worked in management before returning to school. Rudy approaches life with a spirit of determination. "There's always something you can do to not be bored. Go somewhere and do something. Meet somebody new. Turn the day around." Controlling life and shaping it the way he wants is part of his life metaphor.

Life is what you make it, how you want to live it, what you want to do with it. You can't live it to anybody else's expectations of what they want you to do. Life is like totally up to you. . . . Living life the way you want to makes it worthwhile. Accomplishing goals that you set for yourself. Things that you've set out to do and done. The challenges that I've set up and accomplished makes me feel pretty good.

Rudy dislikes being restricted, and the service taught him that he did not like living according to others' rules and expectations. The service also forced him to confront his feelings about authority and power. He equates institutions, such as the military and college, with control. Part of his attraction to the service stemmed from the "sameness," the "regimentation," and the "discipline." At the same time, he equates losing control with "being stuck" and "locked into" one particular life-style. On the one hand, Rudy likes being in situations where an external force (like the military) controls his life. On the other hand, he shuns the idea because he wants to take control himself. In the end, he left the military because he felt it had too much power over his life. By leaving, Rudy felt he took control. Although he misses some aspects of military life, he feels that now he can move forward in any direction he wants.

His feelings about the service reflect his attitude toward control. "If you wanna get locked in for six years, you got good job security. I guess that's a benefit. But the military's got a lot of drawbacks too." One of the drawbacks is "playing the game."

It's like comparing you going to college. You want your degree. You gotta play the game. You gotta attend classes. When they schedule you, you gotta go. When they tell you to do something, you gotta do it. And that's the way the service is. You gotta do what they tell you to do, when they tell you. They totally control your life. To the extent that you've signed up for the service, you're there to do with as they please.

Rudy gravitates toward situations in which control shifts back and forth. He thinks computers are like the service because they also have the potential to "totally control" the operations. He likes working with microprocessors, finding out "how they all work and how to put 'em all together to make 'em work." He is also curious about the potential control that computers have. "A person might stand there and physically do everything, but the computer just totally controls the operations."

Arlene: "A Puzzle"

Arlene, a thirty-four-year-old housewife, values control so much because she has experienced the dramatic effects of losing it. "Struggling" with a weight problem, which she has "fought" all her life, she moves in and out of control. Her life metaphor emphasizes the importance of self-control.

> Life is like a puzzle. You have choices to make. I had a friend tell me one time, "there are two things you have no control over—birth and death." Once you're born that's it. You have to live. And you have a choice. You have things at your disposal to make life what you want it to be. There are side things that come in that you don't have control over, but basically you've got certain things that you can work with. You can make life as happy as you want or as rotten as you want. I think it all depends on attitude.

"Choice" and "attitude" are critical issues. For the most part, Arlene wants to believe that one can control one's choices in life. By treating life as a puzzle she pictures herself as a player trying to fit the pieces together. As her weight goes up, she places the pieces one way. As her weight goes down, she moves them in another direction. She controls the pieces, just as she controls her choices about what to eat. Not surprisingly, she feels frustrated when she makes a mistake or the wrong choice.

She recently lost eighty-six pounds and has maintained the loss for almost one year. She feels in control and able to make choices again: the puzzle is fitting together. She draws strength from people in similar circumstances and does not feel embarrassed about relying on them.

> I'm active in a self-help group here in town. I'm a compulsive overeater. It's the same as Alcoholics Anonymous, only it's for overeaters. We work together. It's a lot of self-help therapy. One-

on-one with people who suffer from the same disease. We do a lot of reading. We do a lot of meditating. We do a lot of writing—anything positive. We try to completely get out of the negative because we feel the negative causes us to be where we are anyway.

Through the group, Arlene learned to like herself and to develop a positive self-image. She overcame inferiority feelings. "The fact that I've always been bigger than everybody else made me feel like I never fit in." Troubled by feelings of "helplessness," she thinks society has misconceptions about overweight people that make the problem more difficult. "People like myself are not just gluttons. We're not just weak people who sit down at the table and stuff ourselves because we don't know any better. We have a disease. We can't help it. I have a compulsion. I have an addiction to sugar. If I start, I cannot stop. It's just like the person who drinks."

Treating her problem, not as one of gluttony, but as one of control, helps her cope better. By renaming the problem, she also reframed it. She explains how it feels to be out of control: "I can't stop. And it's a terrifying thing to be caught up in something that you know is killing you. But you can't stop. You don't have the will. And you just can't do it on your own. This group has really helped me a lot."

No matter how much she values control, Arlene believes it is important to ask others for help if it is needed. "People try to do everything alone. We never want to admit failure because we always want to be perfect. It's very hard for most people to say, 'I made a mistake.' There isn't anything wrong with making a mistake, if you learn from it."

Regarding mistakes as growth experiences reflects the way Enthusiasts are able to turn their lives around. Looking at life as a way to learn about themselves and others gives them a certain amount of control. They know they can use their perspective to get through the rough times. Even though there are periods in Arlene's life when she is "out of control," she keeps on fighting, knowing that eventually she will transform her problem.

Bonnie: "A Game"

Bonnie, twenty-two, works full-time as a postmaster in a drugstore postal station to put herself and her student-husband through college. In almost every facet of her life, she demonstrates the Enthusiast's skill in controlling life events. She deals with impatient patrons at work by treating them pleasantly, which makes it harder for them to be nasty. She confronts obstacles in her job by formulating elaborate ideas about how to increase the efficiency of the postal system. Although she often feels frustrated by her job, she converts that frustration into a positive experience. "It really teaches me patience . . . and when I go into other stores, I am the nicest person."

Bonnie suffered a difficult childhood, mainly because her father abandoned the family. Although it happened many years ago, she still wonders why. After her father left, her mother treated her badly. "I kept asking, why doesn't she like me? What have I done to this woman? I spent many, many, many years of crying and just wondering and just thinking that I did not belong there. I've quit asking myself why. I just vowed that I'd never put my kids through that."

Bonnie's marriage provided an escape from the oppression of her unhappy home, but she still needed to cope with the effects of those bitter years.

> When I got married it was like freedom. I was out, away from my mother. And yet when I got married I felt so guilty that I had left, and I felt like that for about two months. And then all of a sudden, it just left. But I don't think about it anymore. Everything I've gone through when I was young, I just put in the back of my head, and when I'm a parent and it comes to a situation, I promise I'll handle it differently.

Bonnie is convinced that her marriage helped her wounded self-esteem. She believes her husband is her ideal mate. "I couldn't have found anybody better if I'd have put an ad in the paper. It was one of those—I saw him and I knew right then." Much of their compatibility comes from his easygoing nature.

> Before I got married I used to worry about everything. Are we gonna be able to afford this? Can we afford that? Then one day my husband said, "Hey, if the money's gonna be there, it's gonna be there. And if it's not, it's not. All the worrying in the world is not gonna make that amount grow." I don't worry about money at all because it doesn't help. It just makes you more tired.

Bonnie's life metaphor reveals a sense of adventure, a penchant for trying new things, and a desire to be different. "Life is like a game to me. Because you can take a game and you can play the same old routine and never change it, and that's what your life will be. But you can also change the rules or play it backwards or just totally forget about it."

She senses that she needs variety in her life. She cannot tolerate "the same old routine" and knows she would tire of the game or become bored by it. She also implicitly believes she can change her fate. From experience, she knows she could have gone through life with a bad self-image, but her active intervention prevented it. Thinking more about life, she adapted her original ideas.

> But then again, it's like, to me it's gonna be like whatever you put into it. So like, say you're a sculptor and you're making a sculpture, what you put into it is what you're gonna get. To me, that's life in general, because if you sit home all day, that's what you're gonna get. . . nothin'. But if you go out and do crazy things, take risks, go overboard once in a while, it's more rewarding.

Bonnie thinks of herself as a work of art, carefully and lovingly fashioned by its creator. She takes responsibility for making that creation a "rewarding" and meaningful experience.

> I'm not afraid to try anything. A lot of people say, "I'm not very good," or "I'm afraid." Well, how are you gonna get any better if you don't go try it? If I wanna do something I try it. I don't care if I don't do it perfect. I can't stand perfectionists, because everything in your life has to be perfect. You live your life to impress someone else.

Bonnie's eagerness to try new things reflects the Enthusiasts' belief that they can control anything if they want. Each person in this section possesses an ingrained sense of power to direct their lives—the determined baton twirler leading her own band; the ex-Marine obsessed with the controlling forces of the computer; the conscientious problem solver, putting together the pieces of a puzzle; and the fastidious postal worker creating her own rules.

Motivation

"Life is what you make it." "I figured I'm the one that decided I'm gonna do it. And I guess I won't give up. I figure, I'll do anything to survive and not fail." "I somehow feel that we make our own luck."

Interestingly, the most predominant life metaphor in the entire study is life is "what you make it," and it is used most frequently by Enthusiasts. Five people (Teresa, George, Val, Ron, Rudy) explicitly claim "what you make it" as their life metaphor. The word *make* provides the internal driving force that motivates them.[6]

One might think there is not enough difference between control and motivation to warrant two separate discussions. Does motivation subsume control? Or does control subsume motivation? I have separated them because there are shades of difference. You may believe that you have control but not feel motivated to do anything about it; on the other hand, you may perceive little control but try like crazy to change the way things are.

Enthusiasts are success oriented and usually excel at whatever they do. Most are self-starters, motivated by a variety of goals—"to learn," "to achieve," "to fulfill ambition," and to "pursue personal growth." Four of the people I interviewed typify the intensity of motivation characteristic of the enthusiastic orientation. Ron undertook a business venture, which he turned into a success. Teresa, a cosmetologist, changed her attitude toward life following her brother's suicide. Dorcas, who works in the college cafeteria, is a bouncing, energetic woman determined to make the most of life, in spite of humble beginnings. Father Dave's spiritual motivation keeps him moving forward as he invites his parishioners to accompany him on his journey. In their unique ways, each one exemplifies how Enthusiasts are motivated by the belief that life is "what you make it."

Ron: "What You Make It"

Ron owns and manages a popcorn shop. At forty-two, he loves working for himself and loves the rewards it has brought. "My wife and myself have gone from nothing to a very profitable business." In spite of his success, he remembers that things were difficult when he started. During the first year, his wife helped during the day and went home in the evening to be with the children. By the second year, he needed to work another job to meet the financial demands.

> The first year, I came in about nine o'clock in the morning and went home about ten o'clock at night. . . . In the second year, I worked my other job from eight to five. And then I came out here every evening and then worked Saturday and Sunday. I did that for two years. Then the year after that, I started to take evenings off, and Sundays off. It was finally getting to the point where the business was starting to pay for itself, and the bills were covered.

Working long hours and taking work home were necessary sacrifices to make the business work. "To really make your own business go, you gotta be in touch with it all the time." Never losing his determination, Ron taught himself to survive. "I figured I'm the one that decided I'm gonna do it. And I guess I won't give up. I figure, I'll do anything to survive and not fail." Knowing that success comes through hard work, sacrifice, and perseverance, he does not rely on fate or luck.

> When you're successful, people say, well you were real lucky. They say that you happened to be in the right place at the right time. Most people don't know what's involved. How hard a person has to work to get something going. They don't realize that the person made their own luck there. I mean, they could maybe give up and say, to heck with it. But instead they go ahead and visualize that they can make a go of it.

Ron's life metaphor reflects his belief in himself. "Life is what you make it. A lot of people say you have bad luck. But I feel that we make our own luck. The fact, I guess, has to do with your own ambition and willingness to take a chance. You make your own luck. 'Cause you can't sit around waiting for something to happen to you."

His outlook has developed over the years mainly because of the success of his commercial venture, which marked "the biggest change" in his life: "the motivation of wanting to get ahead superseded my negative feelings." The victory and achievement he acquired through his business reinforced Ron's belief that "life is entirely what you make it. You can be or do anything you wanna do. I feel it's fine for anybody to do anything or whatever they wanna do as long as they're not hurting somebody else when they're doing it."

He recalls how he thought about life before his prosperity: "At one time I had more of a tendency to give up. You gotta be smart enough to know when it's time to quit trying something. And frequently I would say I can't do this. But now I never say can't. I changed a lot in that attitude. I can do whatever I want to do. When I'm willing to put the effort out."

Ron attributes his success to enjoying what he does. "To do something you like" motivates him more than anything, and he enjoys working hard on any project that inspires him. "If I'm involved in something that I'm really interested in, I might work twelve or fifteen hours on it. I don't realize it, and I don't feel tired from it. I think if I really get involved I feel relaxed and refreshed."

Teresa: "What You Make It"

Teresa, thirty-four, works as a cosmetologist in a beauty salon. She admits bluntly, "If I didn't like it, I wouldn't do it." Her life metaphor reflects her overall approach.

> Life is what you make it. If you sit around and feel sorry for yourself all the time, you're gonna feel depressed. If you don't go out and find the different things in life, you're gonna feel bad. But you only get out of it what you put into it. If you're only gonna give it half the effort, then you should expect to receive half an effort.

The preceding paragraph repeats many of the themes already discussed. Teresa's life metaphor developed out of a personal crisis that marked a turning point in her life and changed her entire perspective.

> I used to think that everything had to be perfect. Housework had to be perfect. Then one day my brother killed himself. And you always think you're gonna do this tomorrow and you're gonna do that tomorrow and you never did it. I guess when that happened it made me realize, you should do it now because you may not be able to do it. You may not get the opportunity again.

And you're gonna lose out on a lot in life. The housework will always be there. It changed my way of thinking about a lot of things.

Knowing she could either feel bitter and depressed or appreciate life even more, she chose the more positive, active way of coping. Like Sue, she learned that she needs to take advantage of the present because the future is too uncertain.

> You always think you're gonna go see somebody, call somebody. You always think you're gonna stop and do this. Unless you really force yourself, you put it off. People are always doing that. If you wanna do it, take the time to do it. You're gonna put something else off, but it'll be there or you can get to it as soon as you can. People take things for granted. If you can do it you should go do it. Because you may not get the opportunity.

Teresa recalls that her brother's death brought other changes. "I used to be scared. But everybody's gonna die sometime. If that's what you're scared of. There's nothing to be scared of I guess. It's really hard to describe. 'Cause you're all gonna end up somewhere sometime. And there's no use wondering what it would have been like if. . . ."

Comprehending death became a way to understand life. Although a terrible experience, Teresa managed to transform it. Enthusiasts have the ability to turn something negative into something positive, which Teresa clearly demonstrates by aggressively taking control of her life. Instead of being overwhelmed by her brother's death, she used it to motivate her to appreciate life. Now she savors all her relationships.

> Love is one of the scariest things in the whole world. Getting close to a person is frightening. Two people get so dependent on each other. It's good, but you never know. Something could happen to one or the other, and then you're gonna be stuck. And I think, no matter whether it's a man or a woman, they should be able to take care of themselves, without the other one. My children are very independent, which I think is good.

Teresa takes advantage of life, seizing the moment rather than waiting for an opportunity in the future. "You should do what comes along, if you have the time and it seems right." Having asked herself questions about life and death, Teresa believes it is possible to find answers. "Eventually you get an answer. You find out why something was the way it was. It may take you a while to realize why such and such happened. But usually you end up getting an answer." The answer she found to her brother's death strengthens her and helps her cope with day-to-day life.

Dorcas: "My Life's Pretty Good"

Dorcas has worked as a cashier at the campus cafeteria for sixteen years. She constantly talks about life in terms of what she does and where she is going. She has found her unwavering motivation in a loving marital relationship that spills out into her relationships with others. At sixty-one, she and her husband travel together on vacations, driving all over the country to visit friends and relatives. Togetherness is important. "We go everywhere together." She whispers, "I think if you can just find the right man, you and him can cook!" She thinks she and her husband have "got it together," making a "good life," which she states clearly in her life metaphor:

> My life is pretty good. I really feel good about my life. I've been married thirty-nine years, and my husband and I are still together. He's retired. And we have a lovely home. I have a lot of outside interests that I'm doin'—Church work, and I visit a lot of people in the nursing homes. There's always something. I just keep goin'.

Like Peggy, her life metaphor seems to echo her mother's advice. As a young girl, she remembers her mother telling her to be daring.

> My mother always told me, "It's only what you make out of it," she said, "If you don't try to make nothin' out of it, it's not gonna be anything. You got to get up and make things happen." And I believe in that philosophy. If you want things to happen, you got to get out and make 'em happen. Nothing's gonna come to you on a silver platter.

As Dorcas grew up, her family struggled, and many opportunities were denied because there was not enough money.

> My mom had to do everything for us by herself. It was a matter of survival. When you got out of high school you just went lookin' for a job. Nothin' else. You wasn't gonna get to go to college or

things like that 'cause there just wasn't enough money. I wanted to be a high-powered secretary. . . . But I had my children. And I always managed to find a job, so I didn't worry about it too much. Just kept going the way I was going.

Although Dorcas would have liked something different for her life, she moved forward and welcomed everything. She believes things happen for a reason. "I guess everybody has a station in life. Maybe it's not to be some fabulous person or have some fabulous job. But I think all the little things add up to the big things." She feels motivated to share her good fortune, believing people should care for others and share their energy and time. "You think of all the people that need somebody. If everybody just took one or two people, you wouldn't have as many problems. Everybody would be taken care of. So I look at it: you do your little part, then somebody comes along and does theirs, and everybody's taken care of."

Dorcas envisions a large-scale system of care giving. "Everything is in its place. People are not neglected. And they feel that somebody cares about them." She keeps moving to survive. "Each morning that you can get up and get goin', that's good. . . . It's a kinda' rolling thing that goes into one to the other."

There is no time for monotony, and Dorcas follows a "routine that's not boring." Involved in many community activities, she does not sit around when she gets home. She is likely to visit nursing homes, take meals to elderly people who cannot leave their homes, and care for sick children. "My life is just kinda' filled up." Dorcas believes that in addition to making someone else's life a little better, people help themselves by helping others. "When you're doing something for somebody else, you forget about yourself. You don't think about your little aches and pains and all the things that got you going, 'cause you're doing something for someone else."

Father Dave: "A Journey"

At thirty-eight, Father Dave is attuned to the predominantly youthful Catholic college community he serves. Not surprisingly, his story is one of personal motivation and intense desire to become a priest. He vividly remembers his "calling."

My own journey began in the third grade with a priest who really impressed me. I didn't want to be a priest until the seventh grade when I read the scripture passage, "love one another." And at the time I just remember how things were in the world. There were a lot of conflicts and a lot of battles going on. And I thought how the world would be different if everyone loved one another. I know that had a real strong impact on me.

Although not entirely sure that he wanted to be a priest, Father Dave entered the seminary at thirteen and quickly became caught up in the life. "I was kind of dreamy. Kind of idealistic. The seminary is like a boy's boarding school. And I enjoyed that. I was a rowdy kid, and I liked sports and athletics." Continuing his education at a progressive seminary, which emphasized social programs, he found that he liked working with handicapped children and remedial students. He also liked the spiritual atmosphere because the people were "really working together. They had a great sense of ministry and it was exciting."

Father Dave finally realized his calling as he heard an older priest ask, "Why do you stay? Why are you still here?" The audience of young priests gave various answers. The older priest persisted, "What does Jesus have to do with your life?" With that question Father Dave decided to begin his journey. "Nobody had ever asked that question. Such a fundamental question. I hadn't quite made the connection with Christ at that point. . . . Then I had to begin a journey. Just who is Jesus? What is the relationship that I have? What does he call us to?"

Wanting to follow in Christ's footsteps, Father Dave adopted the philosophy that life is a journey, which is his life metaphor.

I would describe life in terms of a journey. But we're walking through it. Sometimes we see clearly, and other times it's dark and hidden. And you can still walk and think through it. And walking through it, in walking through a darkness, you come to a fuller understanding. A sense of it. And sometimes tripping and falling. And yet still "come follow me" is what you have to remember. Get up again and continue on the journey.

Scriptural imperatives motivate Father Dave on his journey. "God's word to His disciples is always 'come follow me.' So I see it as a continuing journey. Walking with Him through life. And He calls us to love one another." Like so many priests who use metaphors, Father Dave uses the image of a gardener tending to his plants to explain the satisfaction that motivates caring for his parishioners. Watching them grow, he is "like a gardener."

> A gardener has a small plot of land and looks after the different needs of the plants. He tries to provide nourishment all year round. He takes an interest in the growth of the different plants. Also, the gardener realizes it's not up to him. He can't provide the sunshine. So a lot of things are beyond the gardener's work. It's also cooperating.

His work counseling students and preparing couples for marriage helps him expand his understanding of human nature. In his firsthand observation of suffering and the human capacity to endure it, he finds monumental inspiration.

> I would say it's the amount of suffering that people have gone through. And yet also, the amount of feeling. I've seen people go through some things that I could not imagine going through. I don't know how people have endured things and still hold together. I just love that they have dealt with it. I'd be a basket case. Very often I see people going through a lot of pain. But they persist through. Usually I see people come through it. And that has amazed me tremendously. I never dreamt of the amount of pain in people's lives.

Father Dave believes that God controls life and destiny, but rather than feeling himself a puppet in the hands of some cosmic stage director, he finds in God's providence the source of his deepest motivations. The sense of external control comforts him and others.

> If someone's having a rough time. I tell them the story about one of my classmates in the priesthood. We were outside in the country. And it was really green and lush. And I said, "Joe, just think. Do you believe that God takes that which the body discards and doesn't have any use for, and is able to really nourish these plants. And make it so rich? Joe, just think, if God can work wonders out of this shit, just think of what he can do with you." That's the bottom line.

Enthusiasts are motivated by a sincere belief that life is "what you make it." Embedded in this statement is a vision of people who actively shape and mold themselves and their lives. Whether in running a successful business, overcoming a brother's suicide, helping others less fortunate, or giving spiritual guidance, Enthusiasts find tireless motivation in life itself.

Many of the stories reflect the ways Enthusiasts cope. Everyone faces problems that must be handled in one way or another, and human nature reflects an enormous range of coping skills and strategies. Some people suffer great losses and survive quite well; others confront smaller problems and manage very badly. The tendency to approach life actively and positively influences the way Enthusiasts cope. In fact, all the qualities discussed so far combine to form a style of handling situations. We find that Enthusiasts face their problems. Even painful experiences can be reframed as "learning experiences." They do not deny that bad things happen, but instead of dwelling on them, they turn their energy toward making the most of the situation. From this perspective, everything contributes to life's goal of self-improvement.

It is important to Enthusiasts to find the most healthy way of coping with any situation. They try to balance the positive and the negative and, in many cases, change negative events into positive ones by imposing their optimistic perspective. Their efforts to be positive and optimistic become part of their way of coping. They believe that they can choose to make life whatever they want it to be and they see no point in making it miserable. The next chapter, "The Fatalist," focuses on people who believe that fate cannot be changed and that the individual cannot be held accountable for what happens in life.

CHAPTER 5

The Fatalist

> As the old Hermit of Prague, that never saw pen
> and ink, very wittily said to a niece of King
> Gorboduc, "That that is is ."
>> William Shakespeare, *Twelfth Night*, IV, 11.
>
> What doctrine call you this, Che sarà sarà. What
> will be, shall be.
>> Thomas Marlowe, *Dr. Faustus*, I, i.

When we hear the word *fate* we think of such things as "destiny," "fortune," "chance," or "luck." We often say, "Let's not cry over spilled milk"; "Take the rough with the smooth"; "What will be, will be"; and "There's no flying from fate." These expressions rest on the implicit idea that, try as one might, it is impossible for the individual to change the course of events.

Not only do references to fate creep into our everyday language, they also influence our actions. Throwing salt over your shoulder, not walking under a ladder, or staying home on Friday the thirteenth are examples of fate that we call superstition. People sometimes think of "old wives' tales" under the heading of fate. Spinning a coin over a pregnant woman's belly, for example, is supposed to predict the sex of the child.

How many people read their horoscopes every day? Even those who do not believe in astrology are mildly curious. If the stars are not for you, there are a number of other ways of having the future forecasted, ranging from gazing into a crystal ball and having your palm read, to finding out what your tarot cards mean. Whatever the form, these "occult sciences" exploit the human proclivity to believe in fate.

Fatalism is often regarded as the popular name for determinism, a word borrowed from physics to describe the movement of billiard balls: as one ball strikes another, its direction is already established based on the way the balls are set up.[1] When applied to human beings, this principle argues that people do not have free will. Just as the movement of the billiard balls is predictable, so is the course of a person's life.

Much like the characters in Greek tragedies who are unable to alter their destinies, Fatalists resign themselves to their lot. The inevitable forces of destiny that characterize tragedy have fascinated audiences for centuries. In most cases, the central character undergoes a change of fortune, usually from prosperity to misery owing to some mistaken act. The unfortunate turn of events comes from the character's "tragic flaw." Indeed, the tragic character's appeal lies in his or her inability to combat the "winds of fortune." In addition, audiences usually identify with the characters. Tragic heroes are just like us in many ways, reinforcing the idea that fate can intervene in anyone's life.

Some of the most memorable tragic figures come from Shakespeare's plays. Macbeth, Hamlet, King Lear, and Othello are figures whose fates were disastrous. Contemporary writers continue the themes. Eugene O'Neill's play *Mourning Becomes Electra* is a revision of Aeschylus's play *Orestia*. O'Neill moved the location from Greece to New York and changed the theme from Orestes's tragic fate to a family's psychological fate. Most of Samuel Becket's characters are trapped by fate: the tramps, Vladimir and Estragon in *Waiting for Godot,* and the elderly, blind, paralyzed Hamm in *Endgame* are caught in a world from which there is no escape. Even the popular soap operas can be thought of as modern morality plays, in which everything has consequences: star-crossed lovers whose destinies seem inevitable; clandestine murderers whose crimes will eventually be discovered. Good acts are rewarded, bad ones never go unpunished.

Fatalists are the antithesis of Enthusiasts, representing the less active and the less positive orientation. They do not evaluate life affirmatively. Although not extremely negative, they seem not to care one way or the other about life. The best way to describe Fatalists is to say that they tend to be less positive. In many cases they are pessimistic, cynical, or sarcastic. They frequently have a gloomy outlook, and some are even sad about life and prone to feeling defeated.

Their activity, reflected by their lack of energy for life, matches their evaluation. Seldom exuberant, they are nonchalant and apathetic. Unlike Enthusiasts or Antagonists, who try to change the course of events, Fatalists succumb to life. Their attitude encourages them to accept what happens, making them passive receivers. They typically say "life just is," believing that life is something that simply exists. More importantly, they believe that life happens *to* them. For the Fatalist, life can be great, or a bowl of cherries, or not. Whatever the case, life is not a big deal, and certainly nothing to get excited about.

On the whole, Fatalists find it difficult to liken life to anything. Of all the people I interviewed, they gave the least clearly defined life metaphors. For most, the subject of life is not something they spend considerable time thinking about. In spite of this, their Fatalistic orientation provides a lens through which they view the world. The lack of enthusiasm and outward signs of pleasure do not mean Fatalists are dissatisfied. On the contrary, they rest comfortably knowing they do not have to worry. As long as their basic needs are met, they feel content.

Like Enthusiasts, they represent a relatively large population. Not surprisingly, people who are less positive are also less active.[2] Seventeen people are classified as Fatalists, and I have arranged this chapter as I did the previous one.[3] The attributes to be covered are activity, evaluation, control, and motivation. As before, each topic will be discussed separately, beginning with activity.

Activity

"I take things as they come." "I just roll along with the punches." "I don't think I've ever actually prepared myself for the future in any way." "I move around slow. I never get in a hurry about doing anything."

Activity refers to one's energy and enthusiasm for life. Fatalists accept whatever happens and have little compulsion to try to change things. Consequently, they gravitate toward the less active end of the continuum. Often submissive individuals, they are resigned to life. They are not usually busy and prefer to spend their leisure time doing nothing. They prefer minimal activity and certainly do not wish they were like the energetic Enthusiasts or the aggressive Antagonists.

The expression of time in people's lives is usually one way to detect how active they are. For Fatalists, time moves slowly as they go about their lives in no great hurry. They show little eagerness to get things done, take their time working on projects, and make slow progress on whatever they do. They experience stable routines; the days, weeks, months, and years remain much the same. They expect few interruptions in the cycle of their lives, and they find that few unpredictable or unscheduled events occur.

Fatalists rarely anticipate the future, preferring instead to look backward. For many, the past is a source of comfort, which helps them cope with the changes they experience. Many lament the past and vividly describe the way things used to be. Others avoid dealing with the future by consciously living in the present. They focus on each day, saying that they take life one day at a time. Since life is already predetermined, they see little point in trying to change the way the next day will be.

The section begins with Steve, a musician, who works as a cook while he waits to become a famous rock star. Edward is a thoughtful college professor who savors the predictability of university life. Claude has worked at the fire station for thirty years and likes his solitary, inactive job answering the phone. Mike, a retired painter, works as an attendant of a parking lot where he sits on his own in a small cubicle. Each person describes the Fatalistic orientation in general and specifically reveals how inactivity marks their lives.

Steve: "A Fine Line Between Frustration and Amusement"

At twenty-four, Steve plays guitar and writes songs for a band. He is not actively pursuing success because he is "not willing to starve just yet." He has been working as a chef for four and one half years to support himself until he becomes famous. "You keep telling yourself, you're gonna save up enough money to do something." Although tired of the job, he needs the money to keep writing songs but does not have the energy to do both. "I would have to give up one thing, and go all out for the other, and I'd rather wait until I move to another town before I do that." His life metaphor explains his predicament.

A fine line between frustration and amusement. We're all constantly in a process of learning. The old cliché, "you're never too old to learn." And I think that's where the frustration and amusement comes in. The frustration that you're still learning about things. The amusement comes from the kinds of things you're learning.

Steve's inactivity is best reflected by his preference for spending time thinking rather than acting. Describing himself as an "armchair philosopher," he contemplates the intellectual meaning of life. "You learn about everything. About yourself and how you relate to changes all around you. . . . The most important thing that anybody can learn is that there's so much to be learned about everything. . . ."

Steve's desire to learn from everything manifests itself through reading, which he enjoys immensely. He thinks his "generation does not read enough." Reading provides the primary way to learn about life through others' interpretations. For Steve, it is an indirect way to encounter life.

Steve thinks that life is largely "a matter of attitude," and he uses music to create any attitude and to experience different sensations. "Music can change a mood depending on what you put on. Or it can reinforce a mood. It gives you some kind of strength to deal with things." He likes the unknown element in music.

It probably should remain a mystery. Wouldn't it be terrible if the researchers came up with a foolproof method of defining what it is, what kind of music makes people do what. There's something so beautiful about it. And so ugly. If I'm in a really black mood or something and get really angry, I'll put on the Sex Pistols. And just blast away. If I wanna calm down I'll put on some Wagner and sit back and listen to that.

Steve manages to transform his relation to the world through his music, either listening or playing. This escape implies a passive approach to life.

Like most Fatalists, he believes things happen for a reason, which prompts him to speculate about his life. He looks for answers but believes they usually come at the wrong times. "You look and look for an answer and then you come up with something when you're not expecting one." Steve believes in the inevitability of a selected course of events.

> It's a thing of knowing that things aren't always gonna be as they are. And knowing that no matter how bad things are, they're gonna change whether you like it or not. . . . It's like, no matter how bad things are, they're gonna change. They're not gonna stay like that. Nothing ever does. No good thing ever stays around forever. No bad thing does either. It's all very interesting to watch. Life. There's so much to learn. As long as you can keep everything in perspective while you're doing what you do. It is interesting. If it wasn't, the suicide rate would probably be a lot higher than it is.

"Watching" and "learning," Steve passes leisurely through life content with the way things are and unwilling to make any major changes that would alter the predictability of his life-style.

Edward: "Walking the Wire"

Edward, a twenty-nine-year-old professor, recently completed his Ph.D.; the memories of hard work and deadlines are fresh in his mind. His life metaphor reflects his tendency toward little action in his life.

> I could probably use other people's metaphors like baseball, a long season, or stuff like that. A metaphor I like comes from *All That Jazz*. It says, "the wire is life and everything else is waiting." And I found that to be very ego-aphoristic. For me, it's nice to anticipate walking the wire, and in between the parts of walking the wire, being fairly tense and bored for something else to do but nothing terribly active.

"The wire" refers to the exciting things in life. Edward thinks of life as a series of intermittent "wires" strung together by quiet periods. On the whole, he prefers the in-between periods when life is predictable, certain, and calm. For the most part, he does not want unforeseen events to interrupt the cycle. Overall, he appreciates a "steady-state" existence.

> It'd be nice if it were a little more varied. But there's a certain comfort in nothing extravagant or extreme happening unless you

want it to. So it's a steady-state thing. Although it's not terribly exciting, it's fine with me because I can always find some excitement. But it's a lot harder to find peace and quiet if things are always exciting. I would rather start from a baseline of calm and then get as exciting as I'd like to get, rather than the other way around.

Although Edward consciously tries to maintain a "baseline of calm," he tolerates a limited amount of excitement. Too much activity, however, makes him feel like he is losing control in his life.

Like your everyday routine I think you oughta have control over. At the same time, it's fun to do the things that are serendipitous and wild. On occasion. But I would not like that to be the daily routine. Most of my weeks are pretty much like the last ones. Except for doing little bits of different things. But at conventions I expect to have everything happen by chance and have to react to things. You know, changes of plan at the moment. And that's moment-to-moment. And that's fine, but I wouldn't want to wake up every day not knowing what kind of weird new thing was gonna happen.

The academic world suits Edward's steady life-style perfectly as he thrives in the analytic atmosphere. "I'll sit and read naturally without any provocation whatsoever. And it's nice to share ideas with other people. Have some smart people around you who you can talk to and have a high-level discussion about ideas and things. Other people who value ideas and knowing about the world."

Getting an education reassured Edward and helped him mature. "The first couple of years at college were hard for me in terms of finding out who I was. Graduate school was very good just because I got a lot of reinforcement for being bright and that sort of thing." Ultimately, his Fatalistic approach helped him put things in perspective.

Life goes on. You can't decide to not *do.* I don't think I put any great effort into self-scrutiny. It's like when you're going to teach. Nobody had taught us how to teach. We struggled through a couple of years, got barely competent, and then a little better and a little better. And now I consider myself a decently good teacher, whereas when I started, I didn't. But I didn't decide I'm gonna get my whole act together, and I'm gonna become a good teacher. The skills you need are so subtle that even if someone told you "do this," you wouldn't just do them and change.

Edward acknowledges that life is not something one learns how to do; instead one does it by living. Just as one is thrown into unknown situations when first teaching, so one faces life.

> A lot of times, getting through days is knowing that you have friends and things that matter to you even though you're doing something terribly boring or stressful. Like you do matter in the wider scheme of things. And this is just an end for being able to do things for them. I can see how people that work in factories every day find it terribly boring. If they had an outside reason, like being the breadwinner and sending the kid to college. Jeez you may as well put the tools down and give up. If the thing itself has no value to you. If you keep that in mind, it's easier to get through boring or difficult times.

Edward makes the point that it really does not matter what people do as long as they can see a point to it. Although not actively pursuing any "ultimate" answers himself, he believes it is enough to find something that matters, and having a sense of where he fits into the "larger scheme of things" helps.

Claude: "Life's Great to Me"

At fifty-eight, Claude has worked at the fire station for thirty years. He answers the phone in a small self-contained office, where he spends the entire time. The room cannot be left unattended. He works twenty-four-hour shifts—three days on, four days off. A window, an old black-and-white television set, and a radio provide some distractions.

> Some days pass pretty fast. And other days there's three days in twenty-four hours. It seems that way but it isn't. . . . I watch the traffic. Of course being confined in this room, that's all I can do. The other guys can sit outdoors when the weather's nice. Time passes faster. In here, why, you gotta face it.

Claude takes his job seriously and respects the isolation as necessary. He has always been a loner, and he likes it that way. "I don't pay any attention to people. I know what I want and how I wanna live, and they can live whatever way they wanna live."

Like other Fatalists, he enjoys working on his own. "I like to be by myself. I'm the only one around. I like to be with my own." Since his two heart attacks, Claude has been forced to reduce the amount of activity in his life. "This is about the only job I can handle right now, . . . about the only thing I can do." His last attack was five years ago. "For two days I didn't know where I lived. I didn't really know where I was at. It happened at work. Then I went to the doctor. And that's when it hit me. I knew I wasn't home. I must have been asleep all the time and I woke up, look around, and everything is different."

Since then, there have been good days and bad days, but Claude is not ready for the undertaker. "I'm not ready to die yet. Got another twenty-five or thirty years in me." He knows his time will come eventually. "You know when you come into this world you're only here for so long. You gotta go sometime. You gotta go with it." Realizing they cannot fight destiny, Fatalists take comfort in the inevitable progression of events. "These days I'm more or less sitting around. Not doing anything. I just go on living. I know I gotta. Just being here." Claude "takes" life as it is, reflecting a more passive approach. His life metaphor supports Claude's easygoing nature.

> Life's been great to me. You meet different kinds of people—all kinds, all types. There are different ways of doing things. I've had a good life, myself. . . . I'm slow. I'm in reverse. I move around slow. I never get in a hurry about anything. Just take it easy. . . . Being able to get up in the morning and being able to move, they're the most important things.

At first, it might seem contradictory to find the idea that life is great in the Fatalist orientation. However, looking more carefully at the langauge reveals that "life" *has been* great *to* the person. The life metaphor expresses the Fatalistic theme that life is something done to the person, making him the receiver of what happens, fostering a less active approach to life.

Living in the past encourages Claude to move slowly through the present. Fatalists typically lament the past, and Claude often recalls the way things "used to be. . . . Back when I was seventeen years old, it was different from what the seventeen-year-olds are now. They're more wild. Course, back then you didn't have what you got today. . . . Times is different. Back when I was a kid, why, you didn't have the money like you got nowadays." Claude almost begrudges today's youth their opportunities.

Mike: "It's Been Great to Me"

At seventy-three, Mike works part-time as an attendant in a small parking lot in the middle of the small downtown area. Before retiring, he was a painter and decorator for fifty-five years. Like Claude, he is grateful to be working. His wife is dead, and because they had no children, his social life revolves around the American Legion, where his companions have become his family.

Life follows a predictable pattern, and the days are always the same. He works at the parking lot in the afternoons where he "sweats it out." Then he usually goes "out to the club. That's all I do. I usually go to the Legion. Poke around. Then go home and go to bed." Although he does not particularly like it, he lives alone. He overcomes his loneliness by getting out. "I'm never there. I don't stay alone that long. I don't cook. I used to. I quit that. Cook for one person? Miserable. I throw it away."

For Mike, the present is probably the hardest time. "The older you get, the harder the years get." But he claims not to be at a loss for entertainment. "Oh, I have fun. Got a million friends." He thinks of himself as "a damned good person. They all like me at the club. One guy out there, he works there, he tends bar, he says I'm the best guy on earth. I'm satisfied with myself." Like most Fatalists, Mike is "satisfied" with most things about his life. "I'm not sayin' that I never made mistakes. But I don't make them on purpose."

His life metaphor, "Life's been great to me," shows his acquiescence. "Like I told you, I'm satisfied. And it's pretty easy for a person to satisfy himself. Don't you think?" Mike's interpretation of life sounds like Cluade's. While neither has any major complaints about life, each has spent his time "taking" whatever life offered. Again, "life" *has been* great *to* the individual.

Mike believes it is possible for a person to satisfy himself. "Be good to yourself. Try to do right. Think about your Father." He accepts life. "You gotta take it as it comes." The emphasis on taking advances the characteristic lack of activity in Fatalists' lives, reinforcing the theme that life is something that a person accepts. By stressing the reception of life in his life orientation,

Mike explains the apparent contradiction between the idea that life is something great and his categorization as a Fatalist.

Like Claude, Mike sits alone in a little office where he collects the money as people leave the lot. There is a radio, a coffee maker, and a portable heater. He says he likes the job because he loves people. "That's the reason when I retired I wanted a job, and this is perfect. That's 'cause I love people. And this is wonderful here." But there is not much communication: a few greetings, perhaps a kind word or two, nothing more.

But Mike is satisfied; he has what he needs and, like so many Fatalists, relies on "the man up above." "I got a home and it's paid for. And I have no sweat. I can make a living here, plus a little social security. It's not much. I get by. Worse comes to worse, when I can't take care of my own, I go out to the Veteran's home."

He has thought briefly about death. "I don't worry about it. That would just make me die quicker. Worrying will kill you. And I don't worry about death, because you know it happens anyway. No need to worry about it. . . . It's like going to sleep for a long while."

This section reveals two "balancing" metaphors—the line between frustration and amusement and the wire stringing together excitement and calm—and two "receptive" metaphors—life's great to me. What do they have in common? They share the Fatalist's ideal self-image as a person who "takes" his time with things and moves slowly and painstakingly through life, preferring calm to activity and solitude to crowds.

Evaluation

"Take the rough with the smooth." "The older you get the harder the years get." "You don't have to work at life. It's just there." "Cherries are sweet, life is sweet. Cherries are also sour and life is sour."

We can think of evaluation as a continuum ranging from positive to negative. Although we regard Fatalists as the opposite of Enthusiasts, they are not extremely negative. It would be more accurate to say that Fatalists tend to move in the negative direction. Individuals who are exceedingly negative are bitter, depressed, and often try to escape through extreme isolation. While

Fatalists exhibit some of these tendencies, they do so to a much lesser extent. Fatalists might be prone to periods of depression and prefer to work in jobs that do not involve people, but this does not make them nihilists, who deny all existing doctrines by rejecting moral or religious beliefs.

An aloof attitude reflects the Fatalistic resignation to life. Their compliant acceptance of the status quo makes them nonassertive, and they have few expectations. They see no point to making a fuss because things cannot be changed. They accept the good and bad and feel no inclination to alter things.

Expressing little enthusiasm for life and being characterized as less positive does not mean that Fatalists are unhappy. For the most part, they are content. They struggle to meet their basic needs and once they have done so are satisfied and live comfortably. They are emphatic in not wanting more than they need.

Fatalists are often drifters who stumble into their line of work. This section describes five such people, beginning with Mac, a college graduate who works at a service station as a mechanic. Next is Dan, a handyman working for a trailer company. Carol started a business after an unhappy divorce. Pat has been separated from her husband for only one week, leaving her indecisive about her future. Finally, Keith started driving trucks in the service and has never stopped. Their stories reveal the neutral or apathetic evaluation of life.

Mac: "An Open-Ended Question"

Going to college was a "foregone conclusion" for Mac. His family expected it, so he went and got a degree in business. After a single interview with a large company he decided that the executive life was not for him. Finding the bureaucracy of a large organization distasteful and unrewarding, he looked for something that would satisfy him.

At thirty-two, he works as a mechanic in a gas station after stumbling across the job. "I just drifted into being a mechanic. And the more I worked at it, the more satisfied I was with it." His work entails "gettin' up early, stayin' out in weather when it's too cold, dragging in cars, fixin' them, arguing with people."

Mac used to manage other stations but prefers working for someone else. He found the responsibility overwhelming and did not like being burdened with the problems. If Mac were an Enthusiast, he would strive to become the owner of the company and would actively seek control. Fatalists, however, seem naturally inclined towards avoiding power and typically hold positions where they are motivated by others.

As one relinquishes control, one also reduces the amount of worrying, and Fatalists love to not worry. Mac is no exception. "I got tired of being where the buck gets passed to last. And I got tired of being the one that does all the arguing and stuff. That's why I've just stuck with being a mechanic."

His life metaphor echoes an ambivalent attitude: "life is an open-ended question. It's what you make with what you got. You plug in your own variables and that's what you get out of it." Just as "plugging in" the correct wires makes the car run, so "plugging in" the appropriate "variables" makes one's life work.

An open-ended question is one that has no answer or perhaps has multiple answers. In any case, life, for Mac is not definitive. "Life isn't any one thing. It's just the sum of what you put into it. For the most part, it's pretty much a direct result of what you do with it."

He proudly avoids thinking about the meaning of life. "I've not really been one to philosophize about purpose. I never thought there was much to it. I was never looking for a divine purpose in my own life. I was never concerned with how my life would affect the world in general. Not concerned with bigger issues, just things that make me most comfortable." He believes that life progresses according to an underlying order, which he calls the "human condition." Like other Fatalists, he can articulate his vision of that condition.

> Nothing unusual is wrong with society. It's just progressing along normal paths. Faster than civilizations used to deteriorate, but deteriorating at a normal rate. I figure that it's good for a few hundred years more at least. And just progressively going the way it is. I don't think government is in unduly bad shape. Draft, corruption, havoc haven't reached unbearable levels yet. I think it's going along as expected. Nothing is shocking.

He does not confuse order with purpose. "I'm not convinced there's any purpose behind mankind other than a progression, biologically—continued evolution. A good one perhaps, but not any more dramatic than that." He gets by in life, not striving to do any more than he needs. "I been able to slide real well in life. I haven't had to confront a lot of big things. My life has been calm. I've sailed pretty calm seas."

Mac thinks about his life on a small scale, believing that he lives a "classic little contented life." The most important things in life are basic needs, such as shelter, food, family, and home. He attends to daily chores and events as the most important things in life.

Dan: "A Progression of Small Events"

Dan, a "service technician" for a mobile-home company, does electrical work, plumbing, carpentry, and driving. Thirty-seven, easygoing, and relaxed, he admits that he likes to "take life as it comes" and believes that you "don't have to work at life. It's just there." His life metaphor emphasizes satisfaction with the smallness of life. "Life is a progression of small events. Just minor things here and there. Every once in a while something isn't so minor. Mainly it's the small events. You don't have any big events. Everybody's got small events. A few people have big events but not that many."

In other words, Dan believes that life consists of events that are connected, marked by a distinct order. "It's all joined together. One leads into another. Small things. You start something and it leads to something else. Nothing major." He uses another metaphor to explain. "It might just be deciding to work in a garden or plant a garden. And you go from there. You take what you're growing and freeze it, or can it, or do whatever. You know just everyday occurrences." Like Mac, Dan emphasizes the "small" things, but smallness does not mean insignificance. On the contrary, the small things are the important ones, and if they are taken care of there is nothing to worry about.

Like the typical Fatalist, Dan does not worry. "I don't worry too much about the future. What comes next? That's about the only thing I ever wonder about. Other than that not too much." He accepts his fate. "You ain't gonna change anything in the past, so there's no sense worrying about it. What's past is past." Because he believes in a predetermined order, he knows "there's a whole lot of major events you aren't gonna change." He takes life slowly.

"There's some times I do rush, but I don't see any reason to get excited for anything really."

After a six-year stay in the service he moved into a house with some friends and did nothing except have "a good time." After a few months, he started to look for work, but that activity was erratic, and he was disinterested. Slowly things changed as he tired of his unpredictable life. He quit the parties, found steady work, and established a routine. "Before, I didn't really care. When I started steady work I settled down to the routine of living." The routine entails "knowing what you're gonna do the next day or the next week, or even the next month. You can plan 'cause you know what's happening. Before I didn't plan ahead for anything." Dan rests comfortably now knowing his life follows a predictable pattern.

Carol: "A Bowl of Cherries"

Carol works in the craft store she co-owns with Glenda, the Enthusiast. They became partners after "a rather distasteful divorce," which left Carol in need of financial support. In addition to economic upheaval, the change left her emotionally distressed. At forty-eight, she decided she better "do something rather than sit around the house doing nothing." Running a business has its disadvantages, and, like Glenda, Carol regrets not having enough time to do everything. "I haven't been dating. When we first started I didn't have time for three children at home plus starting the business plus trying to have a personal life. And so I elected to give up my personal life and devote my time to my children and here."

She resents missing out on a social life to ensure financial stability, and her life metaphor displays her emphasis on the "bitterness" in life. "Judy Garland sings 'life is just a bowl of cherries.' Cherries are bright. Life is bright. Cherries are sweet. Life is sweet. Cherries are also sour. At times life is sour. Cherries have pits, and sometimes life's the pits."

Carol accepts the good and bad in life without feeling any inclination to change things. Thinking about Judy Garland triggers memories.

> It was a song I heard about thirty years ago. When I first met my husband at a fraternity house. It was a few weeks before the

movie *A Star Is Born.* I had never really seen Judy Garland. I
was basically too young at the time she was making most of her
movies. I went over there one night and they had an old radio
that had a deep bass and it just sounded so good. I just got hooked.

She still thinks fondly about that first meeting with her husband. She recollects the painful separation with hostility.

I was not the one that basically wanted out. . . . I had no idea it
was even happening. All of a sudden one day, he says, "I want
out. I don't like the life-style I've been leading and I want out.
You can have the house, the kids, and everything in it. Just set
me free." And that was a hard thing to adjust to. It took a long
time to try to understand what happened.

Her parents and friends helped her through the divorce and she
was determined to not let it destroy her. Although she tried to
understand why the marriage ended, she reached a turning point
when she realized that her husband no longer cared. "I asked him
what his feelings to me were, and he said, 'Nothing. Just blah. I
have no feelings'. And I just started to think and came to the
conclusion that probably the best for all concerned would be a
divorce, but that was not really what I wanted. But there was no
choice."

In spite of the hurt, Carol still loves the man. "If I saw him
today and he said, 'would you marry me?' I'd probably do it all
over again."

Pat: "A Challenge"

I interviewed Pat only one week after her husband had "walked
out" on her. She was upset, uncertain, and angry about everything
in her life.[4] In a matter of days she had been transformed into a
woman unsure of her future.[5] Before she married, she was employed at the university but quit to live in Texas with her husband.
Looking back she regrets the move. "Now I'm back I've lost my
seniority. So I have to start at the bottom again, and that hurts.
It scares me to start something new. Especially at my age. It's
harder as you get older."

The second marriage for both Pat and her husband, she had not
expected anything to go wrong. They had known each other since

high school but married only two and one half years ago. She is forty-one, with four children from her first marriage, and thought herself wise enough to choose a lasting relationship "the second time around." Right now she feels drained. "I don't have the get-up-and-go to do it." Distraught about her husband, caught in the midst of uncertainty, she has no idea whether he will come back. "To me life is terrible. A lot of worries. A lot of stress. A lot of pressure. I don't know which direction to take. . . . I feel so devastated. It's because I'm older, and what am I going to retire on? What am I going to live on? I have nothing. I just didn't expect this to happen to our marriage."

Fortunately Pat has outside interests and is a businesswoman in her own right. She has taken steps to stay on her feet. She just started a new job as an office clerk on the campus and plans to continue managing their rental properties. The "challenge" that she usually finds in real estate parallels her larger view of the world, as indicated by her life metaphor. "Life is like a challenge. I like to get ahead. And I like to be organized and plan and know where I'm going. And I thought I did know where I was going. But you just get a lot of obstacles in your life that you have to overcome. And I'll overcome this too. I s'pose I have to. No choice."

Right now Pat is unable to evaluate things as she ordinarily would. "I thought I had it all together before this." She faces the situation because she has no other options. Again, the feeling of having "no choice" distinguishes Fatalists from the other orientations. They perceive themselves to be trapped by circumstances beyond their control, which they must inevitably go through. Not a total defeatist, Pat knows how to survive even though she is afraid. "New situations scare me and I become afraid and anxious. I keep telling myself that it'll work out and something will happen. It'll just take a little time. You have to have patience and not try to make your way through in one day's time. You have to sleep on it and not make a decision immediately."

In this case, she reflects one of the typical patterns of the Fatalist as she tells herself, "it'll work out." She relies on patience and time to solve her troubles. At the moment, the situation is difficult because her husband is not talking to her, and she fears the consequences. "He's not telling me anything. I'm afraid to ask him if he wants a divorce 'cause I'm afraid he'll say yes. I don't know what I'm gonna do. A woman should be independent and never depend on a man. I resent it. And I'm worried. And that doesn't make me a very happy person."

If her husband returns, Pat wonders if she will have to go through the same thing again. There have been problems before, resulting in his leaving, but she always takes him back. "That's the sad part, I don't have any resistance." She wishes she could tell him to "go to hell" but admits being trapped by the life-style he provides. She worries about lowering her standard of living, being alone, and being unmarried.

More than anything, Pat feels emotionally wounded, admitting that she still loves her husband. Her emotional heartache is matched by a physical ache. "My chest hurt for a solid week after this happened. I mean, I've been through a lot in my life but I've never had my chest hurt like that. It was just so painful. I never realized there would be that pain."

Keith: "An Athlete"

Keith had been on the road for two days, on his way from the South heading for his home. He usually "runs" the eastern thirty-seven states. He likes the work and, like many Fatalists, likes the solitude. "I don't have anybody breathing down my neck. I can stop for a cup of coffee when I feel like it. I'm outdoors. I see a lot of the country." At fifty-two, Keith has driven trucks on and off for thirty years after stumbling into the job after driving in the army. The only thing he would rather be is "retired and fishing."

Like Claude and Mike, many of the modern trends displease Keith, inspiring him to evaluate life unfavorably. He fondly remembers the good old days on the road. "It used to be, you could drive on the road and you wave and they wave back. Now they got their noses in the air. And the radio. I just leave it shut off. Don't need the baloney that goes on." Nowadays, he never picks up hitchhikers. "I don't pick up hitchhikers. Used to be, I would. . . . Used to be, a driver would break down in the road, he'd have four or five drivers stop and try to help him. They're scared to do that now. Scared of getting shot or knifed." Truckstops are another source of frustration.

A truck stop ain't a truck stop anymore. It used to be, that's all the people you seen there. Meals were good for the price. Not

like these places. You sit in a truck and listen to it run long
enough, you don't wanna hear that thing running in here. Want
a little peace and quiet. . . . You get tired of eating.

Deregulation also infuriates Keith. "The people that's running
the state can't see past the end of their nose. Congress passes
these laws. They don't sit down and figure out what happens in
the long run, down the road." Keith manages to ignore the problems and live according to his own rules. "Take it in your stride.
Take it as it comes. Do the best you can do with what you got.
Got your body, your equipment. Everything there. I can't see
where anybody could ask anymore of you." Thinking of himself
as a special kind of person, he expresses his life metaphor in an
unusual way.

I think about me and my life. It's like an athlete. You get your
body built to that type of life. And it doesn't bother you. You
can go out here and drive six, seven, eight, ten hours. Stop and
sleep for an hour, hour and a half, you can get up and do it over
again. But unless you're doing it all the time, if you take two
weeks off, you come back and it's hell getting started again. . . .
I take two weeks off and I gotta take a nap before I can get started.
You gotta get your body accustomed to it. Mind and body both.

Listening to Keith, it is easy to associate him with a long-
distance runner. A truck driver must know the territory he intends
to cover, he cannot afford to become lost; he must be single-
minded, he cannot afford to become sidetracked; and he must
take care of his truck, he cannot afford breakdowns.

Like many athletes, Keith knows the effort is not entirely physical. Runners can be in good shape, but if their minds are not
tuned into the race, they can lose. He emphasizes the relationship
between mind and body.

A lot of hard work. You try to keep the truck running. Fix
anything that needs fixing on it. Or else you got to find yourself
a load. You mind's constantly thinking, did I load it right? Should
I stop and hassle about it? Your hours are changing all the time.
You try to remember what this state is. You gotta know what
the state bridge laws are. You're thinking continually.

Although many of Keith's routes are long, he knows that he
has to do it. "I don't want to, but I got to. Then you think, well

I'll probably see so-and-so up there. You just keep on truckin'. Hell, I know when I get to Atlanta, I'm gonna have me a cold beer. You just push a little harder." Like many Fatalists, sheer determination and the belief that there is no other way help Keith keep going forward.

A question waiting to be answered; a progression of events leading into one another; a bowl of cherries full of pits; a challenge in the midst of a crisis; and an athlete making his "runs"—each life metaphor uniquely expresses the Fatalists' unfavorable evaluation of life. Some Fatalists are dispassionate and unimpressed; others are alienated and detached; and some are critical and depressed.

Control

"I know I have to come back. There's no other way."
"Everything changes and there's not a thing you can do to stop it." "I feel like someone's looking out for me." "I just live each day at a time and thank God for it."

As discussed in the last chapter, "control" refers to a person's perceived sense of power to influence life. Fatalists think that they cannot change the course of events. They believe they are "swept along by the winds of chance," and are likely to say "I am the victim of circumstance," "I may as well flip a coin every time I make a decision," "life is largely a matter of luck," "success is a matter of being in the right place at the right time," and "you really can't change other people's ideas."[6]

In making these statements, the locus of control shifts away from the self, making the individual no longer responsible for what happens. The person attributes everything to luck or to factors that are out of his or her control. Much of the Fatalists' language expresses a sense of lacking control. They typically say, "life's been good to me," "I take life as it comes," or "I don't have any alternative." In these cases, the language clearly differs from that of the Enthusiast, who says, "I've made my life good" and "I make life the way I want."

Fatalists believe that their lives are controlled by powerful forces outside the individual. Although there are different sources of power (such as God or other supernatural forces), all Fatalists rely on some force to control their fate. Feeling that one's life is controlled predisposes that person to believe that life follows a certain order. Embedded in the Fatalist is a sense of organization and a blueprint for life. Amazingly, this pattern is clear in each one's mind.

Fred, Bill, Lynn, and Cheryl illustrate the Fatalist's perception of control. Fred and Bill are both war veterans, survivors of frontline fighting in World War II and Korea, who still marvel at their survival. Lynn is a nurse practitioner who became a nurse during World War II to help the effort. They all believe they are part of a definite plan guided by "someone" who protects them. Cheryl, just out of high school, is filled with questions about her identity and her relationship with her parents. She has been included because she seems to be asking the same questions for which the others have found answers.

Fred: "It's Been Good to Me"

Fred owns a wholesale meat house on the edge of town that has been a family business for thirty years and serves the local farmers. At fifty-eight, he loves farm life and built his business from humble beginnings. There have been many problems with the business: he has been robbed several times, and fire destroyed the whole building. As if not enough, he also suffered personal tragedies. "The hardest years? I lost my little girl to leukemia. Six years old. That was in fifty-seven. Shortly after I got the business. You survive. My first wife passed away in seventy-seven. So that's two losses."

These events might explain the quiet sadness about him. Fatalists typically cope with tragedy by attributing events to forces beyond their control. Fred manages to carry on because he believes in a definite order of things.

> You have to accept it as life. You got hit early. Kind of a hard thing to cope with. I don't think that anyone gets by in life without some tragedy in their lives somewhere. I believe that the Lord giveth and taketh away. I guess that's the way it is. You can't say, why me. Everyone does, but you look around and something else tragic happens to another family. There are so many young boys and girls getting killed at seventeen. The beginning of life.

He looks tearfully at the pictures of his wife and daughter on the desk. There are photographs of his other children amidst pictures of prize-winning livestock. He surrounds himself with the things that mean the most to him.

> You just kind of go ahead. It isn't something that you can ever forget. . . . You know when you bury the animal it's just done. You got to really believe the other way. What's the thing on going to heaven or hell? I feel that it's right here on earth, that you're getting it now. What can be worse than a daughter taken away? A child? And heaven. What is prettier than today? There can't be anything more beautiful than today. I've never talked to a minister, but that's my view of life. And I think everyone suffers, when you feel it can be worse in heaven and hell.

Fatalists believe "someone" looks out for them. Although all of them are not certain exactly who that someone is—it might be God or a mysterious, universal power—this force determines who shall live and who shall die. Fred explains his interpretation in his life metaphor.

> Life's been good to me. The business is successful. But the sadness too. But it's been very good to me. I've been through World War II. I guess I felt the Lord cared for me because during that time I was in combat I was nineteen and got wounded in Okinawa. The boy right next to me got killed with the same shell. I often wondered why it wasn't me. I feel like someone's kinda' looking out for me, caring for me. I don't know why. But someone is right there with me keeping me alive.

Fatalists believe that their lives are "out of their hands" and that survival is not a matter of individual will but of divine intervention. Fred is pessimistic about a future beyond his control. "There's radioactive everything, the atomic bomb. You got so many more problems now. I think we got bigger problems. I lived through World War II. I just see that the problems are gonna be bigger and more massive. . . . World disease. Things in the air that cause cancer. Radioactive waste."

In spite of the tragedies and the course of his life, Fred believes he has "had the average amount of ups and downs." He accepts his fate because that is part of life. Life is something done to the person, who is powerless to control larger forces.

Bill: "A Chance to Really Live"

At fifty-five, Bill has distributed equipment at the recreational gymnasium of the college for more than nineteen years. He treats life as a "chance." "I still say each day is a bonus. For some reason, the man upstairs keeps me on here. Why, I don't know. It'll come out someday. Maybe it's to talk to you. I don't know. And every day I wake up I feel that's another bonus." The idea that each day is a "bonus" ties in with his life metaphor.

> Life to me is a chance to really live. And I live each day. I have four children by a first marriage, and I thought my life was over when my first wife divorced me. I met another lady, and since then we have had another child and life is starting over again. So it's just a continuation. And I can see in my kids how things are gonna keep going.

"Chance" and "bonus" suggest a gamble, but to Bill, life seems more a calculated risk than a gamble. He faced a number of life-threatening situations and somehow survived. He was in an eighteen-hundred-gallon propane truck that exploded. Fortunately, he managed to put the fire out and escape injury. Although he wonders why he came out alive, he says simply, "I figured it wasn't my time, that's all. Because if God had intended for me to go, there were so many different times that I could have went." It might have been when he underwent brain surgery over twenty years ago.

> Back in 1962 I had brain surgery. They gave me a thousand-to-one chance to live through it. And then eight days later they had to operate again. And they gave me no chance at all to make it through the second one. I made it through both of them. Now each day is a bonus. That's the way I feel about it. Every day I got, God gave me an extra day.

Like Fred, Bill believes "someone" watches over him. His descriptions about surviving the war in Korea seem to echo Fred's sentiments about survival.

> My job, when I went to Korea, was, in my estimation, coming home. I wanted to live through what time I had there and come home. I was on the front line for twelve months, and I was very lucky. I came home. A lot of them didn't. I couldn't understand

why I, a single guy, was singled out. Other guys with families were getting killed. But after, I come home, married, and had the four kids and then remarried and had another one. There was reason for it. But at the time I couldn't figure it out.

Like many Fatalists, Bill knew the answer would come with time. Fatalists typically believe that things happen for a reason. They do not need to know the actual reason, just having faith that there is one is enough. Bill does not worry about his inability to explain his survival but knows that eventually he will understand why things happened the way they did. The most convincing evidence to support his belief that God protects him came when he had a heart attack.

About three years ago, they thought I had a heart attack. They took me in to the hospital and started giving me nitroglycerin to quiet the pain. They give me one, and about five minutes later they give me another. And in five or ten minutes they give me the third. When the third one occurred, I felt like I left my body. My blood pressure went to zero and they had an intravenous thing on my arm and they pumped something in there and brought me back. . . . At that time I was floating above it. Now, this may sound screwy but that was the way it was. I was above looking down on it. And when they shot the stuff into my arm again and I come back into my body. Now that's the only real experience I've had of being out of it. And this happened. Why, I don't know. It was something I can't explain. It just happened that way.

Not surprisingly, Bill has thought about death. "I used to fear death until I went through it or close to it. To me it is a beginning of another life. It is whether you have a reward or a penalty for what you've done in this life. That's my idea. You have here to prove whether you're worth going better or worse. Take it each day at a time."

Death means the "beginning of another life," a "continuation," and "part of the order." Like Fred, Bill sees life as reward and punishment, good and bad, happiness and sorrow. One is tempted to think Bill's survival is amazing, but he quickly dismisses the idea. Like most Fatalists, he feels ordinary. "I'm just an average individual. Nothing spectacular. . . . My dad once told me, as long as you can put your feet over the side of the bed and stand up, you're alright." To this day these words guide him.

Lynn: "Flowers"

Lynn works as a nurse practitioner at the student hospital and specializes in women's health. She is fifty-six and likes to share the wisdom she has accumulated over the years. She began nursing during World War II when health-care professionals were in demand. Like all Fatalists, Lynn believes in the covert presence of a powerful, controlling order. According to her perspective, life is organized according to distinct phases through which all people pass if they live long enough. Her life metaphor expresses her assumption about life's progression. "Life is like flowers. It's bud. It's blossom. It's bloom. And it's overblown. It's a process of being and learning and experience." "Flowers" metaphorically represent life. The stages in a flower's growth parallel the stages in a person's development; as the flower grows, it changes from a bud to a bloom before dying. Lynn is very clear about the process.

In the beginning, the budding flower is like the growing child. The individual is exposed to a lengthy stage of "development, learning, education, and experience." Lynn believes people learn most from "experience with others." Other things that educate a person are "reading, having children, and taking responsibility."

The next stage, which Lynn calls "the peak," is the most vital in a person's life. She describes herself as being in the midst of the "peak" and "sustaining." "Everybody must reach a peak in their lives. Probably in their fifties. Peak to me would mean when you can forget yourself and then produce. Because you give to others. You have to first forget yourself."

When people reach the peak, they engage in "service to others." The peak period generally lasts until age sixty-five or seventy, when deterioration begins. This is the "overblown" period, or the time "after the peak," which refers to the end of life when people can no longer take care of themselves. Like overblown flowers, losing their petals, people wither and eventually die. "They certainly do not like their bodies. They can't function as they would like. They are mentally alert, but they get to a point where just being alive and maintaining their health is about all they can think of."

The "flower" framework provides a clear structure and a frame of reference within which Lynn easily locates herself and others. Because she values learning and knowledge so much, she makes them part of her everyday life as well as her professional duties.

> How could I possibly know enough? Medicine is changing almost from month to month. There are new ways of treatment. There are new ideas. I could never know enough. There are other skills I need besides the technical skills. The examination of the patient. The intellectual skills. I have to know what's going on. The emotional skills. How to deal with people. Communication skills. How could I ever excel in those areas? I just keep working.

Lynn's attitude towards work reflects her more general attitude towards religion. Although not a regular churchgoer, Lynn believes in God. Like most Fatalists, she trusts a power greater than herself to direct her life, and her language indicates the importance of fate or determinism.

> For many, many years I asked myself, Is there a God? I determined that emotionally and mentally we don't know enough. We're too ignorant, really, to determine our own fate. Because we are larger than we know. And it was then that I decided that I must have faith. It's my own inability to be as large as I think people are.

Lynn uses the importance of knowledge to explain her relationship with God. By admitting that she can never know everything, she establishes God as the expert and creates a stable framework for herself. She believes that she can expand her potential for largeness by acquiring knowledge, but she can never be as large as God, who is omnipotent. Lynn believes people must have faith to trust in the way their fate is determined. Questioning the existence of God confirmed her belief in fate.

Cheryl: "Change"

Cheryl, a twenty-year-old secretary on campus, was restless during the interview and constantly fiddled with her pen. A similar agitation marks her life. Although uncertain about what she wants to do, she knows she does not want to be a secretary forever. She would like to go to college someday and make a career in public relations but is unsure when she will be able to do so. Her present work is boring. "There's nothing to do. I just sit here and feel like they really don't need me. They just need a body to be sitting at the desk. I feel kinda' useless."

After several years of struggling with her parents, Cheryl gets along well with them now, but she remembers the problems.

> We got into fights. And I wouldn't talk to them and they wouldn't talk to me. We just didn't get along at all. It was really bad there for a while. That was a couple of years ago. I don't know if it's 'cause I've gotten older and realized that you can't fight with them all the time. I just got tired of gettin' in trouble.

Cheryl endured the period of crisis with the help of a close friend who gave her someone to talk to and confide in. "You just have to live through it. There's not a whole lot you can do about it." Like most Fatalists, she accepts what happens, acknowledging that many things cannot be changed. Her life metaphor reflects her belief in the inevitability of events.

> Change. A lot of changes. Everything changes, and there's not a thing you can do to stop it. I feel like I can't stop what is gonna happen. Something's always different. Things have changed so much from how they were two years ago. Right now, I'm in a place where I never thought I would be. . . . I think differently now. I go different places. I'm in a different atmosphere. It's hard to explain.

Although change is usually associated with positive growth, Cheryl equates change with inevitability and limitation. She feels change will restrict her freedom rather than provide her with growing experience. "Change," like "life," signifies something that cannot be controlled and somehow will trap her. "Something that always seems strange to me is how different every summer is. I just keep changing and changing. It's like I'm a different person. I can remember coming home after not being here for so long. Everything was different. My brothers had grown up. And I was different. It was just strange."

Cheryl remembers the times when the problems were overwhelming and how bad she felt about herself. "I didn't care what happened. I was in like, outer space. I was just out of it. It was a really bad time. You just don't care what happens to you. Nothing matters." She thought about suicide, but said "I never had the guts to do it. I never wanted to. I don't like pain." Some of her friends tried to hurt themselves through drinking and drugs, but Cheryl quickly saw that this was not a solution.

> I mean, you'll be okay for a while, but in the end, the same problems are still there. You just have to deal with them. I watched a few of my friends. Watched what happened to them. If you're sitting around and there's people drinking around you and you're not drinking, you see the way they act and how they change. After a couple of hours you can see a big change in people. It makes you realize that what they're doing is wrong and how you act when you're in the same situation.

In an effort to find out about herself she has asked many questions. "Why are things the way they are? There's a lot of things I don't understand. Things that happen every day. Things you don't expect to happen." Like most Fatalists, she believes that somehow things work out.

> I just went through it. There wasn't a whole lot you could do. I been through a lot. You have to learn to live through it. And do the best you can. It's not the end of the world. I knew I just had to get up and go on. Life isn't just gonna end because you want it to. You just have to get up and go on and deal with things. You don't have much of a choice. You just have to keep going.

All the life metaphors in this section reflect an overriding emphasis on the power of fate or luck or some omnipotent force to control what happens—two lives full of hazards: one accepted as "good," the other treated as "a chance"; the life cycle of "flowers"; and ever-present "change." The lack of personal control reflects the Fatalistic orientation toward a life that is governed by powerful but protective forces.

Motivation

"I take life as it is." "Once you have what you need, then you can sit back, relax, and enjoy life." "I come in to work, do what I'm told, and go home." "There's a lot I'd like to have, but I have what I need."

Motivation refers to people's inner drive, their momentum, and the amount of stimulation they need to get things done. The lack of activity in Fatalists' lives makes it easy for them to sit back and take what they find. In addition, the lack of interest in life per se makes it difficult to stimulates a Fatalist's interest. It is hard to get their attention by conventional methods. Rewards, such as status or money, for example, provide little incentive for the Fatalist, who is more concerned with basic needs.

Furthermore, people who do not associate their own actions with what happens to them are likely to be difficult to motivate. If one's destiny is predetermined and beyond individual control, as Fatalists believe, there is no point in trying to change anything. With limited choice and diminished free will, Fatalists are devoid of strong motivating forces, knowing that it is useless to try to fight one's fate.

Lack of motivation takes a variety of forms. Fatalists are not energetic, not adventurous, and not willing to pursue their fortunes. They are much more willing to accept whatever comes their way. They react rather than act; are passive rather than active; and tend to be submissive rather than dominant. Fatalists usually find jobs working for others wherein they can be encouraged, directed, and told what to do. On the whole, they are more likely to be outer-directed and in need of external encouragement to make significant advancements.

Fatalists do not seem motivated to achieve anything beyond the "basics." They distinguish between wants and needs. Needs are essential and wants are extra. Although Fatalists might want some things, they are not worried if they do not have them and are not motivated to go out and get them. Their goal is simply having what they need. Instead of wanting more out of life, Fatalists are satisfied with what they have (whatever that is at the moment). Rather than try to excel at life, they are content with their appointed lot.

Once they achieve their goal of having what they need, Fatalists are content, filled with a feeling of achievement. Life, after all, is a struggle, and it is hard to make a living. They want to meet their basic needs so they can take the time to sit back and rest comfortably. Once everything is cared for, they feel secure and complacent. Why should they be concerned with anything more? Who cares about self-actualization? Such things would require more effort than they wish to put into life. By wanting only the essentials, they avoid the complications associated with success and other people's expectations. They do not want to do well in life but are contented with getting by.

As part of their Fatalistic orientation, they see themselves as "connected," and they sincerely believe that those connections will take care of them. The order outside the individual guides them and organizes their lives, making it unnecessary for the individual to intervene. As always, fate determines what happens.

This section includes Clem, Thelma, Bryan, and Chuck. Clem and Thelma, both illiterate, clearly perceive a sense of order that makes their lives worthwhile.[7] They do not want much in life and are contented—their needs are satisfied. Bryan is discovering his needs and is searching for a way to satisfy them. Chuck works in a bus station and believes there is no purpose to life other than propagation. These people reflect the Fatalistic sense of complacency, with minimal motivation.

Clem: "It Just Is"

Clem, an ironworker, has been cutting steel since 1968. He describes his job as semiskilled because he works with machines that "don't take a lot of brains to operate. You can teach anybody how to run any machine in here in maybe two weeks." At thirty-three, Clem follows the daily routine. "I just come in. Do what I'm told and go home. . . . It's just a job."

At nineteen he enlisted to go to Vietnam because "it seemed like the thing to do. All I know is they told me to go and I went. I put my time in and came back. . . ." Clem seemed barely thoughtful about Vietnam as I asked him if it effected his life. "No, I don't really think so." He believes he was "lucky" to survive but does not know why. "I don't know why I was lucky and they weren't. But I was glad to see it turned out that way."

For Clem "just being here" is the most important thing in life. He uses the word *basically* often. "I just basically take things as they come." He leads a "basic" life with little concern for more than fundamental needs. Few things worry him. "I just take the days as they come. . . . I don't think I've ever actually prepared myself for the future in any way. I just get by." Unable to liken life to anything, Clem approaches life simply. "Life is like. . . I can't think of anything to compare it to. It just is, I s'pose. I can't liken it to anything."

Of all the interviewees, Clem had the most difficulty answering the life metaphor question. Asking what something is "like" usually encourages people to use a metaphor. Clem, however, answered the questions literally. Moreover, most of his answers were neither analytical nor reflective, and at times, he did not understand some of the words I used. In the following verbatim passage, Clem relates his feelings about Vietnam:

Q: How did you survive?
A: Just the best I could.
Q: What did it come down to?
A: Ah, I don't know what you mean by that.
Q: I mean, what was the most important thing you had to do each day to survive over there?
A: Just watch out. Keep down.
Q: Did going to Vietnam affect the rest of your life?
A: No, I don't really think so.

I did not think my questions too difficult nor my language hard to understand, but it seemed that Clem had never thought about the things I was asking. He confirmed my suspicion by often saying, "I never really thought about it," "none that I can think of," or "I don't know." Either he did not understand the questions or he did not want to answer.

Clem is illiterate. Russian psychologist A. R. Luria has done some fascinating studies concerning illiteracy, some of which are described in *Cognitive Development*, in which he examines the cultural and societal bases for the development of an individual's thinking ability.[8] Luria discovered that for illiterates "questions probing for an analysis of personal qualities were either not grasped at all or were related to external material circumstances or everyday situations."[9] For example, Luria asked, "Are you satisfied with yourself or would you like to be different?" and found that an illiterate person might answer, "It would be good if I had a little more land and could sow more wheat." The person related himself to external things. Luria found that on the whole, illiterate people cannot analyze themselves; they think on a literal level, and they confuse categories.[10]

As I read Luria's work I found that the interview with Clem resembled many of Luria's interviews. I was also reminded of Gregory Bateson's discussion of metaphor in his double bind theory. "An individual will take a metaphorical statement literally when he is in a situation where he must respond, where he is faced with contradictory messages, and when he is unable to comment on the contradictions."[11]

Clem may have responded literally because he felt on the spot in the interview situation.[12] Nonetheless, the inability to read and write influences a person's mental activity. Preliterate or oral cultures and children who have not yet acquired language could be described as illiterate. In these cases, metaphor is not absent from their thinking, but works on an unconscious level. It would be untrue to say that illiterate people cannot create or understand metaphors. It would be more accurate to say that they are not identified as such, making them, as Bateson calls them, "unlabeled" metaphors.[13]

Thelma: "A Goal"

Thelma seemed unsure of what to say, and repeatedly answered many of the questions with "I don't know how to answer that"; "I never really thought about it"; or "I don't know what you're looking for." At one point she said, "I don't know what to say, what would be best?" It was difficult to convince her that there were no "correct" answers. Like Clem, she paused often during the interview and seemed thoughtful about the questions. Her difficulty in assessing herself reflects one of the typical patterns of the illiterate.[14]

Thelma works as a janitor for a factory. Only twenty-nine, she looks older. She worked as a secretary for a short time after high school but quit because the pay was not high enough. Before her present job, she worked as a carpenter, and after I commented that it was unusual for a woman to work as a carpenter, she replied, "I don't know. I guess I never really looked at it like that. I feel like if I couldn't get a job, then they shouldn't hire me. You know. I never really thought about it I guess."

Since then she has worked in factories; I asked her what it was like. "I don't know. . . . I guess maybe this is all I know, you know, is factory work. Someday I would like to get out of it and do something." I asked Thelma how other people would describe her and she answered, "I get along good with people. But I really don't know. It doesn't bother me. I don't care what they think." I asked her how she would describe herself and she said, "I'm nice to people. I'm outgoing. And to me I have a nice personality. You know, I don't know what other people think. And I'd give them a hand in any way I could." These answers tend to confirm Luria's observations that illiterate people do not analyze themselves very well and make statements that seem unrelated.[15]

Unlike Clem, however, Thelma could answer the life metaphor question. "Life is like a goal. It's whatever you want to achieve and make out of it. It's whatever you want to be. You know, you can be somethin' if you wanna be somethin'." Then I asked her if she set goals for herself and she answered "Not really. I would like to, but I don't." According to Luria's study, illiterate people often contradict themselves.

Thelma's uncomplicated life satisfies her, and her main concern is to meet her basic needs. Like so many Fatalists, she tries to minimize worrying. "I don't have any worries in life. I really don't. As far as money, really I don't. I have what I want. And I usually do what I want. Don't get me wrong. There's a lot I'd like to have, but I have what I need, let's put it like that. I don't drink or any of that. I have a decent life. I'm not a churchgoer."

In this passage, Thelma makes a powerful distinction, common to most Fatalists, between wants and needs. A want is something nonessential, a luxury, and an extra in life. A need is essential for survival. If Fatalists have what they need, they are content. Different people have different needs. Goal-driven Enthusiasts strive for self-actualization. Angry Antagonists need others to appreciate them. Silent Spectators want to appreciate life. Fatalists achieve satisfaction from merely taking care of their basic needs.

I asked Thelma what she had learned about life, and she said, "I guess how to deal with people. I really haven't learned a whole lot. 'Cause bein' a janitor, you really don't learn a lot." "Being a janitor" means the "daily routine: Come in, punch the time card. You know, you're here. You know what your job is. You do it. You get it done. Then you leave. There's really not a whole lot of future in it. You're here. You get it done."

She works hard, starting the day early by getting her children ready. Her little boy goes to school, and her daughter goes to a baby-sitter. When she gets home, she cleans her house, bathes her children, and prepares dinner for her family; home life follows a routine.

The first thing I do is take a shower. Then I do my dishes. Then I make the beds and stuff like that. Then I usually go and sit down for a while and then start my supper as soon as my kids get their baths at seven. Then they go to bed at eight. Then I'll relax in the evening. I try to get everything done. I go to bed about eleven.

What motivates Thelma? The inevitable daily routine drives her forward. Like so many Fatalists, she cannot escape her fate.

I know I have to come back. I don't have any alternative. It's the same you know. You come here, you know what has to be done, and it's more or less a daily chore. On different days you have different stuff. But as far as every week, it's the same. I just take it one day at a time. I know I have to do it. You get up and you do it. I know I have to have the money. And I know I have to work. So it's just one of those things I know I have to do.

Bryan: "School"

Bryan waits tables at a small cafeteria, trying to save money so that he can go to school. At only eighteen, education is foremost in his mind, and it is not surprising to find the desire for knowledge expressed in his life metaphor. "Life is like school. Because for me, I'm forever learning. I try to learn from experience. I'm always learning something new. Whether it's about people or changing the oil on your car, or anything. I try to."

Bryan devotes his energy to a gradual process of self-education. In many ways, he is like Steve, who says life is "a fine line between frustration and amusement." Both Bryan and Steve are concerned with a passive process of self-education. They do not wish to make any radical discoveries; they only want to find out who they are. As part of Bryan's education, he needs to know that he is "going places" and that his "goals are coming through." Although goal oriented, he does not actively intrude in the course of events and speaks passively about his goals. Bryan is content to sit and watch how things progress.

Part of Bryan's difficulty in getting motivated stems from a self-conscious hesitation to take risks. Peer pressure made growing up difficult as classmates ridiculed him about his large size during his teenage years. He fears he will be humiliated again. Like Arlene, he believes that society places too much emphasis on looks and not enough on personality, and that people make too many judgments. "It bothers me when somebody judges somebody else. Or there's talking behind backs and things like that."

There were family troubles as well, causing Bryan to worry frequently—about many things. "I would say that for me, I've worried about things and tried to figure them out. You know, ask myself why and worry about it. My mother and father are separated now. I worried about what's gonna happen. But I think with time I found the answer."

The answer came through not worrying. Like other Fatalists, Bryan learned that he will eventually find answers to the things that are most important to him. This discovery helps him consciously minimize the stress in his life. "It just took time. I try not to worry. I just think, is it really gonna help, just pacing around and worrying about this and that? I've found it doesn't help anything. I try and work it out and if I can, that's good, and if I can't, then I just go along."

The emphasis on learning and experience represents a recurring theme for Bryan. Even though his high school years were tough, they helped him learn about himself.

> I've learned that people will take me as I am. I thought for a lot of years that I had to be like everyone else. You know, I had to dress like everyone else. I had to act like everyone else to fit in. But I found as I've grown that if I'm gonna have friends, they're gonna take me as I am. You can't live to please others. You have to be happy with yourself first.

Bryan incorporates his need to learn into his major goal, which is "always trying to better myself." Bryan's major incentive in life is self-improvement and self-discovery. By focusing on himself, he tends towards introspection rather than action. He tries to do things "the right way. . . . I just try to take things as they come." Bryan expresses the Fatalistic tendency towards passive motivation by "taking" what life offers.

Chuck: "Roll Along with the Punches"

Chuck, thirty-six, works as a ticket agent at a bus station. Softspoken and shy, he used to sell insurance but likes the bus station much more. "Nobody bugs me. Nobody really puts you under a lot of pressure. It's pretty good." Unable to recall anything in particular he wanted to be when growing up, he describes himself as a drifter. "I didn't have anything I really wanted to be. I was always just kind of drifting along there."

Small-town life seems monotonous to him after California, which he left eight years ago to live near his brother. The Midwest provides much less activity than Los Angeles, but he puts up with it, sometimes traveling to Chicago and the museums. "People think it's crazy but I like the natural history museum. I find it very interesting. The wars. The time of the pharaohs, and the Christians. . . . It all has an appeal to me. The way they did things. The buildings they built. The culture. It attracts me."

Chuck's passion for history provides an escape from everyday reality. He travels to the distant lands and times to combat feelings of being "trapped." Although he dislikes living in a small town, he appreciates its stability and values being able to provide a steady life for his children. "When I was a kid, I moved a lot and I never had just one spot. We used to move once a week. So I wanna try and give my kids some roots. You gotta have something to grasp onto. I like to keep moving and I gotta fight that urge all the time."

Chuck proudly admits that he "never philosophized about how life is. . . . I don't look for a purpose in everything, you know. I think a lot of it's all very unintentional." His life metaphor suggests his purposeful thoughtlessness.

> You roll along with the punches. I just think you're here for so long and then you kick off. Some of my friends say, "well, that's it," you know, it's the end of the ball game. My younger brother, now he believes in the afterlife. I got a sister out in California who thinks you're reincarnated. So I think somewhere in there, there's a grey area that maybe somethin' goes on. At least I'd like to think so.

Not wanting to think that death means the end, he holds onto the hope of something more. "I'd hate to think that you're just here for so long and that's that. I don't know what the other would be like." Although hopeful about an afterlife, he has little faith about the purpose of the present life. "I don't think there's a purpose to this. I think it's pretty well all chance. I say there's no purpose. There is no purpose. You know, we're here. And it just

matters how you feel about things. How you make your life. . . .
I just take it easy. That's about it. Not much I can do about it."
Chuck argues that since life is "chance," it is pointless to intervene. "Propagation is one purpose. But other than that, I don't
think there's really any purpose. That doesn't mean it's necessarily
true. It's just how I feel." Another purpose for life is "knowing
how to surmount the difficulties. If you can handle those difficulties, if you can surmount them, it means you're a better person." He admits it is not an easy task; "it's hard to do. If you live
one kind of life and it's not satisfying and there's some other way,
you gotta find that way and try and change."

In spite of the conspicuous absence of philosophy, Chuck knows
how the world operates and where he fits into the scheme of
things. Unlike most Fatalists, who believe that eventually they
will find an answer, he believes that there are no answers to eternal
questions about life and death.

> There's a lot of questions you ask yourself. There ain't no answer.
> So why even fool with them. It's just the way it is. I never been
> known to do a lot of real deep thinking. . . . The reason or purpose
> for being here—there is none. We're just going along. You have
> no choice on whether you want to be here. You can't get off the
> planet without dying. So I figure there's no real reason or purpose
> for being here. We're just going along.

A literal interpretation of a life that "just is"; two life metaphors
preoccupied with unfulfilled ambitions, "a goal" and "school";
and a passive life metaphor of "rolling along with the punches"—
each indicates an unconditional acquiescence to life. Moreover,
embedded in each metaphor is a compliance with life, as if Fatalists have agreed with their maker not to overstep their lot.

Fatalists share some features with the other orientations. Like
Antagonists, they do not think very positively about life, but they
are not as actively aggressive. Fatalists are the opposite of Enthusiasts on both the activity and the evaluative dimensions. Fatalists
take life; Enthusiasts make life. Fatalists say that "life is OK;
Enthusiasts say that life is fantastic. Fatalists and Spectators rely
on fate; however, Spectators are much more positive about life.
They are characterized as the less active and the most positive.
The next chapter describes six Spectators by presenting a detailed
portrait of each.

CHAPTER 6

The Spectator

> To become the spectator of one's own life is to
> escape the suffering of life.
> > Oscar Wilde, *The Picture of Dorian Gray.*

> The looker-on sees most of the game. English
> proverb, borrowed from the Latin of Seneca, and
> quoted as familiar.
> > Francis Bacon, *Essays.*

> The spectator is not the arbiter of the work of
> art. He is one who is admitted to contemplate
> the work of art. . . .
> > Oscar Wilde, *The Soul of Man Under Socialism.*

The word *spectator* brings to mind a number of associations:
we readily think of spectator sports, such as football, baseball, or
wrestling; perhaps some will think of less raucous pastimes like
tennis or golf. In any case, these games represent various images
of spectator sports. Each one could, of course, be played without
observers, but having someone there seems to enhance the spec-
tacle and change the quality of the action. Part of the excitement
that spectator sports generate stems from the presence of people
watching the game.

There are various kinds of spectators: the football spectator and
the wrestling spectator, and so on. Writer Murray Ross points out
that baseball closes the distance between the spectators and the
players, while football increases it. He argues that football is larger
than life, with the players transformed into ideal images of mas-
culinity. Baseball heroes, on the other hand, are much more down-
to-earth and less godlike.[1]

Wrestling has an appeal different from either football or baseball because it depicts a present-day morality play.[2] The audience judges the relative good and evil of the participants in a weekly ritual. The "bad guy" is greeted with boos and hisses as he enters the ring. Even the children, who do not fully understand the morality, hiss to show their contempt. The "good guy" is applauded, cheered, shrouded in white light, treated like royalty, and accompanied by majestic music.

In contrast to team sports, there are individual sports, which appeal to a spectator who enjoys a more relaxed form of entertainment. Tennis and golf, for example, have fewer players, which encourages a more sedate pace, making the bursts of excitement that interrupt the action seem all the more pleasurable.

Although the range of spectators is broad, they share several qualities. Being a spectator means partaking of the action without having to do the work. By imagining what it might be like to be in the middle of the field, spectators play out their fantasies without having to go through the training and the sacrifice. They can safely interact without bearing the responsibility for the outcome. In spectator sports, the excitement comes from the shared act of watching, which progressively unites the audience as the energy escalates. Being a spectator means participating in a shared drama created by each individual. Spectator sports are appealing because they allow the viewer to dream, to vicariously participate, to identify, or to walk away. Part of the thrill also comes from the anonymity: rarely do the people in the crowd stand out. As soon as they enter the stadium, they become unidentifiable figures blending into a mass of other faces.

For a variety of reasons, Spectators believe that life should be valued. Some acquire this orientation because they have survived traumatic events, while others seem to be naturally inclined towards this disposition. In each case, Spectators are unable to understand why people treat life gratuitously and often become frustrated when they see the reckless abuse of life. For Spectators, life is something that must be appreciated and respected and never taken for granted.[3]

An equally dramatic, though more intense, example of Spectators may be found in people who survive devastating events. One overwhelming example concerns survivors of the Holocaust. They are the spectators of the Nazi horror; they carry the burden of remembering and talking about the nightmare. Indeed, Holocaust survivors call themselves "witnesses" and believe that it is their duty to "bear witness." By virtue of surviving and witnessing what happened, they acquired a mission in life: to tell the world the story.[4] Other forms of survival that entail talking about what they witnessed include people who live through mass murders, natural disasters, or freak accidents.

Like the Fatalist, the Spectator believes in an underlying order that controls life and that must be respected. The Spectator also sees little point in trying to make changes because fate determines one's destiny. However, unlike the pessimistic Fatalist, the Spectator searches for the positive side and is likely to find the "silver lining" in every dark cloud.

Spectators are rated as less active because they take life as it comes, without trying to make significant changes. A benign acceptance of what happens fosters this perspective. Generally content with a slow-paced life, they are in no great hurry. Spectators are also rated as the most positive on the evaluative dimension. Savoring the "gift of life," they are happy to be alive.

Spectators are humble people without the slightest inclination to take advantage of any situation. They know it is possible to make life interesting, but they are not eager to pursue that option. Instead, they are happy to watch others achieve bigger and better things. Spectators do not want a complicated life, preferring to attend to their simple needs.

Most Spectators are eager to help others and usually find jobs working with people. They appreciate human beings and receive great satisfaction from being able to help. Their reliance on others confirms their reality. Psychologist Edward Sampson describes this tendency as "other-directedness." "[A person] understands what he understands and knows what he knows by reference to what others around him understand and know; his judgments of truth and reality are social judgments based on others' judgments of truth and reality. . . ."[5]

Being so consciously "other-directed" helps Spectators acquire a balanced perspective about life. By comparing themselves with others, they learn to love life. They also know that their relationships with people give them their perspective, which allows them to explain inconsistencies and manage difficulties. Spectators understand and accept their inability to change things, while maintaining inner control over how they look at life. This passive control assures them that everything will be alright.

The Spectator, like the Antagonist, represents a relatively small segment of society. As expected, people who are positive are usually more active than the Spectator. Because only six people have been classified as Spectators, it is possible to present more extended interviews. The chapter is not divided thematically (as the last two were). As you read, however, you will find evidence of the four attributes—activity, evaluation, control, and motivation. The interviews are presented in detail to illustrate the scope of interests.

The chapter begins with Margaret, the least active and most positive individual I interviewed. She is diametrically opposed to Harry, the Antagonist (the most active and least positive individual). Margaret's gentleness contrasts with Harry's stark aggression; and her thankfulness contrasts with his ingratitude. She possesses none of the Antagonist's fierce rebellion or adversarial stance. Instead she approaches life as an irreplaceable gift.

Margaret: "A Very Precious Thing"

I enjoy life very much. . . . Life is very precious. . . . It's just something that you should be grateful in having. . . . There's always something that's gonna come along in the day and make it better.

Margaret works at a dilapidated, residential hotel, which had once been a prestigious landmark. An ornate wooden staircase winds up to the first-floor balcony, which overlooks an enormous lobby. The front desk, originally beautifully polished oak, stands uncared for. The walls need painting, and the marble floors are scuffed and dirty. It is easy to imagine another time when the hotel welcomed visitors and provided a lavish rendezvous. In bygone days, the railway marked the center of urban activity, using the hotel as its central station. The train still runs through the town, stopping twice daily, but there is little flourish, and the dwindling number of passengers threatens the service.

In many ways, Margaret is like the hotel. At forty-one, she dyes her hair jet black and wears bright lipstick. She uses some makeup, which barely hides the lines on her face. She is gentle and sensitive, speaking softly in a controlled, thoughtful voice. Her small frame is lost behind the desk. She combines two jobs, one as a receptionist for the hotel and the other selling tickets for the railway.

Lethargic figures scatter the lobby waiting for the bar to open. They are of various ages, disheveled, smoking, not talking; some have canes; all are oblivious to their surroundings. I interviewed Margaret at the reception desk, and as we talked guests passed and stopped to chat as they might an old friend. She was receptive, smiled, and had something pleasant to say to each. She treated everyone with equal respect.

Margaret is classified as least active because she reacts to life. She emphasizes "taking" what life offers, rather than actively "making" it the way she wants (as the Enthusiast would do). She is classified as most positive because her reaction is essentially a cheerful one. Her life metaphor matches her compassionate behavior. "Life is a very precious thing. Very precious. I enjoy living. I enjoy being here. And I enjoy my work. It's just something you should be very grateful in having. Each day should be precious. . . . I've experienced losing a child. And I see other things that happen and how people cannot see how precious life is."

The structure embedded in the life metaphor often guides people's lives. In Margaret's case, the life metaphor not only helps her cope with her son's death but helps frame other important life issues. Her life metaphor also reflects her universal perspective on life and death.

Even though Margaret persists, her son's death is unforgettable, and she looks back at that time with much pain.

> 1976. I lost my son, my oldest son. I lost him in 1976. That year was the hardest year of my life. You never get over it. You just more or less let time help heal it. But you never get over it. I just take each day at a time and look at my other children and be thankful that I have them. And now I have two beautiful grandchildren.

Her life changed when her son died. "I thought I was the strongest person in the world. There wasn't anything I couldn't accomplish. I could do anything until this happened. And then I seen just how weak I really was." Time and perseverance have helped, but she admits she never fully recovered. "Time helps to heal the hole, or help soothe the pain. But as far as gettin' over it. I never heard of anyone ever gettin' over it. Never. . . . It's like time helped me see. And as I've gone down these last nine years, I've seen a lot and I been able to cope with it."

Margaret's grief was more difficult because her son died away from home. In the beginning, she denied it. "For the first two or three years it was a little rough 'cause I kept waitin' for him to come home. Because he wasn't home when he passed away." Without the evidence of death, she secretly hoped it might not be true, and expected her son to come walking through the door at any time. These feelings stayed with her for a long time.

David Dempsey studies people's perceptions of death in *The Way We Die* and comments that the need to see the dead person is critical.

> Far from being barbaric, viewing is seen as an important psychological adjunct to grieving. It is easier to give up the deceased if the body is visible and, equally important, if it is laid to rest in our presence. . . . [Not viewing the body might lead to] disbelief for months and even years afterwards. . . . Something deep within us demands a confrontation with death, a last look that assures us that the person we loved or admired is, indeed, gone forever.[6]

Not seeing her son's body made his death difficult to acknowledge. *Personal Meanings of Death*, edited by Franz Epting and Robert Neimeyer, contains an article by Dorothy Rowe describing the typical stages of grieving.[7] In the beginning

> people try to reestablish continuity by denying that the person has died. Even though they go through the procedures of the funeral, the exchanges of condolences, the practical tasks of disposing of personal effects and carrying out all the legal requirements, all this seems like play-acting or a dream. They expect to waken any moment or to see their loved one walk through the door. Then one day the play-acting ends, the dream vanishes. They know the person is dead. They ask "why?" and there is no answer.[8]

Margaret seems to express Rowe's findings in a more personal way.

> Back in '76, nobody could talk to me. I had several people who tried, but I didn't wanna listen. I didn't have an answer for

nothin.' In other words, I really didn't care about an answer. I was just tryin' to figure out why. . . . It upsets me to talk about this. I still wonder why. I don't think that will ever really leave me. I see so many things around me I don't understand. Like value in life. My son loved life. He was crazy about sports. And I see others around that don't care. That makes me wonder. But I don't have an answer.

When one confronts death, one confronts the meaning of life. Rowe believes that people "try to find a meaning for death that allows them to establish a continuity to life."[9] Margaret searched for a way to understand her son's death so that she could continue living without feeling overwhelmed by futility. She remembers struggling, trying different things, not certain about what to do. She moved out of her home and quit her job thinking they might help. "They did for a little while because there was a different atmosphere. . . . But it all started coming back again. . . ." She finally accepted her son's death. "I had to learn to accept it. And when I learned to accept it, it was easier. I wasn't gonna accept it, but I finally had to accept it." Eventually she conceded that there were other things to live for.

Spectators overcome the pessimistic feelings associated with senseless death by acquiring a perspective that affirms the meaning in life. Like white cells multiplying to heal the wound, the sense of purpose accelerates to prevent the negative feelings from taking over. Spectators become convinced that there is meaning in life. They interpret death as part of life and fearlessly find solace in a peaceful coexistence with death.

During the difficult times, Margaret never gave up completely. "I never thought life was not worth living. Never. Like I said, life is precious to me." Fortunately, her inner strength supported her. Her son's death reinforced her belief that "life is a very precious thing." Had she not have believed life was precious, she might have been more inclined to give in to the negative feelings.

Coping is never a simple process, and it is naive to think that any one thing alone guarantees survival. Instead, a combination of factors seems the most viable way to manage problems. In addition to Margaret's frame of mind, prayer helps. She confides that "sometimes I'll be standing right here and I'll be doing it. People won't even know it so it really helps. If you have the faith to believe and I do have the faith." Although she does not attend church regularly, she incorporates her religious beliefs into her daily routine.

Margaret also survived her son's death because she possesses a remarkable inner strength. She believes survival depends on the individual's self-reliance.

> You get up and do it. I mean, you know that you have to work. It's just like accomplishing or setting a goal for yourself. If you wanna set goals you have to do it. . . . You have to find a way for yourself. No one can tell you how to do anything or tell you how to solve this problem. You have to do it yourself. You can get help. But it's all in you. You have to determine if you want to do it or not. And if you don't want to, you're not gonna come out of it.

Although Spectators rely on themselves, they admit a need for other people. By comparing herself with others, Margaret finds herself extremely fortunate. She looks around and cannot understand why people do not respect life and realize how precious it is. The experience with death taught Margaret the folly in not appreciating life. She questions people's careless attitudes and believes that if they knew how frail life is they would change. For herself, she tries to make time count.

> I just try to make every minute count to accomplish something. . . . Even though we have bad days, there's always something that's gonna come along during that day to make it better. In other words, if you think you're really down and that you're the only one in the world that has problems, look around you. Take a look around you. And that's gonna make you have a different outlook on things. I see it everyday.

"Attitude" is important to Margaret, which she calls a person's "outlook" or "mood." "I work on it each day. If I get up in a bad mood, I can stay in a bad mood all day. But I try to get up in a good mood. 'Cause if I don't, then it reflects on others around me. And I try to take each day at a time. One step at a time."

Margaret appreciates the unique make-up of each individual's problem. "Even if the problem is very small. It doesn't make a difference to them. The problem is big. So I try to take time out to listen." Empathy helps her understand another's perspective. "I feel like if someone would listen to me. Okay, that person feels the same way. I may not think their problem is big, but to them it's big."

Using her own healing process as a guide, Margaret helps others. "I learned that gettin' involved with other people and helpin' other people helps me more than anything. You have to go on." She regenerates her wisdom as she nourishes others.

> I got a goal now for myself. I wanna be able to help people in anything. Listen to 'em, talk to 'em. Just be kind to 'em. Sometimes I don't think you even have to say anything to a person. It's just touching that person's hand or giving them a smile. That means more to that person than you realize. So that's what I'm out for. Just to help people and let them know I care about them. . . . Life is about loving, caring, and sharing with one another. If I can do something for somebody, it makes me feel good inside.

Spectators believe in inherent human goodness. The desire to help others reflects their positive orientation. Margaret thinks of the hotel and its clients as her family.

> This is their home. Things happen here that would normally happen at home. I just try to take each day, just one step at a time. Before there was too much pressure. I left for awhile. But I'm glad I'm back. I love the people here. And I love to work with people. There's a lot of people that live in this building that don't have no one. I mean no one. And a smile and a kind word goes a long way.

She believes her mission is to help people, but she has in mind a passive kind of help. She is not interested in making radical changes, because she knows that often the simple things are the most helpful. She treasures small intangible gestures of caring. "There's so many people here I can help and just give a hand to or a smile or take 'em to the store, be good to 'em. And that way, my problems, the Lord helps me. By taking care of my problems because I'm always willing to help someone else."

Margaret sums up her philosophy: "If you wake up and have a smile on your face, then you can keep that smile all day. I think that's the whole thing right there." Smiling and listening symbolize more than simply polite gestures. They indicate a respectful attitude towards fellow humans and a benevolent philosophy of life. A smile changes the way a person looks, somehow showing their best features. Margaret believes everyone has a good side, and she wants to be able to see that in people. She looks for the "silver lining" in every cloud and finds ways to bring out the best in a person.

A similar appreciation for life can be identified in each Spectator including John, who, like Margaret appreciates life and thinks of it as something precious. Although John did not lose a loved one, he suffered a heart attack and nearly died, which makes him grateful to be alive.

John: "It's Not That Bad"

> *It's not that bad. I wouldn't wanna die, let's put it that way. 'Cause I been there once. . . . My life stays on an even keel. . . . Chanting brings everything in my body in tune with the universe. And it works.*

John is in his early fifties and delivers mail at the college. During the interview, we sat in a tiny room where the workers take their breaks. Personal possessions clutter the room, reflecting a variety of personalities. A clock ticks loudly in the foreground, conspicuously marking time.

John was born in 1931, "right along the depression era there" and has worked at the university for twenty-six years. Although he has delivered mail on the same route for seventeen of those years, he claims it is not monotonous.

> You go from one building to another, and everything is different. Nothin's ever the same in all the buildings. There's always something moved. . . . One time I went to put mail on the desk, and the desk wasn't there. They said you oughta seen the expression on my face when I walked over to the desk, where the desk should have been, and there was no desk.

The interview began slowly. Initially John answered the questions directly, briefly, and with few details. He made little conversation, and at first I thought he was shy. It seemed as though he had nothing much to say and was not eager to elaborate about his life. It was difficult to make eye contact, and I wondered if it had been a mistake to interview him. He proved me wrong when I asked him about his life metaphor.

> It's not that bad. I wouldn't wanna die. Let's put it that way. 'Cause I been there once. . . . When I had my heart attack. When they did the angiogram on me I died and I didn't wanna come back. . . . It was really neat. I was in so much pain, and, ah. . . . All of a sudden the pain just quit, and I mean it felt so good. There was no pain. I was floating in the air. I was floating up to the lights. I was just floating away. And it felt pretty nice. . . .

John became animated and talkative and the shyness disappeared. His expression changed, and his face came alive. He was eager to talk about this part of his life. By asking John the right question, I gained access to another side of him.[10] Had I not asked him that particular question, I might not have found out anything about John's near-death experience. The interview might have continued with little progress and little interaction. Instead, the life metaphor question triggered a series of related beliefs and assumptions about which John could talk at length and with ease. He was not intentionally trying to hide anything or be an uncooperative interviewee, but in all likelihood he would not have volunteered the information simply because he did not consider it remarkable. Prompted by a description of his out-of-body experience, he elaborated on his philosophy of life.

A significant amount of literature has accumulated on out-of-body experiences. People who write about the subject tend to be interested in some of the following topics: astral projection; death and the afterlife; unconscious powers; religious experiences; eastern philosophy; psychic phenomena; memory of survival.

Life at Death, by Kenneth Ring, recounts interviews with people who have survived near-death experiences.[11] Ring observes that "most near-death experiences seem to unfold according to a *single pattern,* almost as though the prospect of death serves to release a stored, *common* 'program' of feelings, perceptions, and experiences."[12] He traces the recurring pattern of the near-death experience. One woman, after a cardiac arrest, is quoted as follows:

> [There was] nothing painful. There was nothing frightening about it. It was just something that I felt I gave myself into completely. And it felt good. . . . One very, very strong feeling was that if I could *only* make them [her doctors] understand how comfortable and painless it is . . . how natural it is . . . I felt *no* sadness. No longing. No fear.[13]

Through extensive interviews, Ring compiled a list of characteristics, discovering that the "core experience" unfolds according to a five-stage process.[14] First, it begins with peace and a sense of well-being. In the second stage, the individual leaves the body. The third stage is characterized by beginning to "enter the darkness," accompanied by a sense of floating or drifting. The appearance of light identifies the transition from the third to the fourth stage. In the fifth stage, the individual actually enters the light. At this point, the person experiences the sensation of being in another world. John's brief account, as well as the previous quotation from the woman, echo this pattern, supporting Ring's hypothesis. Bill, the Fatalist, who also spoke of his out-of-body experience, expresses similar sensations.[15]

I asked John if his heart attack changed his life, and he began to answer at a literal level. "Yeah, I can't climb too many stairs any more 'cause I get weak. I got weak today and I had to sit down. You go home in the evening, and you don't feel like going out. I just go home, I just sit down. I'm exhausted." But at a more philosophical level, he explained that the experience did not change his life because he is a Buddhist.

Seeing John in his cluttered office, in his uniform, eating his lunch, he somehow does not fit my picture of a Buddhist. He clarified his philosophy: "We believe in life. Living your life to your fullest." The belief in life helped him understand his out-of-body experience. Rather than viewing death as distinct from life, Buddhism teaches that death cannot be separated from life: death is the fulfillment of life.

John became a Buddhist in 1967, and vividly recalls the accompanying changes.

A friend of mine was in it. And I seen the change in his life. And I started. I was skeptical about it at first. I used to be an old grouch. . . . I mean all the secretaries were scared of me. Well I been doing this [Buddhism] for about two weeks, and one of the ladies came up to me one day, and said, "What have you done differently?" I said, "Oh, I don't know. Why?" She said, "Whatever it is don't ever go back. 'Cause," she says, "we can talk to you now, and you don't snap our heads off." Before you'd say anything to me and I'd snap right back at 'em. And then I told 'em that I was a Buddhist. And she said, "Don't ever go back. You keep that up."

The transition from an "old grouch" to an approachable person is something John wants to keep. Twenty years later he remembers the conversation as if it were yesterday. He likes to tell the story because it seems to prove that he changed. Somehow, the story helps him hold onto his renewed personality. Memory has the power to preserve a changed identity by reminding one of one's previous personality. The memory lingers to protect the person. John invokes thoughts of what life used to be like so that he does not revert to his old habits.

Other changes followed John's religious conversion. "Everything good started happening. For awhile everything bad was happening. Then everything leveled off and it's been pretty good since. My life stays on an even keel." John's life became balanced, purposeful, and pleasurable. He believes the period of dissatisfaction was a prerequisite to the eventual goodness that surfaced in his life. He thinks of life in terms of levels and stages. For example, John argues that the progression from animal life to human life leads to a higher state of mind. Without a doubt, he believes that humans are superior to animals. "Animal life is a lower form of life and I think I have reached a higher grade of life than that. I really believe that. When I come back in my next life I will be higher than I am now."

Buddhism provides a structure for life, which incorporates an understanding of death. Death is never perceived as something final: within a philosophy of change, it is the ultimate transformation. John's faith teaches him that life progresses toward a clearly marked destiny—death followed by the afterlife. He expects to be reincarnated. "I know I will come back in the next life. I just know it. I feel it. I don't know what my other lives have been. . . . I'll probably come back as a human. In a better state of mind where, you know what I mean. Everything will be more on an even keel than the last life."

The moment of liberation is the moment of death. Jung Young Lee, in *Death and Beyond in the Eastern Perspective*, explains the process of reincarnation as follows:

> Death is the passive side of life, and life is the active side of death. What is experienced in life is to be fulfilled and completed in death. Thus the death experience is the reversal of the life experience. Just as yin is the reverse of yang, death is the other side of life. In this kind of complementary relation-

ship, the process of reincarnation is none other than part of the changing process. Thus reincarnation is the process of renewal and evolvement.[16]

Following Buddhist philosophy, a clearly defined sense of order directs John's life. Order assumes pattern and predictability and is one aspect of control. Some people require a high degree of stability and direction, others do not. Many people, such as Spectators, cope with a chaotic world by believing in an underlying order or pattern of existence.

Staying calm is another aspect of control, and John approaches life calmly. His unhurried speech physically reflects his psychological attitude. Within Buddhist philosophy, calmness is often associated with meditation—it is a way of being, an attitude or a way of relating to the world. Chanting is one part of meditation, which focuses attention by concentrating on one sound, one image, or one idea. The repetition of sounds alters a person's state of mind so that one can engage in surrender, self-expression, and heightened levels of concentration. If John becomes agitated or "disturbed" as he calls it, he stops, takes a few seconds, and chants "namyahorinyago" under his breath. According to him, "that brings everything in my body in tune with the universe. And it works. Then everything is back. I don't get mad no more." He often chants on the job, in much the same way that Margaret secretly prays. Both like the idea of being able to do something that calms them but does not draw attention to their discomfort and need.

One of John's biggest accomplishments is being able to control his temper. Not getting mad is important because it proves to him that he is "on an even keel." Life is as it should be, and everything is in order. Remaining calm is a personal barometer he uses to assess how well he is coping. He uses the following example to explain his pride in not getting mad:

> I raise racing pigeons. A couple of weeks ago five of my pigeons got killed. They got smothered in the track. And I was talking to some guys afterwards and they were all hot under the collar. And I said, "Well, I'm not really mad. I just feel sorry for the poor birds." That's what I told 'em, and they stopped and they thought a little bit. . . . I says, "You have to learn to live with death. That's part of life. That's a part of life. There ain't no use gettin' excited about it, there ain't nothin' you can do about it. Just happened. You just go ahead and keep on going."

Who would suspect that John, who so quietly and diligently delivers mail, had an out-of-body experience, is a Buddhist, chants every day, raises racing pigeons, and has worked for more than twenty years for the university. Spectators often have remarkable lives buried beneath a quiet and undramatic surface.

Joe: "What You Make It"

> *Life is what you make it. You know if you got the will to get ahead. . . . There's nothing really to understand. It's just the way it is I guess. You make it what it is. . . . The only way to go round is being positive. Because positive is happy.*

The omnipresent life metaphor "life is what you make it" appears again in the Spectator's quadrant. This single life metaphor has been the most frequently used and most versatile expression. The adaptability of the phrase underscores language's inherent ambiguity. Language does not always fit our expectations but often presents surprises.

We might hear someone say that "life is what you make it" and assume that they mean life is something terrific, but that is not necessrily so. Not surprisingly, "life is what you make it" is most frequently used by Enthusiasts (five people), which seems to bear out our expectation, but there are some exceptions. We have seen that Rick, an Antagonist, says "life is what you make it," but he harbors a grudge against the government, struggles fiercely to survive, and feels forced to salvage whatever he can from life. His attitude is that of a wounded individualist who is trying desperately to "make" it on his own and to replace what the war took from him.

Now we come to Joe, a Spectator, and find that he too thinks "life is what you make it." He feels good about life, but, unlike the Enthusiasts, he does not feel compelled to act just because he is positive. Joe has no desire or motivation to change anything about his life. He says "life is what you make it" and accepts his fate.

Language does not always establish precise definitions and rigid categories. People have the power to change the meaning of words, as evidenced by the different ways in which "life is what you make it" has been internalized. In the present study, the only life orientation from which the life metaphor is absent is the Fatalist. Although difficult to imagine a Fatalist saying "life is what you make it," it is not impossible. Language must be contextualized to reach a true defintion. To understand how Joe uses "life is what you make it," the following pages examine his language and meanings.

Joe works at the bus station where I interviewed Chuck, the Fatalist. He provides schedule information, sells tickets, and handles the Western Union business. He has had the job for eight years and proudly claims to know eighty-nine hundred bus schedules. "My specialty is knowing the book. I picked it up real quick. Memory is an important thing in this job. I've always had a good memory. Giving out fares and schedules is my specialty. I like doing it 'cause I got the memory for it."

In addition to using his memory, Joe likes the job because he has the chance to "work for the public." He deals directly with people, and his goal is "keeping the passenger happy." He likes what he does much more than factory work. "You stand there and do the same thing for eight hours, no distractions, no nothing. I couldn't handle it. I couldn't handle not seeing the outdoors."

At times, Joe's responsibilities include guarding the station, removing vagrants, and maintaining order on the premises. He knows he can handle himself in difficult situations. He is thirty-four years old, six feet tall, and well built. "Luckily I'm big enough that if someone gives me trouble I can tell them how to control themself." He remembers a blizzard in the winter of 1978.

We had two bus-loads of people stranded here. They stayed for forty-eight hours before we got the Red Cross to put them up. We didn't have the facilities. We had eighty-six people and only sixteen seats. They were sitting on the floor and everywhere. I worked through the night, after working twelve hours already. The people got to yelling. There was a fight. I smiled, and I says, "If you give me any trouble I'll kick ya." And they didn't give me any trouble. I told them in a friendly way, which they knew was serious. It's just knowing how to handle people I guess. It's not that it's an ability. It's just an instinct.

In spite of Joe's apparent aggressiveness, he is really gentle, describing himself as friendly, helpful, and caring. "I'm the type of person that if I see somebody broken down on the highway, I usually stop and see if I can help 'em. 'Cause I've been in that situation myself." Like Margaret, Joe easily puts himself in the other person's position. Spectators empathize so effortlessly because they can imagine what it would be like to be in the situation themselves.

Spectators also enjoy helping others, and Joe does odd jobs for friends and family in his spare time. He helps people fix cars, move to new houses, and even lends them money. His wife thinks he helps too many people.

> I got burned out on helping people there for a while. I was helpin' so many people, and they was stabbing me in the back. Old high school friends wantin' to borrow money. . . . I have a rule. If a student comes in and they're a dollar short, I'll help 'em. But after I help three students and none of them comes back to pay me, I won't help 'em 'til I get my money back.

Not surprisingly, he has mixed stories about helping people— some good and some bad. There have been times when people have taken advantage of him.

> There was a kid, got thrown off the bus 'cause he couldn't find his receipt. He gets on the phone and he's talkin' to his mother. So he asks if I can go over and talk to her. She took my name and address and said if I would send him on the next bus that she would put a money order in the mail to me immediately. So I put fifteen bucks out of my pocket. Got that kid on the bus. Never did get that money. That really burned me up.

In spite of what he finds around him, Joe wants to believe that people are basically good and honest. Like Margaret, he wants to see the best in people. There are many heartwarming stories that make the job worthwhile. For example, Joe organizes tour groups and has developed friendships with many of the participants. They send him postcards and photos from the trip and return each year to plan the next one.

Joe believes that the way a person approaches life is largely a matter of opinion. "It's all in your perspective. If you enjoy your job and working with people, then it's a good perspective." Just as Margaret emphasizes her "outlook" on life, Joe stresses his "perspective." Like many Spectators, he talks himself into adopting a positive perspective. Again sounding like Margaret, he says:

It's all in the attitude. If you wanna be sour, you can go around sour every day. It's against my nature to be sour. It comes back to the attitude. . . . It's all in your perspective, in your outlook. If you wanna be bitter, then everything's gonna be sour, and you're gonna be upset all the time. You make people upset around you. So the only way to go round it is being positive because positive is happy.

Joe believes he can take control of events. Hearing this, one might be inclined to think him quite active and wonder why he has been placed in the Spectator category. The subject of control is complex, and Spectators do not think about it the same way Enthusiasts do. Indeed, the Spectator's perception of control is more akin to the Fatalist's. Spectators believe, as Joe comments, that "fate hands you what it wants." He acknowledges that he does not have to take control actively or intervene in life in any significant way. On one hand, Spectators believe that fate determines their destiny; on the other hand, they believe that they control their perspective.

The distinction points to two types of control—active and passive. *Active control* is the kind of control we have seen demonstrated by Enthusiasts, who strive to change not only their perspectives but also their lives. *Passive control* refers to less assertive control, which involves only the individual's perspective. Influenced by fate, Spectators exert a passive control over their lives. They emphasize the importance of their perspective and believe it to be a powerful force, maintaining that personal direction comes from their perspective. Spectators know what they can and cannot control; they know when their perspective becomes obsolete and when fate steps in to take over. Joe describes it as follows:

It all comes down to your attitude and how you wanna be. I mean, maybe you can't control your destiny as far as money goes. That's the trouble, really, with the world. Money's become too important. It all boils down to what you make it. And how you're gonna enjoy life. Sure money plays an important role in how happy you are. Obviously, the more independent you are, the happier you are.

Joe planned to be a doctor and worked at a hospital in high school to prepare himself. "When I got out of high school I went to college for one year and ran out of money, and back in those days you had to have parents to cosign a loan." Since he had no parents, he did not get the loan resulting in a change in his life's direction. He interprets the change fatalistically. "I had nothing to do with the fact that I couldn't get a loan for college, but maybe fate played a hand." Joe spoke easily about his life metaphor. "Life is what you make it. You know, if you got the will to get ahead. Sometimes I don't think I done as good as I could. Since it turned out that I wasn't supposed to go to college."

Again, embedded in the life metaphor we see the way Joe combines fate and personal control. Not getting the loan meant he was not destined to be a doctor. In spite of his claim that "life is what you make it," he knows that fate often intrudes. Joe can control his perspective, and in that sense he makes life the way he wants. His interpretation of control points out that it is never an absolute—as long as he believes he is in control, he acts accordingly.

Joe's life is sprinkled with many unexpected events. He grew up believing his mother was dead. He also knew he had a sister whom he had never met. One day, a girl approached him and said, "I'm your sister." Her next question was, "How come you never go and see Mom?" And so, at eighteen Joe found out his mother was alive and living in a neighboring town. He recounts what happened after meeting his sister:

> The next day, I got on my motorcycle and went out and saw 'em. She had four kids, younger than me. It turned out that a friend of the family had been giving her my picture every year. I drove in the yard, and these little kids came running out and went screaming back in the door, "It's the guy whose picture is on the fireplace." It was really strange. But when I saw her, there was no doubt that she was my mother.

Still somewhat confused about parts of his life, Joe accepts it as providence. His parents divorced when he was a baby, and his father remarried (the first of three remarriages). Apparently, his new stepmother convinced his father to tell Joe that his mother was dead. This particular stepmother also mistreated him as a child. Although the next stepmother was not as harsh, Joe felt the emptiness of not having a mother. The feeling of loss was compounded by the death of his father, for which, as a teenager, he was teased.

I used to be real bitter. Fact is, when I was in high school and my dad died. There was this one kid every day on the way out from school, he'd say, "There's that lucky Joe, doesn't have no dad tellin' him what to do." And I just ignore him. Then one day, I had a real bad test and he told me that and I just threw the books down, hit him, and he kicked at me and I took his leg and people thirty feet away said they could hear his foot snap. I broke the bones in it. Anyway I got kicked out of high school on that. And then, that night, I went to work at the hospital and I had to put him on the bed and put traction on him for breaking his leg. His dad came up to me two days later and asked why in the world I did that to him. I told him my dad died Christmas day, and every day on the way home he told me I was lucky I didn't have a dad yellin' at me. And he stood there and looked at me. The next day I was called down to the high school and met with the principal. And the principal said, on this man's recommendation, "We're kicking the son out of school and you're reinstated."

Listening to Joe, I was struck by the series of tragic events, and I asked him how he felt. He likened the way he coped to a person trying to overcome shyness.

I had to work at it. You know how shy people have to sort of put their self forward to get over their shyness. I had to just finally put it in my mind that I was gonna quit being bitter. Plus I got beat up a couple of times in bar fights. I mean, I did my share of beating up too. But I thought this isn't the life.

Spectators share a closeness with death. Already, we have seen that Margaret experienced losing a son, and John had a near-death experience. Joe also experienced death a number of times, in a number of ways. He believed his mother was dead. His father died tragically in a fire. He remembers one brush with death himself. The closeness to death seems to explain the special appreciation for life that characterizes Spectators.

After Janet's mother was diagnosed with cancer, the family prepared for her death. The illness carried on and on, and they spent years thinking she might be taken away at any time. As it turns out, her mother did not die, but the effect on Janet was great.

Janet: "A Game"

The whole idea of the game behind life keeps me enter-
tained. . . . A loss here will be counteracted with a win
some other time. . . . It's just a game. I see what I can do
to change the situation to win. . . . I think problems are
something to be gotten through.

Janet manages a delicatessen and, although she has only worked there for about three months, already loves the independence and power. She is twenty-three and recently graduated from college with a degree in marketing. Straightforward, forthright, and determined to assert herself, she cannot think of anything she would rather be doing. "I love it that much. I'm very happy. Most jobs don't have this kind of freedom. I'm not at a desk. I'm working with people. I'm using my college degree." She has come a long way from her youth growing up on a farm, which she remembers fondly.

One of the really nice things is that you could run and scream and nobody cared. 'Cause nobody was around for a mile. We had cats, lots of cats. As many as you wanted. We had a big house, big yard, and everything. And it was always nice to be alone. And yet not alone. Lots of green, fresh growth around you.

Troubled high school years led Janet to develop a strong sense of self at any early age.

In junior high, kids can be real mean. Especially if you're not the prettiest but you are the smartest. My mom was a teacher too, and I had her in class, which meant I got a really hard time from my classmates. "Teacher's pet, teacher's pet." But I lived with it. Went through it. . . . It just set up a whole situation where cruelty came in, and I learned that it doesn't matter what they say about me or what they think or how they try to hurt me, I'm me. It doesn't matter. All that matters is how I see myself. And how those that are really close to me see me.

Like Joe, she survived the ridicule. If anything, it strengthened her outlook. Like other Spectators, Janet understands the impor-

tance of perspective. "What's important today may not matter at
all tomorrow. So I just enjoy it for now and see what tomorrow
brings. Or endure it for now and wait for what tomorrow brings.
Whatever the situation is." Future-oriented Spectators believe
that tomorrow will be better.

By the time she reached college, she was prepared for the challenge. She enjoyed her time there, likening it to a game. "College
is a big game because everybody there's working for degrees to
get their job. And we are all competing against each other. So you
have competition within the game. It's sort of like a race." Competition is an important theme in Janet's life. "I think of development. I can see competition. And I can understand motivation."
She likes the game because it keeps her amused. "I can't just sit
and listen to a dull sermon if it doesn't keep me entertained. I'm
always doing something else—if it's playing word games on paper,
practicing handwriting—anything to keep me entertained. The
whole idea of the game behind life keeps me entertained so that
I don't get bored."

Janet does not picture herself playing the game, or winning the
game. Instead, her vision is more passive, one in which she wants
to be entertained by the game. Although she got her degree and
played the game, she does not think of herself as an active com-
petitor. She describes herself as "going through" life: more a pas-
serby than a participator; more acted upon than acting; and more
watchful than performing. Instead of actively making her way
through life, she passively takes it in her stride. Not only does
Janet treat school as a game, indeed, she approaches life as a game,
as expressed by her life metaphor.

> A game. For better or worse, it's a game. Each day there are so
> many problems that you have to go through, to figure out. And
> you figure it out. And if you did that one right or wrong, it really
> doesn't matter. But you've got it done. That's all that matters.
> And then you can go onto the next part of the game and see if
> you can compete in the job market, see how you can do there.
> You just move on.

Janet enjoys the predictability of a game within which people
play clearly specified roles. According to Janet, the game consists
of a series of moves (problems in life) and parts (stages in life).
The idea of a game leads her to expect certain moves, just as she

expects certain problems. Her task in life is to solve the problems and develop strategies for playing the game. She is the kind of person who says that "it doesn't matter if you win or lose, it's how you play the game."

Spectators like being in positions of dealing with the public and take pride in understanding people. They believe work is an important part of life, which provides critical reinforcement that they are good people. John is pleased because there is no "trouble" with any of the people where he works. Margaret and Joe pride themselves on "pleasing the public." Janet also believes her ability to get along with people makes her a good salesperson.

> I have enough enthusiasm, enough willingness, to set my personal feelings on the line by saying, "This is my favorite cheese." Some people won't and can't open up enough to do that. The customers appreciate it. And I always try and listen to them. If you listen to them, you make a friend. And that's the nice part about his job. I've made a lot of friends with people that come in.

Again, Janet uses the underlying principles of a game to help with her job.

> You have to play the game to see who can figure out how to get past the last obstacle to get what they really want. I came to this place, and I have in a strange sense thought I can do what I want. What price can I put on the brick cheese to make it sell? It's just a game. See what I can do to see if I can change the situation to win.

While she seems to get along well with the customers, she has more difficulty with her employees. She works with an essentially older staff, the closest in age is sixty-four. Although much younger with much less experience, Janet is willing to assert her authority. She readily reprimands the women and has already fired one. "Once I got through firing the girl, it was over. I don't have to mess with it anymore. The other employees know what will happen if they break the rules. So I'm not gonna have a problem from them anymore. It's just a matter of time. I know in my heart that eventually everything will be alright."

Although difficult to fire someone, Janet feels justified. Drawing from her experience as a student, she uses an academic analogy to explain the task of having to fire someone. "It's like taking a final. It only lasts two hours, and when it's done, it's over. The grade will effect your life for three years maybe. And after that nobody cares. It's just something you go through."

The relationship with the older women can create difficult situations, which Janet feels she is slowly resolving. She follows clear guidelines and standards, which form the "rules" of the "game." "If it's a rule that's been broken and I've already told them what the punishment would be and they still choose to break the rule, I follow through on the punishment. If it's a problem where they say they'll do something and then they won't because they don't wanna take time. I just live with it."

Just as one must play by the rules to be permitted to continue the game, so must one adhere to certain regulations on the job. The rules are so clear for Janet that she cannot make any exceptions. The rules are as much a part of the game, as they are of life: they must be followed or the game collapses. Amidst Janet's frustrations, she knows she cannot force her coworkers to behave a certain way, she shrugs, "It's their choice, and I live with it."

Assuming responsibility comes naturally to Janet, since she learned to be dependable at an early age. After her mother was diagnosed with cancer, she suddenly found herself with many duties. "When I was thirteen it was kinda' weird. My mom had cancer. We have a farm and a huge garden. Enough to fill two freezers full. My job, when I was thirteen, was to run the household and get all that food from the garden into the freezer. And I grew up and I learned to take responsibility."

She does not resent the burden placed on her at an early age. "I'm a very practical person. I didn't think of what I was losing or giving up. It was something to do and I did it. It was something to be gotten through. I look at it that way. It will eventually be over. Life will be better."

Janet coped with her mother's illness the same way she manages everything in her life, by "living with" it or "getting through" it. Death, or the proximity to death, is central in the Spectator's life. Janet's mother did not die, but the family prepared and waited. The reality of death changes an individual's perspective about life—it becomes treasured and rare. Time becomes more valuable, and the moments are special. Life is no longer something that can be taken for granted.

Anticipating what "tomorrow will bring," Janet waits for things to get better and accepts life as it is. She goes through the present, passively hoping that the future will be better and that things will improve: "The knowledge that eventually it will turn around, or it doesn't really matter. Or a loss here will be counteracted with a win some other time. If I'm losing in my work situation I may be winning at home, or vice versa."

Janet's "it-doesn't-matter" attitude reflects a belief in fate. Spectators maintain order in life and expect it to follow a predetermined pattern. In part, their passivity stems from their fatalistic inclination. They know that life contains events that cannot be changed, so they do not attempt to make those changes.

Dave, an Antagonist, also uses the expression "life is like a game." Dave and Janet both strive for equilibrium, believing that winning and losing counteract one another. They both expect to follow rules in life. However, Janet and Dave differ in their evaluation of life: Dave feels trapped by the same inevitability that comforts Janet.

Janet uses parts of the life metaphor to describe other issues in her life. For example, she remembers the difficulty with college and the prospect of getting a job:

> College can be infuriating. We all trained in marketing, and then three weeks before graduation, they come in and tell the marketing class that "by the way, you can't get a job doing what you were trained to do." You just forget it. That's like the gag at the end of the game. And everyone's sitting there wondering why they spent four years doing this.

Like Margaret, she attributes her survival to independence. The quiet reliance on the self characterizes the Spectator. While independence provides comfort, it also has its drawbacks.

> It's like building a wall around yourself. And that makes it hard sometimes to reach other people or to have other people get close to you to build a friendship. . . . There are pros and cons. It's nice to be safe. 'Cause I really need that security. But it makes it hard with other people sometimes. Other people reach out to me, and it's hard to feel like they aren't trying to trick me. A lot of mistrust is left in that wall. And I wish I could get rid of it. . . . I'm just starting to make an effort. I'm still terribly

insecure. And as I get older, I may break it down, I don't know. Time will tell.

Although Janet has encountered some major issues in her life, she admits to a nonconfrontational style of coping.

> I've only asked myself a few questions. I know it's not that I have all the answers, it's that I haven't asked the right questions. Some of the big questions. And being a Christian, you run into them all the time. And I must admit I take the coward's way out on it. I will not confront it. Later on, I'll say it's real to me and that's all that matters. So I just sort of avoid a lot of major questions.

The nonconfrontational style characterizes Spectators, who prefer not to disrupt the order of life. They do not like to rock the boat, believing that everything will be alright. They know that they cannot make any difference anyway. Janet asks questions but is contented if there are no answers. Leonard is another individual who is content if the answers are not forthcoming. A fire fighter, facing death and devastation regularly, he knows that there are often no explanations for the tragedies.

Leonard: "A Challenge"

> *I just try to get ahead. . . . You know, you get through. . . . Life has its ups and downs. It's a struggle. . . . Whatever you do, you should do it so well that people know you do it well.*

Leonard is a twenty-four-year-old fire fighter who, like Dennis the Antagonist, had romantic boyhood dreams about what he would be. "When I was young, I wanted to be a fireman. When you're young, you want to be a lot of things. But then I forgot about it." Although fire fighting was not a driving ambition, Leonard saw an add in the paper and thought he would try it.

A novice fire fighter works like an apprentice and is trained by a resident "house officer" who teaches theory and practice. Leonard says, "It's more or less books, and most of the fire fighting is on-the-job training. You just get your feet wet." Studying books, reading maps, and learning the streets make up a large portion of the predictable daily routine. Fighting the fires constitutes the unpredictable part.

Leonard likes shift work. "Every other day for three days, and then you get four days off. It's much better than a regular job." He describes the fire station as "home away from home. It has a kitchen and bathroom and bedroom—just like a home—TV, radio." During the quiet times, the job gets monotonous. Leonard plays guitar, sometimes plays cards, and manages to get through the day. "We motivate ourselves. Talk about different things. You get through. There's always something to do, something to talk about." He describes an average day:

> We report to duty at seven in the morning, and we have a radio check. Then we usually eat breakfast, then sit back and watch some TV, do some studying. Then around noon, eat lunch. Maybe take a nap. Like me this afternoon, I'll probably play some guitar, watch some more TV, eat supper, and then just kind of relax in the evening and go to bed about ten. And hope it's quiet.

The city's fire fighters undergo some of their practical training at a separate firehouse called the "smoke house." "We do repelling. High-rise rescue, I guess. They train us for air masks. You gotta feel comfortable with those. And it's got a fire hydrant out there where you can do a lot of pump practice." Other practical training comes with on-the-job experience.

> You can be out all night. [That's when] time goes the fastest, I guess. You really don't notice the clock as much as you do sitting around. . . . I remember one time, I think it was one in the morning. We went to bed about eleven thirty. There was a call about an apartment full of smoke. It just looked like a normal home, but it was full of smoke. I think there was three people in the house. They were coming out as we got there. So we did rescue. We found a house that had hidden walls. It had a hidden ceiling, which really is a fire hazard. Then before you know it, it comes out of the roof. We lost that house. We were there till six in the morning.

Time speeds as the fire fighter battles the flames. "You really don't have much time to think about it. Once you get to work." Leonard showed me a photograph of a raging fire—"This is an action shot. . . . I guess after a while it gets in your blood and you get into your work." Driven by the excitement, he remembers his first fire: "When I first came on, I'd never even seen a fire. The first one kinda' makes you wonder; it's scary. But now it's a competitive thing, you know, to put it out, the best you can, with as little amount of water as possible." Like a professional fighter, Leonard adds elements of expertise to the competition: speed, precision, conservation. "Your adrenaline is running full on. It's really flowing. It's full of excitement. The smell is something you never forget. It gets your blood pumping. You're all fired up. That's what you're here for. You hate to see it happen but you gotta do it. You just do the best you can."

Helping people and serving the public are familiar themes in the Spectator's life. The thing that makes Leonard's job worthwhile is "to know you're needed, to feel that people need you. It's serving the public. And after, when you do save a house or get somebody out of a home, it's worth a million bucks." Spectators enjoy helping people because it makes them feel good about themselves.

In the line of duty, helping people sometimes results in success and sometimes in failure. Facing death is part of a fire fighter's work. Tragedies are to be expected, and whoever chooses the profession must be a special kind of person. Although witnessing fatalities comes with the job, Leonard is not used to it.

That's something that you never accept. It's the hardest thing to deal with. To see that happen. Time helps. My wife's a big help on that. It's really hard to deal with. But then again, it goes along with your job. In the heat of the moment, you don't have time to think about it. It's afterwards it really gets you.

Leonard's life metaphor and his comments about it suggest his reliance on others. "A challenge. Making a good name for yourself. Whatever you do, you do it so well people know you do it well. They remember you. Doing the best you can at whatever you do. Doing the best you can for others." His advice to his daughter emphasizes the central idea of his life metaphor. He plans to tell her to "do the best you can all the time, be honest, help people, things like that."

The metaphor "life is like a challenge" has already been used by Pat, a Fatalist. Now the same life metaphor is used in another context, to represent another orientation. Such duplicating of life metaphors reinforces the need to be well-informed about each person's overall perspective. It is imperative to understand the context surrounding the life metaphor. Both Pat and Leonard perceive life as a challenge. Both have similar ratings on the activity dimension (neither is particularly active); however, they differ on the evaluative dimension (one is optimistic, the other pessimistic). Pat's pessimism probably stems from her recent separation from her husband. Leonard, on the other hand, appreciates life, enjoys his work and family, and optimistically looks forward to the future.

His most difficult years came when he finished high school: "You know, getting established in a job where you can have some income and something to rely on. Some security, I guess." But he managed. "I got through it, I guess. Just take it as it comes." Like Janet and other Spectators, Leonard relies on a strategy of getting through something. Again, the language of taking life as it comes confirms the passive predisposition of the Spectator.

In spite of the happiness in Leonard's life, he is a realist who believes that life is hard. "It's a struggle. It has its ups and downs. Like bills and the price of food. It's pretty hard for a young couple now to own their own home. It's a struggle." He perseveres because he wants to save some money and see what the future will bring.

The prospect of what life will bring reflects the Spectators' natural inquisitiveness and appeals to their hopeful spirit. They usually anticipate the future and look forward to their destiny. Joan, the final person in this section, is an explorer and an adventurer who is eager to find out about other cultures. Her work as a travel agent permits her to pursue these fantasies.

Joan: "Very Ordinary"

> *I think life is very ordinary. . . . Life is the same everywhere, even if it's on a grand scale or on a very poor scale. I still find it interesting. . . . Life is what you make it. If you want to make your life interesting you have the opportunity to do so.*

Joan was born in England, spent her early years in India (where she grew up under British rule), then moved to the United States. As a child, traveling so much caused some problems. Possessions were discarded because of the practical impossibility of carrying them. Now, fifty-eight, Joan recalls her thoughts as a girl, migrating to other countries:

> The most difficult thing when we were actually moving was the fact that you were very careful [about] what you accumulated. You were constantly making a home and then disbanding it and not keeping a lot of things that you would like to keep, that had some kind of meaning to you. That was always a very difficult thing to do. But it was very necessary because of the great distances that we were moving.

In addition to tangible belongings, psychological attachments were abandoned. This early pattern of dissolving personal relationships has followed Joan throughout her life. "I haven't formed any really great friendships over my lifetime, very few, because of the fact that I've moved around so much. . . . When you move around it's hard to continue those types of relationships without having the contact that you would like to have."

Despite the drawbacks, traveling added a rewarding dimension to life.

> It's been a very educational experience. You learn a lot about people in other parts of the world. Which is very important. You learn that everybody is really pretty much the same. We all have the same desires out of life, so to speak. We like to work. Most people are industrious everywhere. At least if they can be. In poor countries, the people don't have the education or the chance to do anything but they're still willing to work to make a living. Life is the same everywhere, if it's on a grand scale or on a very poor scale. I still find it very interesting.

The discovery that life is the same everywhere helped formulate her life metaphor, "I think life is very ordinary. That's a good way to describe it. Life is what you make it. If you want to make your life interesting you have the opportunity to do so. This opportunity really comes everywhere. If you've got a desire to get out and do something and make it interesting."

When she uses the word *ordinary*, Joan does not mean boring. She means usual, normal, commonplace, and customary. Life is ordinary because everyone encounters it. Remembering that life is ordinary helps her keep things in perspective. Knowing that life in India goes on in more or less the same way as it does in the United States, forces one to recognize the smallness of the universe and the insignificance of the individual. Things are not blown out of proportion because one realizes that everything is relative. Joan's outlook in this respect is like Janet's "relative" perspective: "what's important today may not matter at all tomorrow."

When she says "life is what you make it," she means the same thing Joe does. Both exert passive control, which means they believe themselves to be responsible for controlling their perspective. Neither is an aggressive, overachiever trying to change the course of life radically. They are content with the order of things as long as they can control their perspective.

Although a long way from India, Joan remains connected to her early roots through her work at a travel agency, which she has managed for more than twenty years. Her job includes everything having to do with travel. She is very down-to-earth, practical, and opinionated. "I'm a friendly person. I don't dislike people without having a reason to dislike them. I'm not an overly outgoing person. I'm very, very much business. During my business hours, I conduct things in a businesslike way. I don't like wasting time."

Growing up in India strongly influenced her life. She was part of a regime in which women were treated like second-class citizens and expected to be subservient. "My father thought I would just get married and be a lady. So there was never any thought in my mind when I was younger that I was ever going to make a career. I didn't really have any desire to do so." It was not until much later in life that Joan became aware of wider possibilities for women. Her pursuit of a career evolved. Although the travel agency was not a deliberate decision, looking back, it seems fated that she should find such a suitable career. Even though her raised consciousness came later in life than she would have liked, she is glad to have established a profession.

Like most Spectators, Joan likes meeting people, and her job permits her to encounter a variety.

> You're working with all kinds of people. The different destinations around the world. It's something new all the time. You never do the same thing over twice. . . . I think more than anything, one has to be tactful. To recognize that we are giving a service and we do not have a product to sell. The only way we

stay in business is by giving service and trying to make it a good service. So you learn to handle everybody as they come along.

Spectators rely on others to help themselves, and Joan expresses her need for others in "life" and "death" terms.

I think it's very important that people continue to do something with their lives so that you're needed. It's important to be needed. And if you literally sit at home doing nothing, not helping anybody, nobody's helping you. I don't think that you get anything out of life, and I think most people who retire in that manner don't last very long. I think it's a matter of time before they talk themselves out of life, literally.

Part of Joan's work includes training employees. She follows a clear agenda, indicating the precision she requires.

I tell them how I wish them to greet people when they come in. I don't like the casual "hi" and "hello." I like to say "good morning" or "good afternoon." I do insist that everybody address our clients as Mr. or Mrs. unless they are invited to do otherwise. And not to address people by their first names.

Joan believes that good manners and appropriate, suitable behavior are signs of an efficient business. She never loses sight of her professional responsibility. "I think it is very important to keep a business relationship as a business relationship. We cannot afford to make mistakes. Mistakes cost money, and they usually end up costing big money."

Joan is a private person who enjoys a quiet night at home entertaining a few friends. She also enjoys going to the theater, and her hobbies include cooking, sewing, and knitting. She likes to be involved with her son's family and be a part of their lives. She loves being with her two grandchildren very much. Her early experiences left an impression that influences her present relations with her family.

My parents were divorced when I was very young, and I resented the fact that I didn't have a good home life. And that often comes up now, even at my age. I'm very careful because of that to really encourage my son and his family to have a good home life. It's extremely important for children. . . . I like to see interaction in the family. If it's just playing games, or being out shoveling the sidewalk, or washing the car or doing something. Doing things together I think is most rewarding.

She appreciates traveling, and the three most memorable trips Joan made were to China, Russia, and East Africa. Each held a different charm. In China, she learned how people live under communism. In Russia, she observed that "you really knew you were being watched. People weren't happy. They weren't friendly either." Her favorite trip was to East Africa where she discovered the beauty of wild animals on a camel safari through the parks.

Ironically, Joan's exotic travels reinforce her life metaphor. She believes that life is ordinary precisely because one can travel to remote places and find basic human nature unchanged. Regardless of one's culture, one's economic status, or one's religion, people are basically alike.

> People live the same kind of life whether you live in one room or whether you live in a flat or whether you live in a house. Everybody gets up in the morning, you go to work, you have a lunch hour, you go home in the evening. Whatever sort of social life you have, that still happens everywhere. As I say, whatever scale it's on.

One might think Joan's adventurous spirit inappropriate for inclusion in the Spectator category; she seems more like a participator. Indeed, she is the most active Spectator and at times verges on exhibiting many of the Enthusiast's qualities; however, from her perspective she is not an active individual. In particular, she regrets not being more career oriented. "When I look back on it, knowing what I know now, I really would like to have been a career person and done much more with my life." Joan thought about possible reasons for not having pursued her aspirations more aggressively.

> Possibly the fact that you stay in a smaller town, and, for one reason or another, I probably haven't been willing to take the chances that I could have, or should have. But, if circumstances were different, then I would like to do something on my own. . . . It was due to my family life. And I didn't have the opportunity, and I was insecure, I think.

Joan attributes her lack of action to fate. Growing up in India, being educated under the rule of the Empire were things beyond her control but of great influence. Overall, she responds favorably to fate's intervention. "I think on the whole, everything falls into its own place." Joan looks to the future as a possible source of happiness. "I think life is something that if you're interested in it, you continually think about it. I do often compare past and present. That's the nice thing. It's always nice to look forward to what's going to happen in the future. Sometimes it looks awfully grim, but we hope for better."

Her perennial hope for something better comes by way of her appreciation of other countries. Having seen changes in cultural values, such as India, she knows that progress can be made. In addition to helping a person's outlook, Joan believes that travel educates a person, increases understanding, broadens a perspective, and precludes hasty moral judgments.

> I don't think that the average person, who's never traveled, never been anywhere, has any understanding of other countries. They can't understand what it's like to live in India. Or understand what it's like to live in the Middle East. What it's like to live in China or Africa. Because they just literally don't know. . . . They can't compare those people to themselves. I think people who travel get a glimpse of that. Even if they don't travel a lot. They get a little glimpse of what goes on somewhere else and therefore they can use that as a judgment when they listen to what's going on in the world. I think that they usually can better determine if that is right or wrong.

Joan carries the Spectator's vision of sharing to the extreme through her image of a "world language." "I think one of the greatest things that could happen in this whole world is if we could have a world language. That would lead to communication between people, which would do a great deal more good than anything." Her vision of Esperanto would make communication easier, which would expose a person to views and ideas that might otherwise be unattainable. "If you were literally posted overseas, for example, and lived in a country, you would by desire and by necessity learn to communicate. Then once you've done it one place, you will do it in other places."

Joan's secret to life reflects the benevolence of the Spectator. She offers her best advice:

> Take an interest in what's going on in the world. And if you can, don't judge people without having good reason to say what is right or wrong. Don't judge people as a whole, which is oftentimes done. People are people all over the world. And everybody's an individual. And on the whole, you'll find most people are like yourself. They have a desire to be friendly. They want to know as much about you as you do about them.

Like Margaret, Joan stresses each person's individuality. Spectators respect that no two problems are the same and try to evaluate each situation uniquely. In spite of the difficulties, Joan is positive, which reflects the Spectator's ultimate optimism.

> Life in general has probably not been as rewarding as I think the amount of effort I've put into life. Monetarily, or something like that, I haven't got out of it what I put into it. But that's beside the point as far as I'm concerned. The self-satisfaction is more important. My work and what I do is most important.

As a postscript to Joan's interview, a brief word should be mentioned about her association with death. Although we did not discuss the subject during the interview, after I turned off the tape recorder, she told me her first husband committed suicide in India. She rarely discusses the subject and remains quietly angry because she felt so abandoned.

The Spectator marks the last of the four life orientations. I have now covered the major combinations of the active and the evaluative dimensions. Although people are grouped together as Fatalists or Spectators, Antagonists or Enthusiasts, each individual does not necessarily possess the same weightings on the two dimensions. There are differences within each orientation, and no two people possess identical proportions of activity and evaluation.

Kenneth Burke writes that a "monstrous, or inhuman character does not possess qualities not possessed by other men—he simply possesses them to a greater or lesser extent."[17] Burke assumes that people share certain qualities, to a greater or lesser degree. In the same way, people manifest activity and evaluation in varying proportions. The combination of the dimensions forms an interactive ratio, which marks each person as unique. Burke connects language with identity by suggesting that our vocabulary is a metaphor for who we are. Within this framework, people communicate by a "weighted" vocabulary, which reveals the substance of their personality.[18] By emphasizing certain words, we accentuate certain aspects of our character. By omitting other words, we exclude corresponding values and behaviors. Language identifies us and helps others learn how to communicate with us. The cry to find someone who "speaks our language," translates into a search for someone to understand who we are.

CHAPTER 7

Conclusion

> I come with stories—not just a supply of stories
> to deliver to the analyst but stories built into
> my very being. The patterns and sequences of
> childhood experience are built into me.
>
> Gregory Bateson, *Mind and Nature.*

Stories hold this book together just as they hold life together. We learn who we are, where we come from, and where we have been by sharing stories. They form the building blocks of life, helping us lay the foundations for our identity. If the structure is strong, the individual will thrive; if it is weak, the individual falters.

Michael Polanyi and Harry Prosch describe the durability of artistic forms as "infinitely superior to that of our personal experiences, for the coherence of their parts is so much firmer and more effectively organized."[1] Stories, like works of art, are uniquely created by each individual to integrate chaotic, disorganized events. They enable one to organize experience.

Historically, stories have shaped individuals and cultures. In *The Republic,* through the voice of Socrates, Plato constructs an elaborate story within which the characters discuss the creation of the ideal government.[2] The story of *The Republic* frames the dialogue wherein the characters decide which stories are appropriate for the construction of the perfect state. The canons of the constitution must be founded on stories, expressed through stories, and maintained by stories. Through the dialogue, Socrates proceeds to construct the ideal city—the republic—and the ideal individual—the philosopher. The city in the making parallels the individual in the making. For the healthy city to be created and progress, it must be founded on stories. For the healthy individual to grow and develop, one also depends on stories. In his wisdom, Socrates proclaimed that the primary task of the founders of the city is to devise stories.

> Our first duty then, it seems, is to set a watch over the makers of stories, to select every beautiful story they make, and reject any that are not beautiful. Then we shall persuade nurses and mothers to tell those selected stories to the children. Thus will they shape their souls with stories far more than they can shape their bodies with their hands.[3]

Plato valued the power of stories to provide pragmatic instructions about how to live. He believed that stories help the individual learn how to proceed through life, overcome difficulties, and manage conflicts. Times have changed since ancient Greece, and modern critics question the preservation of the narrative. In *The Minimal Self: Psychic Survival in Troubled Times*, Christopher Lasch writes, "The survivor cannot afford to linger long in the past, lest he envy the dead. He keeps his eyes fixed on the road just in front of him. He shores up fragments against his ruin. His life consists of isolated acts and events. It has no story, no pattern, no structure as an unfolding narrative."[4]

While psychic survival and emotional coping are universal human concerns, I argue that given the potential loss of self, the threat of alienation, the inexact promise of what tomorrow will bring, the possibility of there not even being a tomorrow, people become empowered by the narrative ability they possess. In a world of fluctuating material possessions, stories provide psychic possessions, representing one aspect of life over which one has control. The story belongs to the individual, providing a means of achieving stability and equilibrium.

Telling a story organizes an individual's impressions of experience. Consider the impulse to bear witness, which characterizes and motivates survivors of devastating events and personal tragedies.[5] The urge to speak out about the tragedy helps the survivor extract significance from absurdity and meaning from meaninglessness. Without the story, there is nothing on which to stand, no context from which to organize meaning. By telling the story, one organizes meaning in a way that makes it possible to cope with what happened. This organization does not imply understanding. People who survived Hiroshima, Nagasaki, the Holocaust, and Vietnam may never understand why the events took place, but they are able to organize what happened to them in a way that helps them cope.

Russian psychologist A. R. Luria treated a memory-loss patient for twenty-five years. He reports the treatment in *The Man with a Shattered World*,[6] in which he incorporates analytic and diagnostic comments into fragments of the patient's own account. The patient, Zasetsky, suffered a severe brain injury from a bullet, resulting in a shattered world and a fragmented vision of life. Luria writes:

> Before he was wounded, words had distinct meanings which readily occurred to him. Each word was part of a vital world to which it was linked by thousands of associations; each aroused a flood of vivid and graphic recollections. To be in command of a word meant he was able to evoke almost any impression of the past, to understand relationships between things, conceive ideas and be in command of his life. And now all this had been obliterated.[7]

The loss of memory affected every aspect of the patient's life: in the process of formulating an idea, he forgot the thought he wanted to express; as he tried to remember a word, he would forget why he needed it. His amnesia affected his physical being as well. Not only would he forget the word for parts of the body, but he would also forget their functions. With no context from which to organize meaning, Zasetsky could barely cope. "The bullet fragment that entered his brain had so devastated his world that he no longer had any sense of space, could not judge relationships between things, and perceived the world as broken into thousands of separate parts. As he put it, space 'made no sense'; he feared it, for it lacked stability."[8]

Luria urged Zasetsky to write a story about his illness, including his daily experiences, his recollections and his difficulties. By writing a diary, the patient kept track of his own progress.

> Writing his journal, the story of his life, gave him some reason to live. It was essential in that it was his only link with life, his only hope of recovering and becoming the man he had been. . . . That is why he undertook this exhausting labor, spending hours,

days, years searching for lost memories. . . . This work became the most important thing in life to him—his reason for living: to write his story and possibly overcome his illness, pick up his life again, become a man like other men.[9]

Zasetsky's case is an extreme example of how stories help people survive. In a less dramatic way, telling stories helps organize our impressions of daily life. As we move through the process of telling a story, we make sense of experience. We fix things up, change some things, rearrange the parts until the story is the way we want it to be. We choose what to tell, what not to tell, and how to tell it; we select the style, pace, persona, and mood we desire. It may not be that the events in the story are the way we want them to be, but our arrangement is. The organization transforms the experience we are trying to describe.

Social Model of Coping

To understand the relationship between language and coping, this book presents four different life orientations—the Antagonist, the Enthusiast, the Fatalist, and the Spectator—each reflected by a variety of life metaphors. I have not evaluated the life metaphors, therefore I cannot argue that any one orientation affords a person a better way of coping than another. Some people cope precisely because they approach life actively or positively; while others manage by being relatively inactive or negative.

Although some of the people in this study face difficulties, they are trying to cope and, on the whole, are succeeding. I have deliberately excluded people who are not coping. I did not visit prisons or mental institutions or other places where we expect people might have more difficulty. It is interesting to speculate about how the factors of activity and evaluation would fit in such cases. Based on the two dimensions, it should be possible to develop a hypothetical model that would cover a broader range of life orientations and include coping and noncoping behavior. A more generalizable social model would be anchored by the oppositional adjective pairs: active and passive, and positive and negative. Figure 7–1 represents the expanded model.

If the dimensions were to be extended to encompass a wider context, each life orientation would become transformed. When

Figure 7–1.   Social Model of Coping Types

Active-Negative   Active-Positive

ANTAGONIST	ENTHUSIAST
Terrorists	Doers
Anarchists	Actors
Activists	Workers
Survivalists	Producers
	Professionals
	Artisans
	Hackers
FATALIST	**SPECTATOR**
Cynics	Pacifists
Misanthropes	Procrastinators
Pessimists	Waiters on Providence

Passive-Negative   Passive-Positive

compared with society as a whole, the Antagonist described in these pages would not seem quite so extreme. Extending the dimensions, the Antagonist would be transformed into the terrorist, the activist, or the revolutionary. Groups that frequently resort to violence come to mind: the Irish Republican Army and the Palestine Liberation Organization. Jim Jones and Charles Manson are vicious individuals who staged atrocious acts to shock the world. Often acting brutally and out of control, these people are very negative about life and act on their hatred.[10] Quadrant I contains people who actively demonstrate antisocial behavior.

The Enthusiast is the most positive and most active individual. If we were to consider these qualities in the extreme, the individual would be transformed into a fanatic or a zealot. Television evangelist Jim Bakker, who uses his charismatic personality to lure people into his ministry, represents the extreme version of the Enthusiast. Exuberant individuals, operating on the how-to-win-friends-and-influence-people model developed by Dale Carnegie, are another example.[11] In the entertainment field, Ed McMahon is a popular, good-natured, outgoing, and excited cohost of Johnny Carson's "Tonight Show" who typifies the excessive Enthusiast. Quadrant II includes individuals who express extremely active and positive behavior.[12]

If the qualities of the Fatalist were carried to the extreme, the individual would change into a defeatist, a pessimist, or a misanthrope. The character in the infamous Peggy Lee song who asks, "Is that all there is?" is skeptical, and cynical about life to the point of having given up, and unwilling to take any action. Comedian, Rodney Dangerfield presents a humorous and exaggerated version of the Fatalist. In some cases, the Fatalist might change into a recluse. In his later years, Howard Hughes hid himself away, paranoid and distrustful of everyone.[13] Quadrant III includes people who express extremely negative and passive outlooks.

When the passive and positive dimensions are carried to the extreme, the Spectator becomes transformed into the pacifist, the conscientious objector, or the "waiter on providence." This individual is the opposite of the terroristlike figure, passively affirming the goodness of life through benevolent behavior. Dr. Martin Luther King, Jr. is immortalized as a supreme pacifist, working to instill his "dream" in a nonviolent way.[14] Another historic figure, representing the extreme Spectator, is Anne Frank. Remembered because of her famous diary, she was a heroic witness to Nazi horrors as she and her family hid in a small attic.[15] Quadrant IV contains people who express extremely positive and passive behavior.

This model is purely speculative and remains to be tested. The next series of interviews should target extreme populations—the prisons, the mental institutions, and the world of the homeless—to find out what they think "life is like . . ." The future agenda should include portions of society that offer alternative life-styles.

Control

The present sequence of interviews recounts the words of "ordinary" people. After reconsidering the model used in the present study, I would revise it to include the dimension of control. In the beginning, the dimensions activity and evaluation emerged quickly and strongly as important factors. After the model was developed, I realized how much the subject of control subtly penetrated the interviews. Every life metaphor implicitly articulates an individual's perception of control.

In the future, I would directly ask people how much control they think they have or where they would rate themselves on a continuum of perceived control. I would expand the life-orientation model into a three-dimensional model, consisting of activity, evaluation, and control.[16] One's perception of control should be part of the information that explains the process of coping. Herbert Lefcourt, who pioneered psychological research of control, describes the relationship between control and coping:

> Whether people, or other species for that matter, believe that they are actors and can determine their own fates within limits will be seen to be of critical importance to the way in which they *cope with stress and engage in challenges.* In other words, what Skinner believes to be an irrelevant illusion [the myth of individual freedom] will be shown to be a very relevant illusion— one that seems to be central to man's ability to survive, and, what is more, to enjoy life [emphasis added].[17]

People cope differently depending on whether they believe they control their lives or whether they believe an outside force is in control. David Brenders studies the impact of control on interpersonal relationships in health-care settings and believes that "perceptions of control help the person to act in proactive, goal-directed ways as opposed to reactive, self-limiting, and self-destructive ways."[18] How you look at life influences how you will get through it.

Life generally involves facing two kinds of problems: those that can be changed and those that cannot. In any situation, elements emerge over which the individual has little or no control. Neither a healthy perspective nor an unhealthy perspective can change immutable events; however, a healthy perspective can make life more tolerable and transform one's relation to the world. For example, in cases of nonmedical treatment of cancer patients, studies indicate that talking positively about cancer improves their quality of life.[19] There is no proof that language guarantees a prolonged life or the destruction of the disease, but there is evidence that it promotes a more healthy attitude.[20] While the cancer may never be stopped, it may be possible to change the person's perspective about the disease by creating a healthy, productive metaphor.[21]

Lefcourt speculates that the important element in the relationship between control and coping is "the manner in which individuals come to terms with their difficulties and, more specifically, how they explain their difficulties to themselves."[22] Very often people rationalize their problems based on their perceptions of control. Some people face obstacles by saying that it could happen to anyone, in which case they relinquish control, and accountability becomes externalized. Others, who say, "It's my fault, I should have known better," assume direct control over the problem and internalize the responsibility.

Psychologist J. B. Rotter explains the types of control in the following way:

> [An event may be perceived by an individual] as the result of luck, chance, fate, as under the control of powerful others, or as unpredictable because of the great complexity of forces surrounding him. When the event is interpreted in this way by an individual, we have labeled this a belief in *external control*. If the person perceives that the event is contingent upon his own behavior or his own relatively permanent characteristics, we have termed this a belief in *internal control*.[23]

People who express an *internal* locus of control generally answer the life metaphor question quickly, easily, and in detail: the life metaphor is salient and guides their life. People who express an *external* locus of control have more difficulty answering the life metaphor question: the life metaphor is not as salient and functions more as a reflector of their lives.

In *Freedom and Destiny*, Rollo May considers personal freedom and its threats.[24] According to him, destiny can be placed along a continuum. Events that are scarcely susceptible to human change lie at the extreme left—these might be earthquakes and volcanoes or a belief in determinism. In the middle, May places "the unconscious function of the human mind, since it is partly determined and partly influenced by human activity." Moving towards the right end, are "the cultural aspects of destiny," which include the culture, the society, and the historical period in which a person lives. One has no choice about being born into these aspects, but they can be used freely. On the extreme right lies "talent," because although in some sense it might be a given, there is "considerable freedom with respect to how to use it."[25] Most people can be located somewhere along this continuum of destiny. May goes on to describe the ways in which people relate to destiny: ranging from passive to active, an individual can (1) cooperate, (2) be aware and acknowledge, (3) engage, (4) confront and challenge, and (5) encounter and rebel.[26] In the present scheme, we could say that the Antagonist rebels, the Enthusiast challenges, the Fatalist accepts, and the Spectator engages.[27]

Self-Fulfilling Prophecy

Regardless of how much control people think they have, the life metaphor expresses the perceived relationship between experience and perspective. In many cases, the relationship becomes a self-fulfilling prophecy, because the expectation leads the individual to act in a way that makes the prophecy come true. In *Pragmatics of Human Communication*, Paul Watzlawick, Janet Beavin, and Don Jackson define a self-fulfilling prophecy as

> behavior that brings about in others the reaction to which the behavior would be an appropriate reaction. For instance, a person who acts on the premise that "nobody likes me" will behave in a distrustful, defensive, or aggressive manner to which others are likely to react unsympathetically, thus bearing out his original premise.[28]

Because the relationship is circular and difficult to interrupt, it is almost impossible to say where it begins. Do people's experiences influence their perspective? Or does the perspective influence what and how the individual experiences?

Pragmatically, the life metaphor functions like a self-fulfilling prophecy, guiding and reflecting an individual's life, just as the self-fulfilling prophecy guides and reflects reality.[29] If one believes that life is like a journey, one behaves as if one is on that journey. One is curious, adventurous, and inquisitive, projecting associations of a journey onto the world. In turn, the idea of a journey guides one's life. One expects people to react by helping, answering, and guiding, which bears out the original life metaphor and the prophecy is fulfilled.

Strategic Coping

The capacity to cope involves developing strategies to manage everyday life issues. In chess, the players set out to achieve the goal of getting the opponent into check. A beginner proceeds in an unsophisticated fashion, guessing where to move on the board. Sometimes the advances will be successful and other times they will not. With little or no knowledge of the game, the novice attempts random moves. By contrast, an expert in chess, someone like Bobby Fisher who has played thousands of games, can select from hundreds of moves. He selects the most effective strategy to achieve his goal. His moves are extremely strategic.

A game of chess requires knowledge of the purpose of the game and knowledge of the appropriate moves to make. In life, the same two components are required. An individual needs a sense of purpose and a repertoire of moves from which to choose. If people possess little sense of purpose and confront situations reactively, they cope unstrategically. If they possess a great sense of purpose and actively confront situations, they cope with life strategically. Avery Weisman explains:

> Those who cope well tend to use a wider range of strategies, while specializing in the strategies they know most about. Self-instruction depends on discovering new resources and perfecting what has worked reasonably well in the past. How we cope with any problem, what action we take, will inevitably change the nature of that problem, recasting it in copable or at least familiar terms.[30]

What constitutes a problem is defined from the individual's perspective and is relative to that perspective. One person's dilemma might be another's challenge. One person sees a situation within personal control, while another sees the same situation beyond control. Throughout this book there has been an overwhelming emphasis on perspective. The stories teach us that ordinary survival is a matter of perspective. One person says with disdain that "life is deteriorating," while another says with excitement that "life is what you make it." Metaphors express perspectives. Kenneth Burke argues that "metaphor" is commonly recognized as "perspective," because "metaphor is a devise for seeing something *in terms* of something else."[31]

This collection of interviews has demonstrated that metaphor is not an abstract linguistic device employed solely by poets. Metaphor is alive and used by people in everyday life to express their perceptions of the world. People possess metaphorical structures that define the way they cope. Paul Ricoeur describes the "maker of metaphor" as a "craftsman with verbal skill."[32] Metaphor subtly empowers people with the ability to change their identities, their lives, and their interactions with others. As people craft metaphors they also craft their lives. Ricoeur evocatively suggests that "the metaphor is not the enigma but the solution to the enigma."[33]

Appendix
Notes
References

Appendix: Methods

The approach of qualitatively studying the relationship between language and everyday life has its basis in a variety of disciplines, such as anthropology, sociology, psychology, communication, and linguistics. These fields explicate viable theories of interpretation based on qualitative methods of analyzing data.

Barney Glaser and Anselm Strauss argue in *The Discovery of Grounded Theory: Strategies For Qualitative Research* that sociological inquiry should proceed through grounded theory.[1] The authors explain that grounded theory is inductively generated. "Generating a theory from data means that most hypotheses and concepts not only come from the data, but are systematically worked out in relation to the data during the course of research. *Generating a theory involves a process of research.*"[2]

The major benefit of conducting research this way lies in the preclusion of "the opportunistic use of theories that have dubious fit and working capacity."[3] Sociologist Richard Brown examined the process of interpretation and proposed a "cognitive aesthetic theory of metaphor" as an alternative to the logic of discovery.[4] This approach forms the basis of his poetic approach. *Sociology as an Art Form,* by Robert Nisbet, examines the influence of creativity in the production of knowledge.[5] He argues that the process of discovery or invention, whether in science or in art, relies on similar psychological processes.

Qualitative methodology usually proceeds by the methods of participant observation and intensive interviewing. Anthropology, which relies almost exclusively on these methods, has traditionally examined the patterns, customs, and rituals of different cultures. Such procedures adopt an introspective theoretical stance, which assumes the vantage point of the data and studies phenomena from a subjective point of view to uncover the internal perspective.[6] For example, Gregory Bateson studied the Naven ceremony in the Iatmul culture in New Guinea.[7] Margaret Mead worked extensively in Samoa and described patterns of behavior in that culture.[8]

Anthropologists who examine the practical actions of everyday life often employ ethnomethodology as a research tool, producing ethnographies. Clifford Geertz's classic definition of ethnography is "thick description" because it recounts and interprets the daily activities of different cultures.[9] Michael Agar describes the process as "a social science metaphor within which the richness and variety of group life can be expressed as it is learned from direct involvement with the group itself."[10]

In the field of psychology, Robert F. Bales has developed the interaction process analysis, which provides an elegant interpretive and diagnostic theory.[11] His analysis of group interaction relies on a natural observational approach in which he utilizes subjective impressions to analyze the data. He then systematically discusses how empathic identification, detachment, associations, memories, and feelings can be used to make predictive statements.

Projective psychological tests operate in much the same manner to discover an individual's perception of the world.[12] The tests assume that one projects one's personality through the spontaneous expression of one's feelings. Projective questions ask a vague question that requires some form of interpretation on the part of the respondent. The Rorschach inkblot test asks the respondent what the inkblot means. The thematic apperception test (TAT) asks people to construct stories about a series of pictures. Projective tests presume that the way one organizes a relatively unstructured stimulus reflects one's perception of the world and one's response to it.

These disciplines share a focus on making statements about the interpretive process using qualitative methods. In the communication field, qualitative analysis is becoming a viable research alternative.[13] The present study relies on the interview as the central method of gathering information. The data were not transformed into empirical measures at any stage and remain qualitative. In accordance with many qualitative models of research, the entire study, including the interviews and their analyses, was conducted by myself.

Metaphor

Research about metaphor is prolific. Contemporary approaches have extensively defined its role in shaping human thinking.[14] Metaphor has been examined for its influence on reality.[15] Conceptual schemes have been developed to explain the relationship between metaphor and thought.[16] Models have identified the components of metaphor and how it operates.[17]

Most scholarly works ask, what is the best theory of metaphor?[18] Should one conceive of metaphor according to a word approach? Should one adopt a comparison view, an interaction view, or a substitution view? While in theoretical disagreement, most researchers agree that the salient questions are (1) what is metaphor? and (2) how does it work?

Unfortunately, theoretical examinations of metaphor often exclude its use in everyday life, from the perspective of the everyday users. One notable exception is *Metaphors We Live By*, by George Lakoff and Mark Johnson.[19] They examined the thesis that "metaphor is pervasive in everyday life, not just in language but in thought and action."[20] I wanted to extend their ideas and explore how metaphor functions for people by asking them to talk about their lives, from which it would be possible to develop a scheme that subsumes every possible metaphorical interpretation about life.

PURPOSE OF THE STUDY

My objective was to explore how metaphor functions for people by asking them to talk about their lives. I proceeded to (1) examine the use of metaphor by people in their daily lives and (2) generate a category system. The entire research process (including sorting, rating, and coding) and the findings were not recorded as part of an investigative team. Working on one's own causes certain limitations and introduces the issue of reliability; however, single-case histories (such as those written by A.R. Luria and Milton Erickson) yield valuable information, often derived from no more than the researcher's notes.[21] The interview schedule was designed in accordance with the underlying rationale for the study. It was assumed that an examination of a person's life metaphor and life orientation, based on language, would reveal that person's perspective on coping.

Research Design

PILOT TEST

The interviews were pilot tested on eleven people, providing an opportunity to test the interview schedule and to reformulate the overall goals of this research. From the pilot study, the major issues, appropriate questions, and suitable probes were refined so that detailed discussions of individuals' lives would result.

The eleven people who comprised the pilot study fell into two groups: (1) individuals with regular jobs; and (2) individuals living at a Veterans' Administration hospital. The first group was included in the main study, the second group was not.

It was hoped that the people at the veterans' hospital would expand the range of life metaphors by including a predominantly older, wiser, and more experienced population. However, I soon discovered that rather than reveal strategies for coping with life, the questions encouraged people to talk about their boredom, their loneliness, and their closeness to death. Talking about life exacerbated their limitations, their frustrations, and their pain. The inappropriateness of the questions was apparent from the outset. For example, a number of questions address the issue of a person's work—these people are not working. Another series of questions addresses the issue of monotony—these people face monotony every day, and most of them do not know how to deal with it.

In addition, there were physical limitations. Sometimes their minds wandered; they were easily distracted and unable to focus on the questions or forgot them entirely. At other times, they could not hear me, and I could not be sure about what they thought I said, or about what they were actually answering. It became clear that I would need a different set of questions if I were to include this group in the study. Overall, people from the hospital would best be included in a larger social model of coping.

PARTICIPANTS

The main study consists of forty-six interviews, which were conducted over a seven-month period from September 1983 to

March 1984. The ages of the interviewees range from eighteen to seventy-four. Twenty-five men and twenty-one women constitute the sample.

The population was drawn from four convenient environments in a Midwest college community: (1) ten faculty and staff members from the academic environment; (2) nine self-employed people; (3) five people with managerial positions; and (4) twenty-two people from diverse occupations, such as a beautician, a bus station attendant, several factory workers, a truck driver. Figure A–1 presents a demographic summary.

PROCEDURE

The interviewees were approached at or near their places of employment. This criterion for selection was derived from the practical need to find people and the desire for a diverse sample. It was relatively easy to make contact with people where they worked, and I could select a range of different occupations.

At first, I invited the people to participate in the study. They were initially informed that the purpose of the interview was for communication research. After they agreed to the interview, I asked them if they objected to it being tape recorded.

The interviews lasted approximately one half hour to one and one half hours; the average interview lasted about forty-five minutes. For most people, this was as much time as they could spare. Three people refused to participate in the study: one said he was too busy, another said she would not be interesting enough; and one said she did not want to talk about her life. Apart from these people, everyone participated willingly and answered the questions helpfully. To the extent that people answered honestly and sincerely, the data are reliable.

RATIONALE AND LOGIC OF THE INTERVIEW SCHEDULE

Figure A–2, the interview schedule, was formulated to encourage people to talk about their lives. It specifies major questions and provides a repertoire of possible probes. The major questions were structured openly to permit sufficient freedom to elaborate.

Because I needed to examine the individual's life orientation, the topics covered life issues and life experiences relating to the following ten dimensions: work, interest in work, survival strat-

Figure A–1. Demographic Summary

Name	Age	Occupation
Bill	55	Distributes equipment at gymnasium
Fr. Dave	38	Priest
John	53	Delivers campus mail
Lynn	56	Nurse practitioner
Val	24	College student and drum majorette
Cheryl	21	Secretary in campus department
Sue	30	Cosmetic consultant
Jan	30	Director of Crisis Program at YWCA
Peggy	26	Manager for photocopying company
Bonnie	22	College student and postmaster in drugstore
Pat	41	Owns rental property
Dorcas	61	Cashier at campus cafeteria
Chuck	36	Ticket agent at bus station
Joe	34	Ticket agent at bus station
Joan	58	Manager of travel agency
Margaret	41	Receptionist at hotel
Dave	25	Laid-off factory worker, employed at adult bookstore.
Rudy	25	College student
Bryan	18	Works at candy store
George	47	Owns restaurant
Mac	32	Works at gas station
Arlene	34	Housewife
Karen	34	Owner of bar
Rick	35	Owns restaurant
Carol	48	Co-owner of craft store
Joanna	31	Works in craft store
Glenda	55	Co-owner of craft store
Edward	29	College professor
Janet	23	Manager of delicatessen
Ron	42	Manager of popcorn store
Phil	74	Retired engineer
Clem	34	Ironworker in factory
Mike	73	Parking lot attendant
Leonard	24	Fire fighter
Claude	58	Answers phone at fire station

Figure A–1. Continued

Name	Age	Occupation
Keith	73	Truck driver
Dennis	29	Captain at fire station
Norman	29	Car salesperson
Dan	37	Handyman
Steve	24	Cook and musician
Becky	39	Works in massage parlor
Thelma	29	Janitor in factory
Fred	58	Owns wholesale meat house
Harry	27	Works in factory
Teresa	34	Beautician
Evelynn	27	Attorney

egies, other work, purpose of life, difficult times, personality, life metaphor, view of life, and core life issues. Each area was selected to provide evidence of how a person copes. Taken together, these dimensions constitute each individual's life orientation.

The primary goal was to secure as much information about the person's life as possible to provide a context to understand the life metaphor. A secondary goal was to gather a number of examples of an individual's method of coping. Each question implicitly asks for evidence of coping by examining how people manage various dimensions of their lives.

CODING PROCEDURES

Having gathered a sample of interviews, they were ready to be analyzed. Two preliminary levels of analysis were involved.

Level 1. Notes about each individual's life orientation were recorded, using four major identifiers as guides. (1) Word patterns are indicated by frequently or rarely used words and phrases. For example, Dennis, an Antagonist, repeatedly stated that when he encounters problems it is "like running into a brick wall." (2) Psychological repetition and absence are indicated by silence or emphasis. For example, Fred's silence, when I asked him what had been the hardest years, was followed by the story about his daughter's death from leukemia. On other occasions during the

Figure A–2. Interview Schedule

What is your name?
What is your age?
Tell me about your job.
How long have you worked here?
What does your work entail?
Have you had the same job?
What do you like about the job?
What do you dislike about the job?
Why?
What keeps you going?
How do you survive the day?
What things motivate you to get up in the morning?
What do you look forward to about the day?
What does this job mean to you?
Do you have ways of breaking the monotony?
What kinds of rewards does this job bring you?
What is absent from the job?
Is there something else, some other kind of work you
would rather be doing?
What did you want to be when you were younger?
Do you feel you were put here for a reason?
What is your main purpose in life?
What kinds of changes have you seen?
If you could do it all again, would you do the same things?
What would you keep?
What would you change?
If there were one thing in your life right now that you
could change, what would that be?
What were the hardest years for you?
What do you do in your free time?
When confronted with a new situation, what do you use as
a guideline?
If you were to take a picture of anything that would de-
scribe you, what would that be?
What animal best represents your personality?
What is the first thing that comes to mind when you hear
the word *Life?*

Figure A–2. Continued

If I say to you, "Life is like ___ (blank)," how would you fill in
that space?
   Why?
   What do you mean by that?
   When you say (blank), that brings to mind certain things.
   Are these things important in your life?
   What do you get the most pleasure from in life?
   What makes life worth living?
   What things are important to you?
   What does the concept of time mean in your life?
   If I asked you, "What is your secret of life?" what would
   you say?
   Are there any questions that you have asked yourself, that
   you have found an answer for?
   Do you have any questions for me?
   Is there anything you would like to add to this interview?

---

interview, when he remembered something painful, he would
again grow silent before speaking. (3) Unusual or surprising statements are noteworthy. Harry, an Antagonist, stated that when he
gets really angry he likes to "beat people up." (4) Contradictory
statements are identified by deviations from the apparent logic of
the individual. Clem, a Fatalist, used the word "philosophical,"
which seemed too sophisticated in comparison to the rest of his
vocabulary. The record of this information constitutes the dominant content of the life orientation.

Level 2. A one-page summary statement was made for each
individual. The focus of this summary was on the answer to the
question, "If I say to you, 'life is like ___ (blank),' how would you
fill in that space?" This answer constitutes an individual's life
metaphor.

The summary page also included information from an individual's life orientation (based on the notes from level 1), which
directly related to coping. Specific questions addressed this issue:
"What have been the hardest years for you?" "How did you manage
those years?" "How do you survive the day?" "What motivates

you to get up in the morning?" The data were being framed in such a way as to make explicit the connections among an individual's life metaphor, life orientation, and coping.

Next, a list was made of the life metaphors to secure categories across all of the responses. Initially, it seemed that the life metaphors could be grouped according to topics. Seven categories were created, based on the content of the life metaphor question. Figure A–3 provides a breakdown of these seven metaphor categories by person and specific metaphor. The initial framework consisted of the following thematic groups:

1. **Life Is a Process**
   Life is perceived as constantly changing, adapting, and following a progression of events. Individuals are motivated by the excitement of learning.
2. **Life Is What You Make It**
   Individuals believe they are responsible for taking action in life and making it whatever they choose.
3. **Life Is a Game**
   Each individual imposes the idea of a game on life, stressing various parts, such as winning and losing, rules, choice, and competition.
4. **Life Is Action**
   The group emerged because its members do not fit anywhere else. When examined, each person emphasizes action as an important part of their life metaphor.
5. **Life Is Precious**
   Individuals express the belief that life is something for which people should be grateful. Life can never be taken for granted because it is too special.
6. **Life Is the Way It Is**
   People find it difficult to liken life to anything. The dominant impression of life is that it is something that happens to the person.
7. **Life Is Decay**
   Each member shares the belief that life is something negative. They are not optimistic about life in the present or in the future.

Figure A–3.   Breakdown of Metaphors

GROUP	NAME	METAPHOR
It's the Way It Is	Clem	It just is
	Chuck	Roll along with the punches
	Dan	A progression of small events
	Mike	It's been great to me
	Claude	Life's great to me
	Dorcas	My life's pretty good
	John	It's not that bad
	Fred	It's been good to me
	Cheryl	Change
Precious	Bill	A chance to really live
	Margaret	A very precious thing
Game	Bonnie	A game
	Dennis	A military game
	Janet	A game
	Dave	A chess game
What You Make It	Mac	An open-ended question
	Thelma	A goal
	Joan	Very ordinary
	Teresa	What you make it
	George	What you make it
	Rick	What you make it
	Val	What you make it
	Ron	What you make it
	Joe	What you make it
	Rudy	What you make it
	Norman	A red delicious apple
	Arlene	A puzzle
	Sue	A ball
	Pat	A challenge
	Leonard	A challenge
	Edward	Walking the wire
Decay	Harry	A straight line
	Phil	It's deteriorating
	Becky	It stinks
Learning Process	Jan	A process
	Steve	A fine line between frustration and amusement
	Bryan	School
	Lynn	Flowers
	Carol	A bowl of cherries
	Joanna	A wheel
	Fr. Dave	A journey
	Evelynn	A lesson for the future
Active	Keith	An athlete
	Karen	An adventure
	Glenda	A bird
	Peggy	The ocean

CRITIQUE OF THE CATEGORY SYSTEM

While this seven-part system provided an initial organizational framework, it also presented some problems. The development of any category system usually entails some difficulties and may require several revisions. Robert Bales took twenty years to develop the interaction process analysis and describes the problems one typically finds:

> The decision as to how many classes to put into a system like the present one is a matter of judgment: more classes give more precision, as one goes in the direction of continuous quantitative measurement, but to go very far in this direction puts a heavy strain on memory and intuitive understanding. The present scheme in its practical form is categorical rather than quantitative, hence it is much easier to handle intuitively.[22]

First, overlapping categories within the framework do not distinguish boundaries sharply enough. For example, individuals whose life metaphors fall into the category life is action could also fit into the category life is what you make it. People in the category life is precious have some elements in common with those in the category life is the way it is.

The problem is that any given life metaphor might be classified as "a game," as "what you make it," or as "precious," and so on. What is needed is a category system in which a particular life metaphor can be classified in only one category. The necessary or core dimensions must be specified.

Second, the category system must be comprehensive enough to classify all possible units of analysis. In this sense, the model must be exhaustive; otherwise, the researcher would generate a new category for each new life metaphor encountered.

Given the present sample, seven categories were created. Had the sample size been larger, there might have been a greater number of categories. The intuitive ease of this type of categorization must give way to precision, making the search for the necessary conditions more compelling. The system must minimize individualized categories that limit the generalizability of the framework.

Accordingly, a revision of the categories must fulfill two criteria: (1) the categories must be mutually exclusive, which means specifying the necessary conditions for the inclusion of a particular life metaphor in a particular category; and (2) the category system must be exhaustive, which means accounting for any conceivable life metaphor.

A MODEL

Considered on its own, the life metaphor information yielded an inadequate category system. A model was needed to provide a context within which to place the life metaphor, as well as to represent the content of the entire interview. With this realization, the unit of analysis shifted from the life metaphor to the life orientation. This meant returning to the interview as a whole to provide the context. Based on this information, two recurrent dimensions were indicated: activity and evaluation.

First, every life orientation can be described according to an activity dimension, representing the energy and work an individual puts into life. Second, every life orientation can be described according to an evaluative dimension, indicating the enthusiasm, excitement, and degree of liking with which an individual judges life.

It is not surprising that these dimensions should surface since they represent two factors in a tripart model—consisting of activity, evaluation, and potency—which have been used repeatedly to discover people's attitudes.[23] The two dimensions satisfy the criteria of mutual exclusiveness and exhaustiveness. If treated orthogonally, they characterize four quadrants of coping. Figure 7–1 is the visual representation of this social model of coping.

The model, anchored by the adjective pairs active-passive; and positive-negative, accounts for a range of coping styles, including functional and dysfunctional coping.[24]

CHARTING LIFE METAPHORS

Having established the model, the life metaphors were charted along its dimensions. The only variation concerns the anchoring of the dimensions by the adjective pairs. Instead of the oppositional adjectives active-passive and positive-negative, the pairs most active–less active and most positive–less positive were chosen to best represent the present sample. Individuals who participated in this study are described as coping with life. They are neither extremely passive nor extremely negative when compared with a larger social model of coping.

EVIDENCE INFORMING LIFE METAPHOR CLASSIFICATION

The life metaphors were rated according to a Q sort procedure by a single rater, which established a six-point continuum for each dimension ranging from most active to less active and most positive to less positive. Instead of evaluating the life metaphors according to absolute values, this sorting technique, outlined below, permits each life metaphor to be rated relative to its location within the sample. Figures A–4 presents the ratings for each person for each dimension.

Cards were made for each of the forty-six interviewees. Each card noted the individual's name and his or her life metaphor. The cards were then divided into two equal piles, representing most active and least active. The first pile, most active, was then sorted into three smaller piles according to most active, medium active, and least active. The same sorting procedure was followed for the least active pile.

For each of the piles, seven individuals were sorted into most active, nine into medium active, and seven into least active. These six piles comprised the continuum from most active to least active. Each dimension was numbered accordingly from one to six, with one indicating the least active and six indicating the most active.

These ratings were recorded on the backs of the cards. The cards were then reassembled, and the same procedure was followed for the evaluative dimension. Cards were intially sorted according to most positive and least positive. Each individual then had two ratings—one for the activity dimension and one for the evaluative dimension.

RESULTS

The charting of the life metaphors indicates four quadrants. Quadrant I, the Antagonist, represents the most active–less positive dimension (14%). Quadrant II, the Enthusiast, represents the most active–most positive dimension (36%). Quadrant III, the Fatalist, represents the less active–less positive dimension (36%). Quadrant IV, the Spectator, represents the less active–most positive dimension (14%).

Five findings emanate from this model. First, the model indicates a strong relationship between the active and the positive

Figure A–4. Ratings for Each Person for Each Dimension

The following figures show where the individuals fall using the sorting procedures on the activity demension. Then they were independently sorted on the evaluative dimension. Finally, the scores based on the respective sortings were used to plot the combined dimensions. For example, Harry scored a 6 on the activity deminsion and a 1 on the evaluative dimension. The names with the dot beside them represent those individuals who scored the same value on both dimensions. For example, Cheryl scored a 1 on both dimensions.

Activity Dimension

Least Active	Second Least Active	Third Least Active	Third Most Active	Second Most Active	Most Active
• Cheryl	Claude	Joan	Becky	Rick	Harry
• Chuck	• Edward	Leonard	Rudy	Phil	• Val
Mike	• Mac	Janet	Norman	Dennis	• Bonnie
Steve	Bill	Keith	Karen	• Dorcas	• George
Thelma	Bryan	Lynn	• Fr. Dave	• Sue	• Teresa
Dan	Fred	Carol	• Evelyn	• Joanna	• Ron
Clem	John	Pat	Dave	• Glenda	• Jan
	Joe			• Arlene	
	Margaret			Peggy	

Evaluative Dimension

Least Positive	Second Least Positive	Third Least Positive	Third Most Positive	Second Most Positive	Most Positive
Claude	• Edward	Bill	Joan	Margaret	• Val
• Cheryl	• Mac	Bryan	Leonard	• Arlene	• Bonnie
• Chuck	Mike	Fred	Janet	• Glenda	• George
Harry	Dennis	Steve	• Fr. Dave	• Joanna	• Teresa
Phil	Dave	Clem	• Evelynn	• Sue	• Ron
Rick	Keith	Dan	Joe	• Dorcas	• Jan
Becky	Lynn	Thelma		Karen	Peggy
	Carol			Norman	
	Pat			Rudy	

dimensions. The less positive individuals are also less active; and the most positive are also most active. The arrangement of the data in this way links the activity in people's lives with their evaluation of life. Figure 2–1 presents the locations of the individuals within each quadrant.

Second, six individuals surprisingly fall outside the general tendency of the data. The locations of these people run counter to the expectations established by the model. Margaret, a Spectator, ("life is precious") was rated as Active 2–Positive 5. The other five people, all Antagonists, fall into the most active–less positive quadrant, where the expectation is that the ratings should be closer together. The individuals are Harry ("life is a straight line"); Rick ("life is what you make it"); Phil ("life is deteriorating"); Dennis ("life is a military game"); and Becky ("life stinks"). The information provided by the life orientation explains these deviations by pointing to inconsistencies. By highlighting discrepant ratings, the model draws the researcher's attention to the mismatches between the life metaphor and the life orientation.

Third, it is possible to assess how well the life metaphors fit within each quadrant. Figure 2–2 provides the specific life metaphors by quadrant. For the most part, the locations of the life metaphors seem appropriate; however, two stand out. Thelma states that "life is a goal," but she is a Fatalist (the less active and less positive quadrant). Joe states that "life is what you make it," but he is a Spectator (the less active and most positive quadrant). The expectation is that each of these life metaphors should be rated as more active. Again, the information in the life orientations explains these contradictions.

Fourth, the model can be described according to the spatial relationships and the relative proximity of the life metaphors. For example, the education and learning metaphors remained fairly close together, suggesting that those who use this life metaphor approach life in much the same way. By contrast, the game metaphor is scattered over three quadrants, which means that the idea of a game is subject to a variety of interpretations.

Fifth, the model can be considered according to its horizontal and its vertical dimensions. If the model is examined vertically, the researcher can compare the characteristics of disconfirming and confirming life metaphors. If examined horizontally, the model can be discussed according to the qualities of the actors and the reactors.

The following suggestions indicate ways to expand the scope of the present study. First, more internal cross-validation to increase reliability is needed. This could take the form of more and better questions. For example, better questions would ask the individual to explicitly identify a life metaphor. People who answer that "life isn't all that bad" could be asked exactly what they mean.

Additional questions could also help internal reliability. For example, during the interview, people could be asked to rate themselves according to activity and evaluation. Such questions would ask how active they rate themselves and how positive they rate themselves.

Second, more cross-validation is needed to assist external reliability. Studies might involve returning to the interviewees shortly after the interview to ask them to select from a list of life metaphors the one that best represents their life. Their selections could be compared to their original answers.

Studies at different times could be helpful in determining patterns of life metaphors. It would be interesting to trace the progression of an individual's life metaphor over time. Do some people possess the same, unaltered life metaphor throughout their lives? Or do life metaphors frequently change?

Third, the rating procedure at present relies on one rater. Coders could be trained to identify and rate the dimensions, which would increase reliability. A research team could be established to gather a national or international sample of interviews for greater cultural diversity.

Fourth, the comprehensive social model needs to be tested. The present study focuses on people who are coping. Noncoping behavior needs to be studied to determine if the active and positive dimensions remain valid. Studies are also needed to investigate whether individuals located in the extreme quadrants require different or additional dimensions to explain their life metaphors.

Fifth, the present model excludes the issue of salience, which needs to be specifically addressed in the interview. People differ in their consciousness about how they deal with situations. Highly active and highly positive seem to know consciously what they do in difficult life situations. On the other hand, less active and less positive people seem to have little awareness of what they do when they confront a difficulty.

People for whom a life metaphor is salient usually answer the life metaphor question easily, quickly, and in detail and are probably guided by that life metaphor. In contrast, people for whom a life metaphor is not as salient seem to have more difficulty answering the question. In these cases, a life metaphor might be more accurately described as a reflector of their lives.

Sixth, control, like salience, is a complex subject and seems integrally related to the study. The emergent control dimension was much less obvious than the dimensions activity and evaluation. In retrospect, every life metaphor indirectly expresses the amount of perceived control in a person's life. In the future, the indirect element control ought to be explicitly examined. The interactions between these three dimensions would make a more elegant and interesting model. Specific questions need to address an individual's perception of control.

Seventh, in a generalized way, the notion of a life metaphor can be useful to the variety of people who are interested in self-help, self-understanding, personal enhancement, and individual development. People increasingly want to take responsibility for the quality of their lives. Understanding how their life metaphors work in conjunction with their overall life orientations can help people develop their coping abilities.

Notes

Introduction

1. Beckett, *Waiting for Godot.*
2. Terkel, *Hard Times; American Dreams; Division Street; Working; World War II.*
3. Terkel, *Working,* p. xiii.
4. For a discussion of the ethnographic relationship see Agar, *Professional Stranger.*
5. Terkel, *Working,* p. xiii.
6. Galloway, "Probing the Private Life of the Public Studs Terkel," p. 9.
7. Mead, *Sex and Temperament;* and Bateson, *Naven.*
8. Lewis, *Five Families.*
9. Lewis, *Children of Sanchez.*
10. McCrindle and Rowbotham, eds., *Dutiful Daughters.*
11. McConville, *Sisters.*
12. Gornick, *Women in Science.*
13. Fishel, *Men in Our Lives.*
14. Bellah, et al., *Habits of the Heart.*
15. de Certeau, *Practice of Everyday Life,* discusses how language relates to practical everyday matters.

1. Life and Metaphors

1. Clichés are called "dead metaphors" because the freshness of thought originally expressed has become assimilated into the language, making the phrase no longer surprising. Although technically dead, in many cases, clichés actively guide an individual and make life understandable. A

discussion of the difference between metaphors and clichés can be found in Abrams, *Glossary of Literary Terms*, 25.

2. Burke, *Philosophy of Literary Form*, pp. 293–97.

3. There are a number of books that examine how people cope with disastrous situations, including personal narratives, such as Frankl's autobiography *Man's Search for Meaning*. Others discuss the personality of the survivor, for example, Des Pres, *Survivor*.

4. See, for example, Goffman, *Stigma*.

5. Milton Erickson developed techniques of therapy that focus on behavioral change through the use of metaphor. For a discussion of his work see Haley, *Uncommon Therapy*; and *Problem-Solving Therapy*. See also Watzlawick, Beavin and Jackson, *Pragmatics of Human Communication*.

6. For a discussion of metaphor see Abrams, *Glossary of Literary Terms*, p. 61.

7. Hans Vaihinger devised a theory of fictions, which depended on the creation of an "as if" reality. See Vaihinger, *Philosophy of As If*.

8. Aristotle, *Rhetoric*, 1457.

9. Ong, *Orality and Literacy*, p. 33.

10. Lakoff and Johnson, *Metaphors We Live By*.

11. Richards, *Philosophy of Rhetoric*, pp. 94–95.

12. Although technically a figure signaled by *like* constitutes a simile, both metaphor and simile function to compare elements. In *Rule of Metaphor*, Ricoeur points out that the difference between metaphor and simile is a matter of degree.

13. The title of Ricoeur's book, *Rule of Metaphor*, reflects his interest in "the discovery of living metaphor." Although the translator decided to call the book *Rule of Metaphor*, its original French title is *La Métaphor Vive* which could be interpreted as "The metaphor lives" or "The living metaphor."

14. Madanes, *Strategic Family Therapy*, p. 227.

15. I have adapted this phrase from Cloe Madanes's work. Philip Barker also talks about "relationship metaphors" in Barker, *Using Metaphors in Psychotherapy*, pp. 57ff.

16. The movie *Kiss of the Spiderwoman* subtly illustrates the complexity of interactional metaphors. The protagonists are two inmates of a South American prison: one has been convicted of corrupting a minor and the other has been imprisoned for revolutionary activities. Each is an outcast from society and initially from each other. The homosexual (William Hurt) survives the reality of the prison cell by escaping into an illusory world, which he creates by "telling" memorable movies. The movies change, but their characters and themes remain the same: they are always trapped, motivated by forces beyond their control, expressing

unfulfilled dreams and tormented passions, searching for the freedom to express their true selves, and seeking the commitment to pursue personal identities. The illusory roles of the screen characters match the prisoners' reality. A ritual discussion follows the recounting of each movie. The prisoners avoid explicitly talking about their own relationship but manage to confront the salient issues by discussing the movie characters' relationship. As the film progresses, the men grow more attached to each other, discovering a vision of identity, commitment, and destiny through the other. However, we learn that Hurt is an informant, whose parole depends on acquiring information about the revolutionary activities of his companion. Hurt wants to admit everything but cannot because doing so would jeopardize his chance for freedom. In a poignant moment he recounts a special film about a "spiderwoman" caught in a web of her own making. By recounting the plot, Hurt admits everything to his companion without directly confessing. The patterns of interaction conveyed within the imaginary film parallel the real-life relationship between the two men.

17. For a discussion of this idea see Norton, "Communicator Style Theory in Marital Interaction: Persistent Challenges."

18. Lock, "Emergence of Language," p. 43.

19. For a discussion of children's language development see Garvey, *Children's Talk*.

20. Weisman, *Coping Capacity*, p. 50.

21. See Bettleheim, *Uses of Enchantment*. He presents a Freudian perspective as he examines the relationship between child development and fairy tales.

22. See Eliade, *Myth and Reality*.

23. Von Kranz, *Creation Myths*.

24. See Levine and Ursin, eds., *Coping and Health*.

25. See for example Field, McCabe, and Schneiderman, eds., *Stress and Coping*.

26. Some corresponding titles are as follows: Moos and Schaefer, *Coping with Life Crises*; Burish and Bradley, eds., *Coping with Chronic Disease*; Moos and Tsu, *Coping with Physical Illness*; Levi, *Preventing Work Stress*; Hopfoll, *Stress, Social Support and Women*.

27. Haan, *Coping and Defending*.

28. Other studies that use interviewing and participant observation include Gerry Philipsen's articles, "Speaking 'Like A Man' in Teamsterville," pp. 13–22; and "Places for Speaking in Teamsterville," pp. 15–25. See also Owen, "Interpretive Themes in Relational Communication," pp. 274–87.

29. I also tried to balance the individual expression of coping with general societal guidelines for coping. The people I interviewed were not

in prisons, mental institutions, or living destitute lives on the streets. By all visible evidence they appeared to be coping.

30. I have worked with Jim Hughey and Robert Norton tracing the progression of the media's presentation of AIDS. See for example, Hughey, Norton, and Norton, "Insidious Metaphors and the Changing Meaning of AIDS"; see also Hughey and Norton, "What the AB Test Means: The Consequences of an Innovation," pp. 1–15.

31. I am grateful to Robert Norton for this idea, which he elaborates in his unpublished play *AB Negative.*

32. Aristotle, *Rhetoric,* 1405.

33. Aristotle, *Rhetoric,* 1408.

34. Weisman, in Lenrow, "Uses of Metaphor in Facilitating Behavior Change," pp. 145–48.

35. MacCormac, *Metaphor and Myth in Science and Religion,* p. 82.

2. Life Orientations

1. The technique of using rating scales anchored by bipolar adjectives, devised by Charles Osgood, is generically known as the semantic differential. See Osgood, Suci, and Tannenbaum, *Measurement of Meaning.*

2. Osgood, Suci, and Tannenbaum, "Measurement of Meaning," p. 64.

3. Hundreds of scholars have employed a range of different concepts (such as prominent persons, geometrical forms, and commercial products), across a variety of people, in different countries and with countless adjective pairs. Nunnally, *Psychometric Theory,* p. 609, points out that "The numerous factor-analysis studies of semantic-differential scales leads to the conclusion that there are three major factors of meaning involved. The factors do not always have exactly the same content in different studies, and in some studies more than three prominent factors are found. The remarkable fact is, however, that three factors with similar content have occurred in so many analyses under such varied conditions."

4. Nunnally, *Psychometric Theory,* p. 609.

5. Nunnally, *Psychometric Theory,* p. 609.

6. Bales's model is based on positive-negative, forward-backward, and up-down. These dimensions do not exactly correlate with Osgood's semantic differential, however, speculating about the relationship Bales, p. 53, writes: "His [Osgood's] good versus bad dimension is probably the same as my positive versus negative. My best guess is that his fast versus slow dimension passes from upward-backward to downward-forward in my space, and that his powerful versus weak dimension passes from upward-forward to downward-backward of my space."

7. Bales, *Personality and Interpersonal Behavior,* p. 161.

8. Bales, *Personality and Interpersonal Behavior,* p. 161.

9. Lefcourt, *Locus of Control,* pp. 152–53.

10. I am grateful to Dr. William Foster Owen for discussions and suggestions about possible titles.

11. These ratings derive from my analysis. The appendix includes the precise ratings for each individual (one is the lowest and six is the highest). Not being not part of a team or larger project, this work represents the efforts of a solo researcher. I conducted the entire study on my own—including the interviews, the transcripts, the ratings, and the analysis. Again, the reader is referred to the appendix for a more detailed discussion about the procedure.

12. People who do not use figurative language extensively in their discourse may still be guided by a life metaphor.

3. The Antagonist

1. Although there are five men and one woman in my study, this proportion is not generalizable to a larger population. There were no conclusions based on gender for any of the life orientations.

2. Terkel, *Working*, p. xiii.

3. A helpful book to consult is Clarke, *It's Cancer*, wherein Dr. Clarke examines the language used to describe the stigma associated with cancer.

4. Des Pres, *Survivor;* see also Dimsdale, ed., *Survivors, Victims, and Perpetrators.*

5. Des Pres, *Survivor*, p. 34.

6. Des Pres, *Survivor*, p. 33.

7. Des Pres, *Survivor*, p. 35.

8. Des Pres, *Survivor*, p. 31.

9. Des Pres, *Survivor*, p. 43.

10. Penton, *Apocalypse Delayed.*

11. Penton, *Apocalypse Delayed*, p. 7.

12. Penton, *Apocalypse Delayed*, pp. 4–9.

13. Berne, *Games People Play.*

14. Steiner, *Scripts People Live.*

15. Steiner, *Scripts People Live*, pp. 35–36.

16. Billig, *Arguing and Thinking*, p. 18.

17. Billig, *Arguing and Thinking*, p. 17.

18. Billig, *Arguing and Thinking*, p. 10.

19. Diana, *Prostitute and Her Clients.*

20. Diana, *Prostitute and Her Clients*, p. 33.

21. Diana, *Prostitute and Her Clients*, p. 37.

22. Diana, *Prostitute and Her Clients*, p. 31.

4. The Enthusiast

1. Norton, *Communicator Style*, p. 240.

2. Norton, *Communicator Style*, p. 67.

3. Bales, *Personality and Interpersonal Behavior.*

4. Refer to Figures 2–1 and 2–2 for the overall picture.

5. If I were to conduct the interviews again I would ask more questions directly related to control and include it as a third dimension in the model. The final chapter presents a more complete discussion of control.

6. Like control, motivation was not one of the dimensions by which the life metaphors were rated, it did, however, emerge as a common attribute.

5. The Fatalist

1. For a discussion of this principle as it relates to human control see May, *Freedom and Destiny,* p. 86; and Briggs and Peat, *Looking Glass Universe,* p. 49.

2. Although it is difficult to deny the societal predisposition to evaluate Fatalists less favorably than other orientations, the following section is not intended to judge those who fall into the category.

3. The reader is again referred to Figures 2–1 and 2–2 for the overall picture.

4. I suggested we cancel the interview but she wanted to continue, thinking it might take her mind off things.

5. At another time in her life, Pat might be classified as an Enthusiast, but at the time of the interview her difficulties are overwhelming. She is like Arlene, the Enthusiast, who has maintained a weight loss for one and one half years. At another time in Arlene's life, when she might not be in control, she might be classified differently. These scenarios indicate that life metaphors likely change over time.

6. The locus of control literature reflects many expressions that convey a fatalistic orientation. See, for example, Phares, *Locus of Control;* and Lefcourt, "Function of Illusion of Control and Freedom," pp. 417–25.

7. There is no evidence to suggest any causality between illiteracy and Fatalism. One is not intended to indicate the other, or vice versa.

8. Luria, *Cognitive Development.*

9. Luria, *Cognitive Development,* p. 151.

10. Luria, *Cognitive Development,* p. 161.

11. Bateson, *Steps to an Ecology of Mind,* p. 209.

12. An exaggerated example of taking literal statements metaphorically may be seen in Kozinski, *Being There.* The major character, Chauncey (Chance) Gardiner, makes literal observations based on his occupation (gardener), which are then interpreted metaphorically by those around him.

13. Bateson, *Steps to an Ecology of Mind,* pp. 56, and 205.

14. Through a series of tests with Russian peasants, Luria examined many facets of cognitive development including perception, representation, reasoning, deduction, imagination, and self-awareness. He compared three groups: illiterate peasants, a transitional group, and students

in technical schools. Luria was not interested in the content but in the capacity and awareness of self-analysis.

15. Luria, *Cognitive Development*, p. 151.

6. The Spectator

1. Ross, "Football Red and Baseball Green," pp. 211–12. The article comments on the myths and rituals of two major spectator sports.

2. See Barthes, "World of Wrestling," pp. 15–25.

3. In Hopper, "Taken-for-Granted," pp. 195–211, the "taken-for-granted" refers to "'between-the-lines' information." That is, information that is understood by people although not explicitly stated. People do not generally discuss taken-for-granted subjects because they assume that others know what they are talking about. In the present context, taking life for granted means not appreciating it.

4. Holocaust survivors want to keep the story alive so that it is not forgotten. Their goal is to prevent the crimes from being committed ever again. The National Holocaust Memorial Council meets annually to preserve the memory of those who lost their lives in the concentration camps and to encourage those who survived to speak out about the terrible tragedies and injustices.

5. Sampson, *Ego at the Threshold*, pp. 53–55.

6. Dempsey, *Way We Die*, p. 176.

7. Epting and Neimeyer, *Personal Meanings of Death*.

8. Rowe, "Constructing Life and Death," p. 15.

9. Rowe, "Constructing Life and Death," p. 16.

10. One wonders what happens if the interviewer asks the wrong questions and how the answers are classified: "negative replies," "no significant response," "unable to be interpreted," or "not interesting enough." Asking the right question helps a person open up and may influence the findings.

11. Ring, *Life at Death*.

12. Ring, *Life at Death*, p. 15.

13. Ring, *Life at Death*, p. 41.

14. Ring, *Life at Death*, p. 39.

15. Ring, *Life at Death*, p. 39, describes such accounts or stories as the "basic thanatomimetic narrative," which means "the experiences of (apparent) death in its developmental form."

16. Lee, *Death and Beyond in the Eastern Perspective*, p. 58.

17. Burke, *Towards a Better Life*, p. xviii.

18. Burke, *Permanence and Change*, p. 162.

7. Conclusion

1. Polanyi and Prosch, *Meaning*, p. 87.

2. Plato, *Republic*.

3. Plato, *Republic*, 377.

4. Lasch, *Minimal Self*, p. 96.

5. See Norton, "Transcending Everyday Life Through Narrative Communication."

6. Luria, *Man With A Shattered World*.

7. Luria, *Man With A Shattered World*, p. 89.

8. Luria, *Man With A Shattered World*, p. 60.

9. Luria, *Man With A Shattered World*, pp. 76–77.

10. See some representative books: Mills, *Six Years with God*; Bugliosi, *Helter Skelter*; Burton, *The Politics of Legitimacy*.

11. Carnegie, *How to Stop Worrying*; *How to Win Friends*.

12. The sample of people interviewed for the present study would all fit into this quadrant. On the whole, this quadrant consists of "life copers": individuals who manage life experiences and negotiate life issues for all practical purposes of living.

13. See Phelan, *Howard Hughes*.

14. Dr. Martin Luther King, Jr. has written a number of books including: *Strength to Love*; *Stride Toward Freedom*; and *Why we Can't Wait*.

15. See Goodrich, *Diary of Anne Frank*.

16. Although a significant attribute of each life orientation, motivation is not strong enough to warrant a separate dimension on the model. Motivation can be discussed as it relates to control.

17. Lefcourt, *Locus of Control*, p. 2.

18. Brenders, "Perceived Control: Foundations and Directions for Communication Research," p. 90.

19. See, for example, Clarke, *It's Cancer*. Dr. Clarke presents stories of women talking about coping with a cancer diagnosis.

20. The creation of support groups testifies to the strength that people gain from talking about the disease. Studies have shown that communicative interventions greatly satisfy patients. See, for example, Sacks, *Man Who Mistook His Wife for a Hat*; and Siegel, *Love, Medicine and Miracles*.

21. Milton Erickson skillfully employed a "tomato plant" metaphor to help an aged and dying patient reevaluate his reality and harmoniously live his remaining days. For a detailed discussion see Haley, *Uncommon Therapy*, pp. 301–4. See also my discussion on therapeutic metaphors in "The Therapeutic Functions of Metaphor," pp. 138–63.

22. Lefcourt, *Locus of Control*, p. 16.

23. Rotter, "Generalized Expectancies," p. 1.

24. May, *Freedom and Destiny*, p. 94.

25. May, *Freedom and Destiny*, p. 91.

26. May, *Freedom and Destiny*, p. 91.

27. Interestingly, the more active orientations relate to destiny more actively, suggesting a close relationship between activity and control.
28. Watzlawick, Beavin, and Jackson, *Pragmatics of Human Communication*, p. 99.
29. Smale, *Prophecy, Behaviour and Change*, describes three stages in a self-fulfilling prophecy: "First the prediction is formed; action and subsequent behavior are then taken as a result of this prediction; this behavior then brings about the prophesied event or behavior."
30. Weisman, *Coping Capacity*, p. 50.
31. Burke, *Grammar of Motives*, p. 503.
32. Ricoeur, "Metaphorical Process," p. 232.
33. See Ricoeur, "Metaphorical Process," p. 230.

Appendix

1. Glaser and Strauss, *Discovery of Grounded Theory*. See also Glaser, *Theoretical Sensitivity*.
2. Glaser and Strauss, *The Discovery of Grounded Theory*, p. 6.
3. Glaser and Strauss, *The Discovery of Grounded Theory*, p. 4.
4. Brown, *Poetic for Sociology*.
5. Nisbet, *Sociology as an Art Form*.
6. See the discussion of theoretical perspectives in psychology in Rychlak, *Psychology of Rigorous Humanism*.
7. Bateson, *Naven*.
8. Mead, *Sex and Temperament*.
9. Geertz, *Interpretation of Cultures*.
10. Agar, *The Professional Stranger*, p. 11.
11. Bales, *Personality and Interpersonal Behavior*.
12. See the discussion of projective tests in Rychlak, *Introduction to Personality and Psychotherapy*.
13. For the field of organizational communication see for example, Putnam and Pacanowsky, eds., *Communication and Organizations;* and McPhee and Tompkins, *Organizational Communication*. For interpersonal communication, see Owen, "Interpretive Themes in Relational Communication," pp. 274–87; and Jones and Yarbrough, "Naturalistic Study of the Meanings of Touch," pp. 19–56. Scholars have used qualitative analysis in cultural studies, such as Gerry Philipsen's series of articles about the Teamsterville culture, most recently, "Mayor Daley's Council Speech," pp. 247–60. Dwight Conquergood's work with the Hmong refugees while living in Camp Ban Vinai, Thailand reveals extensive use of qualitative methods. See Conquergood, "Culture, Communication and Narrative Performance," pp. 42–55.

14. Hawkes, *Metaphor*; MacCormac, *Metaphor and Myth*; Ortony, *Metaphor and Thought*.

15. Langer, *Philosophy in a New Key*; Wheelwright, *Metaphor and Reality*; Burke, *Permanence and Change*; Ricoeur, *Rule of Metaphor*.

16. Sapir and Crocker, eds., *Social Use of Metaphor*; Lakoff and Johnson, *Metaphors We Live By*.

17. Black, *Models and Metaphors*; Richards, *Philosophy of Rhetoric*; Turner, *Dramas, Fields, and Metaphors*.

18. See for example, Johnson, ed., *Philosophical Perspectives on Metaphor*.

19. Lakoff and Johnson, *Metaphors We Live By*.

20. While their work is innovative and contributes to contemporary dialogue about metaphor, there are some shortcomings. First, Lakoff and Johnson generalize their findings to a large audience, but the source of most of their data comes from anecdotal information. They state that their claims stem from "evidence of linguistic examples. Many if not most of these have come out of discussions with colleagues, students, and friends" (*Metaphors We Live By*, p. xii). Second, they cannot subsume every metaphor they encounter within their category scheme. They argue, for example, that certain "body" metaphors "are idiosyncratic, unsystematic, and isolated, . . . and hence are not metaphors that we live by" (*Metaphors We Live By*, p. 55). Third, the authors state that metaphor creates realities but they do not examine the created reality in relation to everyday life.

21. See Luria, *Man With A Shattered World*; and *Mind of a Mnemonist*. See also Erickson and Rossi, *Hypnotic Realities*; and Erickson and Rossi, *Experiencing Hypnosis*.

22. Bales, *Personality and Interpersonal Behavior*, p. 458.

23. Nunnally, *Psychometric Theory*, p. 609.

24. Again the issue of perspective is critical. Individuals have been placed on the model to suggest societal definitions of what constitutes coping. For example, society in general would agree that terrorism is active-negative behavior. From a militant group's perspective, the same behavior might be considered positive and active. The following quadrants are suggested as tentative illustrations with the proviso that any interpretation of coping is relative to the individual's perspective.

References

Abrams, M. H. *A Glossary of Literary Terms*. 3d ed. New York: Holt, Rinehart and Winston, 1971.

Agar, Michael H. *The Professional Stranger: An Informal Guide to Ethnography*. New York: Academic Press, 1980.

Aristotle. *The Rhetoric*. Trans., W. Rhys Roberts. New York: Modern Library, 1954.

Bales, Robert Freed. *Personality and Interpersonal Behavior*. New York: Holt, Rinehart and Winston, 1970.

Barker, Philip. *Using Metaphors in Psychotherapy*. New York: Brunner/Mazel, 1985.

Barthes, Roland. *Mythologies*. London: Granada Publishing, 1973.

Bateson, Gregory. *Naven*. 2d ed. Stanford: Stanford University Press, 1958.

———. *Steps to an Ecology of Mind*. New York: Ballantine Books, 1972.

———. *Mind and Nature*. New York: Bantam Books, 1980.

Beckett, Samuel. *Waiting for Godot*. New York: Grove Press, 1954.

Bellah, Robert N., Richard Madsen, William M. Sullivan, Ann Swindler, and Steven M. Tipton. *Habits of the Heart*. New York: Harper and Row, 1985.

Berne, Eric. *Games People Play: The Psychology of Human Relationships*. New York: Grove Press, 1964.

Berry, Thomas. *Religions of India*. New York: Bruce Publishing, 1971.

Bettleheim, Bruno. *The Uses of Enchantment*. New York: Vintage Books, 1977.

Beyer, Stephan. *The Buddhist Experience: Sources and Interpretations*. California: Dickenson Publishing, 1974.

Billig, Michael. *Arguing and Thinking: A Rhetorical Approach to Social Psychology*. Cambridge: Cambridge University Press, 1987.

Black, Max. *Models and Metaphors*. New York: Cornell University Press, 1962.

Blanchard, Kenneth, D. W. Edington, and Marjorie Blanchard. *The One Minute Manager Gets Fit*. New York: William Morrow, 1986.

Brenders, David A. "Perceived Control: Foundations and Directions for Communication Research." In *Human Communication Yearbook 10*, edited by Margaret McLaughlin, pp. 86–116. California: Sage Publications, 1987.

Briggs, John P., and F. David Peat. *Looking Glass Universe*. New York: Simon and Schuster, 1984.

Brown, Richard. *A Poetic for Sociology: Toward a Logic of Discovery for the Human Sciences*. Cambridge: Cambridge University Press, 1977.

Bugliosi, Vincent. *Helter Skelter: The True Story of the Manson Murders*. New York: Norton, 1974.

Burish, Thomas G., and Laurence A. Bradley., eds. *Coping with Chronic Disease*. New York: Academic Press, 1983.

Burke, Kenneth. *Permanence and Change*. 2d ed. Indianapolis: Bobbs-Merrill, 1977.

――――. *The Philosophy of Literary Form*. 3d ed. California: University of California Press, 1973.

――――. *A Grammar of Motives*. Los Angeles: University of California Press, 1969.

――――. *Language as Symbolic Action: Essays on life, Literature, and Method*. California: University of California Press, 1968.

Burton, Frank. *The Politics of Legitimacy: Struggles in a Belfast Community*. London: Routledge and Kegan Paul, 1978.

Carnegie, Dale. *How to Stop Worrying and Start Living*. New York: Simon and Schuster, 1948.

――――. *How to Win Friends and Influence People*. New York: Pocket Books, 1964.

Clarke, Juanne Nancarrow. *It's Cancer*. Toronto: IPI Publishing, 1985.

Coehlo, G. V., D. A. Hamburg, and J. E. Adams., eds. *Coping and Adaptation*. New York: Basic Books, 1974.

Conquergood, Dwight. "Culture, Communication and Narrative Performance." In *On Narratives*, edited by Helmut Geissner, pp. 42–55. Germany: Scriptor Verlag GmbH, 1987.

Crescimanno, R. *Culture, Consciousness and Beyond*. Washington, D.C.: University Press of America, 1982.

de Beaugrande, Robert. *Text, Discourse and Process: Toward a Multidisciplinary Science of Texts*. New Jersey: Ablex Publishing, 1980.

de Certeau, Michel. *The Practice of Everyday Life*. Trans. Steven F. Rendall. California: University of California Press, 1984.

Deikman, A. J. "Deautomization and the Mystic Experience." *Psychiatry* 29 (1966): 324–38.

Dempsey, David. *The Way We Die: An Investigation of Death and Dying in America Today*. New York: McGraw Hill, 1975.

Des Pres, Terence. *The Survivor*. New York: Oxford University Press, 1976.

Diana, Lewis. *The Prostitute and Her Clients: Your Pleasure Is Her Business*. Illinois: Charles C. Thomas, 1985.

Dimsdale, J. E., ed. *Survivors, Victims, and Perpetrators: Essays on the Nazi Holocaust*. Washington, D.C.: Hemisphere, 1980.

Dinitz, Simon, Russell R. Dynes, and Alfred C. Clarke. *Deviance*. 2d ed. New York: Oxford University Press, 1975.

Eliade, Mircea. *Myth and Reality*. New York: Harper and Row, 1963.

Elliott, Albert Pettigrew. *Fatalism in the Works of Thomas Hardy*. Pennsylvania: Folcroft Press, 1935.

Epting, Franz R., and Robert A. Neimeyer. *Personal Meanings of Death*. Washington, D.C.: Hemisphere, 1984.

Erickson, Milton, Ernest Rossi, and Sheila Rossi. *Hypnotic Realities*. New York: Irvington, 1976.

———. *Experiencing Hypnosis: Indirect Approaches to Altered States*. New York: Irvington, 1981.

Field, Tiffany M., Philip McCabe, and Neil Schneiderman, eds. *Stress and Coping*. Hillsdale, N.J.: L. Erlbaum, 1985.

Fishel, Elizabeth. *The Men in Our Lives*. New York: William Morrow, 1985.

Frankl, Victor. *Man's Search for Meaning*. New York: Pocket Books, 1963.

Galloway, Paul. "Probing the Private Life of the Public Studs Terkel." *Chicago Tribune*, 9 September 1984, 7–10.

Garfinkel, Harold. *Studies in Ethnomethodology*. New Jersey: Prentice Hall, 1967.

Garvey, Catherine. *Children's Talk*. Massachusetts: Harvard University Press, 1984.

Geertz, Clifford. *The Interpretation of Cultures*. New York: Basic Books, 1973.

Glaser, Barney. *Theoretical Sensitivity: Advances in the Methodology of Grounded Theory*. California: Sociology Press, 1978.

Glaser, Barney, and Anselm L. Strauss. *The Discovery of Grounded Theory: Strategies for Qualitative Research*. New York: Aldine, 1967.

Goffman, Erving. *Stigma*. New Jersey: Prentice-Hall, 1963.

Goodrich, Frances. *The Diary of Anne Frank*. New York: Random House, 1956.

Gornick, Vivian. *Women in Science*. New York: Simon and Schuster, 1983.

Gumperz, John. *Discourse Strategies*. Cambridge: Cambridge University Press, 1982.

Haan, Norma. *Coping and Defending: Processes of Self-Environment Organization*. New York: Academic Press, 1977.

Haley, Jay. *Problem-Solving Therapy*. New York: Harper and Row, 1978.

———. *Uncommon Therapy*. New York: W. W. Norton, 1973.

Hawkes, Terence. *Metaphor*. New York: Harper and Row, 1972.

Hopfoll, Steven E. *Stress, Social Support and Women*. Washington, D.C.: Hemisphere, 1986.

Hopper, Robert. "The Taken-for-Granted." *Human Communication Research*, Vol. 7, No. 3 (1981): 195–211.

Hughey, Jim D., and Robert W. Norton. "What the AB Test Means: The Consequences of an Innovation." *AIDS Reporter* (1987): 1–15.

———. Robert Norton, and Catherine Sullivan Norton. "Insidious Metaphors and the Changing Meaning of AIDS." Paper presented at the Annual Speech Communication Association Convention, Boston, 1987.

Johnson, Mark, ed. *Philosophical Perspectives on Metaphor*. Minnesota: University of Minnesota Press, 1981.

Jones, Stanley E., and A. Elaine Yarbrough. "A Naturalistic Study of the Meanings of Touch." *Communication Monographs* 52 (1985): 19–56.

King, Martin Luther, Jr. *Strength to Love*. New York: Harper and Row, 1963.

———. *Stride Toward Freedom: The Montgomery Story*. New York: Harper and Row, 1958.

———. *Why We Can't Wait*. New York: Harper and Row, 1964.

Kinser, Bill. *The Dream that Was No More*. New York: Harper and Row, n. d.

Kozinski, Jerzy. *Being There*. New York: Bantam Books, 1970.

Lakoff, George, and Mark Johnson. *Metaphors We Live By*. Chicago: The University of Chicago Press, 1980.

Lal, Kanwar. *The Hawk and the Pigeon*. India: Naresh Verma for Arts and Letters, 1970.

Langer, Suzanne. *Philosophy in a New Key*. New York: New American Library, 1951.

Lasch, Christopher. *The Minimal Self: Psychic Survival in Troubled Times*. New York: W. W. Norton, 1984.

Lee, Jung Young. *Death and Beyond in the Eastern Perspective*. New York: Gordon and Breach, 1974.

Lefcourt, Herbert. "The Function of Illusion of Control and Freedom." *American Psychologist* 28 (1973): 417–25.

———. *Locus of Control: Current Trends in Theory and Research*. New Jersey: Lawrence Erlbaum, 1976.

Lenrow, Peter. "Uses of Metaphor in Facilitating Behavior Change." *Psychotherapy: Theory, Research and Practice* 3 (1965): 145–48.

Levi, Lennart. *Preventing Work Stress*. Reading, Mass.: Addison Wesley, 1981.

Levine, Seymour, and Holger Ursin, eds. *Coping and Health*. New York: Plenum Press, 1980.

Lewis, Oscar. *Five Families*. New York: Penguin, 1959.

———. *The Children of Sanchez*. New York: Penguin, 1961.

Lock, Andrew. "The Emergence of Language: On Being Picked Up." In *Language Development*, edited by Andrew Lock and Eunice Fisher, pp. 39–48. London: Croom Helm, 1984.

Luria, A. R. *Cognitive Development: Its Cultural and Social Foundations*. Trans. M. Lopez-Morillas, and L. Solotaroff. Massachusetts: Harvard University Press, 1976.

———. *The Man with a Shattered World: A History of a Brain Wound*. Trans. Lynn Solotaroff. England: Penguin Books, 1972.

———. *The Mind of a Mnemonist*. Trans. Lynn Solotaroff. Massachusetts: Harvard University Press, 1968.

MacCormac, Earl. *Metaphor and Myth in Science and Religion*. North Carolina: North Carolina University Press, 1976.

MacIntyre, Alasdair. *After Virtue: A Study in Moral Theory*. Indiana: University of Notre Dame Press, 1981.

Madanes, Cloe. *Strategic Family Therapy*. San Francisco: Jossey-Bass, 1983.

Maslow, Abraham. *Motivation and Personality*. New York: Harper and Row, 1954.

May, Rollo. *Freedom and Destiny*. New York: W. W. Norton, 1981.

McConville, Brigid. *Sisters*. London: Pan Books, 1985.

McCrindle, Jean, and Sheila Rowbotham. *Dutiful Daughters*. New York: Penguin, 1977.

McPhee, Robert D., and Philip K. Tompkins. *Organizational Communication: Traditional Themes and New Directions*. Beverly Hills: Sage Publications, 1985.

Mead, Margaret. *Sex and Temperament in Three Primitive Societies*. New York: Morrow, 1935.

Miller, B. F., and C. B. Keane. *Encyclopedia and Dictionary of Medicine, Nursing and Allied Health*. 3d ed. Pennsylvania: Wm. Saunders 1983.

Mills, Jeannie. *Six Years with God: Life inside Reverend Jim Jones's People's Temple.* New York: A & W 1979.

Moos, Rudolf H., and Jeanne A. Schaefer. *Coping with Life Crises.* New York: Plenum Press, 1986.

Moos, Rudolf H., and Vivien Davis Tsu. *Coping with Physical Illness.* New York: Plenum Medical, 1977.

Naranjo, Claudio, and Robert E. Ornstein. *On the Psychology of Meditation.* New York: Viking Press, 1971.

Nisbet, Robert. *Sociology as an Art Form.* London: Oxford University Press, 1977.

Norton, Catherine Sullivan. "Transcending Everyday Life Through Narrative Communication: Stories that Help Us Cope." In *On Narratives*, edited by Helmut Geissner, pp. 116–29. Germany: Scriptor Verlag GmbH, 1987.

———. "The Therapeutic Functions of Metaphor." *Journal of Communication Therapy* 3 (1986): pp. 138–63.

Norton, Robert. *Communicator Style: Theory, Applications, and Measures.* California: Sage Publications, 1983.

———. "Communicator Style Theory in Marital Interaction: Persistent Challenges." In *Handbook of Research in Personal Relationships: Theory, Research, and Intervention*, edited by Steve Duck, pp. 307–23. West Sussex, U.K.: John Wiley, 1988.

———. "AB Negative." Unpublished play.

Nunnally, Jum. *Psychometric Theory.* 2d ed. New York: McGraw-Hill, 1978.

Ong, Walter J. *Orality and Literacy.* New York: Methuen, 1982.

Ortony, Andrew. *Metaphor and Thought.* Cambridge: Cambridge University Press, 1979.

Osgood, Charles E., George J. Suci, and Percy H. Tannenbaum. *The Measurement of Meaning.* Urbana: University of Illinois Press, 1957.

Osgood, Charles E., George J. Suci, and Percy H. Tannenbaum. "The Measurement of Meaning." In *Semantic Differential Technique: A Sourcebook*, edited by James G. Snider and Charles E. Osgood, pp. 56–82. Chicago: Aldine, 1969.

Owen, William Foster. "Interpretive Themes in Relational Communication." *Quarterly Journal of Speech* 70 (1984): 274–87.

Penton, M James. *Apocalypse Delayed: The Story of Jehovah's Witnesses.* Toronto: University of Toronto Press, 1985.

Phares, E. Jerry. *Locus of Control: A Personality Determinant of Behavior.* New Jersey: General Learning Press, 1973.

Phelan, James. *Howard Hughes, The Hidden Years.* New York: Random House, 1976.

Philipsen, Gerry. "Speaking 'Like A Man' in Teamsterville: Cultural Patterns in Role Enactment in an Urban Neighborhood." *Quarterly Journal of Speech* 61 (1975): 13–22.

———. "Places for Speaking in Teamsterville." *Quarterly Journal of Speech* 62 (1976): 15–25.

———. "Mayor Daley's Council Speech: A Cultural Analysis." *Quarterly Journal of Speech* 72 (1986): 247–60.

Pirandello, Luigi. *Six Characters in Search of An Author.* In *Three Plays.* New York: Duttin, 1934.

Plato. *The Republic*. Trans. A. D. Lindsay. New York: E. P. Dutton, 1957.

Polanyi, Michael, and Harry Prosch. *Meaning*. Illinois: University of Chicago Press, 1975.

Putnam, Linda L., and Michael E. Pacanowsky, eds. *Communication and Organizations: An Interpretive Approach*. Beverly Hills: Sage Publications, 1983.

Reid, David, and Edward E. Ware. "Multidimensionality of Internal Versus External Control: Implications for Past and Future Research." *Canadian Journal of Behavioral Science 6* (1974): 131–42.

Richards, Ivor Armstrong. *The Philosophy of Rhetoric*. New York: Oxford University Press, 1965.

Ricoeur, Paul. *The Rule of Metaphor*. Toronto: University of Toronto Press, 1981.

———. "The Metaphorical Process." In *Philosophical Perspectives on Metaphor*, edited by Mark Johnson, pp. 228–47. Minneapolis: University of Minnesota Press, 1981.

Ring, Kenneth. *Life at Death: A Scientific Investigation of the Near-Death Experience*. New York: Coward, McCann and Geoghegan, 1980.

Ross, Murray. "Football Red and Baseball Green." In *The Riverside Reader*, edited by Joseph Trimmer and Maxine Hairston, pp. 211–22. Boston: Houghton Mifflin, 1981.

Rotter, J. B. "Generalized Expectancies for Internal Versus External Control of Reinforcement." *Psychological Monographs* Vol 80, No. 609.

Rowe, Dorothy. "Constructing Life and Death." In *Personal Meanings of Death*, edited by Franz Epting and Robert Neimeyer, pp. 11–28. Washington: Hemisphere, 1984.

Rychlak, Joseph. *The Psychology of Rigorous Humanism*. New York: John Wiley and Sons, 1977.

———. *Introduction to Personality and Psychotherapy*. Boston: Houghton Mifflin, 1981.

Sacks, Oliver. *The Man Who Mistook His Wife for a Hat*. New York: Summit Books, 1985.

Sampson, Edward E. *Ego at the Threshold*. New York: Delta, 1975.

Sapir, J. David, and J. Christopher Crocker, eds. *The Social Use of Metaphor*. Pennsylvania: University of Pennsylvania Press, 1977.

Schank, Roger C., and Robert P. Abelson. *Scripts, Plans, Goals and Understanding: An Inquiry into Human Knowledge Structures*. New York: John Wiley and Sons, 1977.

Siegel, Bernie. *Love, Medicine and Miracles*. New York: Harper and Row, 1987.

Smale, Gerald G. *Prophecy, Behaviour and Change*. London: Routeledge and Kegan Paul, 1977.

Steiner, Claude M. *Scripts People Live: Transactional Analysis of Life Scripts*. New York: Grove Press, 1974.

Terkel, Studs. *Hard Times: An Oral History of the Great Depression*. New York: Pantheon Books, 1967.

———. *Division Street: America*. New York: Pantheon Books, 1970.

———. *Working*. New York: Avon Books, 1972.

———. *American Dreams: Lost and Found*. New York: Ballantine Books, 1980.

———. *World War II*. New York: Pantheon Books, 1986.

Totman, Richard. *Social and Biological Roles of Language*. London: Academic Press, 1985.

Turner, Victor. *Dramas, Fields, and Metaphors*. New York: Cornell University Press, 1974.

Vaihinger, Hans. *The Philosophy of As If*. Trans. C. K. Ogden. 2d ed. New York: Harcourt, Brace, 1935.

Van Deuk, Teun A. *Text and Context: Explorations in the Semantics and Pragmatics of Discourse*. New York: Longman, 1977.

Von Krantz, Marie-Louise. *Creation Myths*. Dallas: Spring Publications, 1972.

Watzlawick, Paul. *The Language of Change*. New York: Basic Books, 1978.

Watzlawick, Paul, Janet Beavin, and Don Jackson. *Pragmatics of Human Communication*. New York: W. W. Norton, 1967.

Weisman, Avery. *The Coping Capacity*. New York: Human Sciences Press, 1984.

Wheelwright, Philip. *Metaphor and Reality*. Indiana: Indiana University Press, 1962.

Catherine Sullivan Norton was born and raised in Brisbane, Australia. After graduating from the University of Queensland, she traveled to Europe and worked in London for two years. After returning to Australia, she decided to continue her education in the United States. She completed her Masters degree in speech communication at San Diego State University, and her Ph.D. in communication at Purdue University. She lives with her husband and son in Memphis, where she writes and lectures. This is her first book.